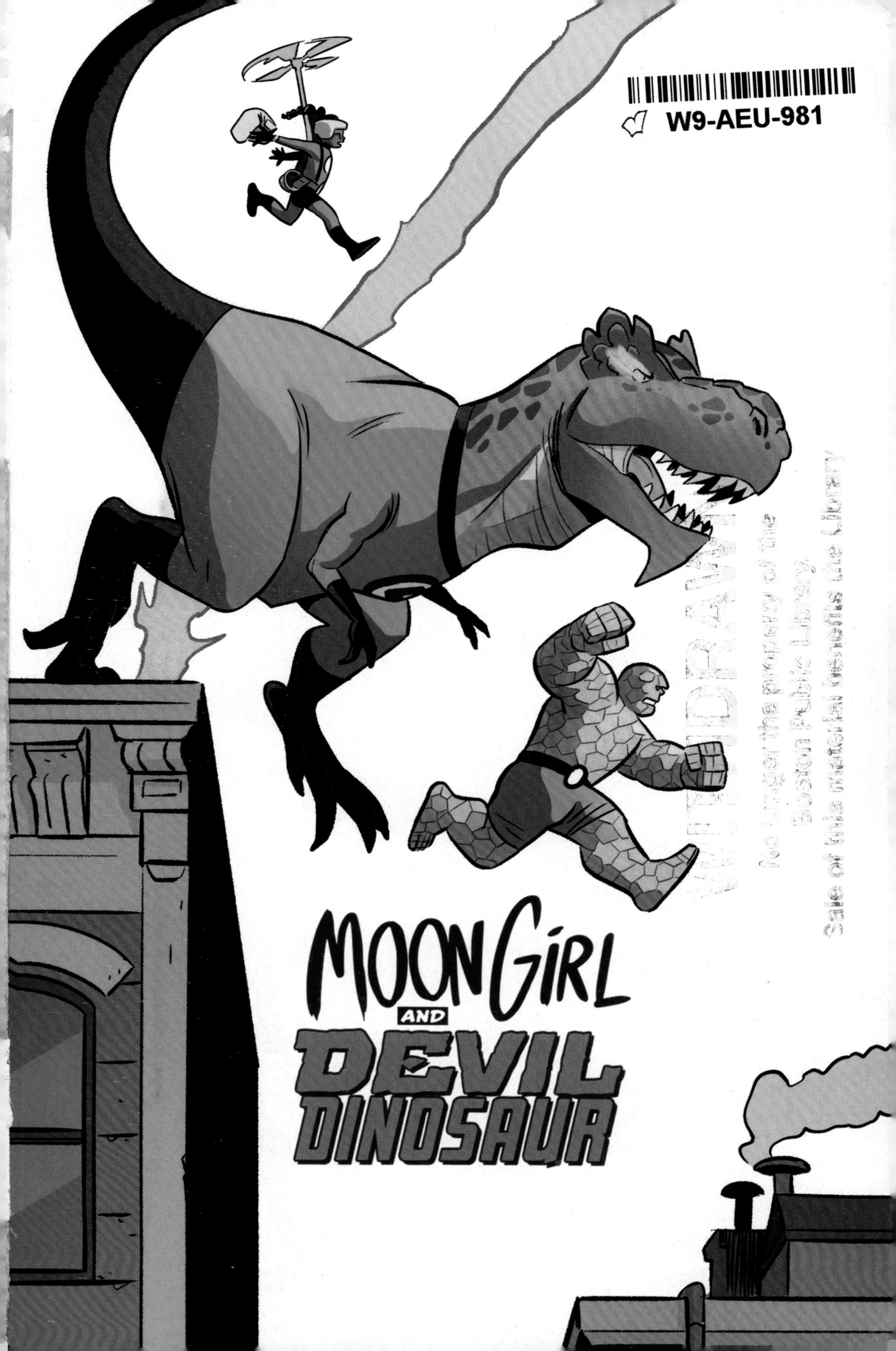
MOON GIRL
AND
DEVIL
DINOSAUR

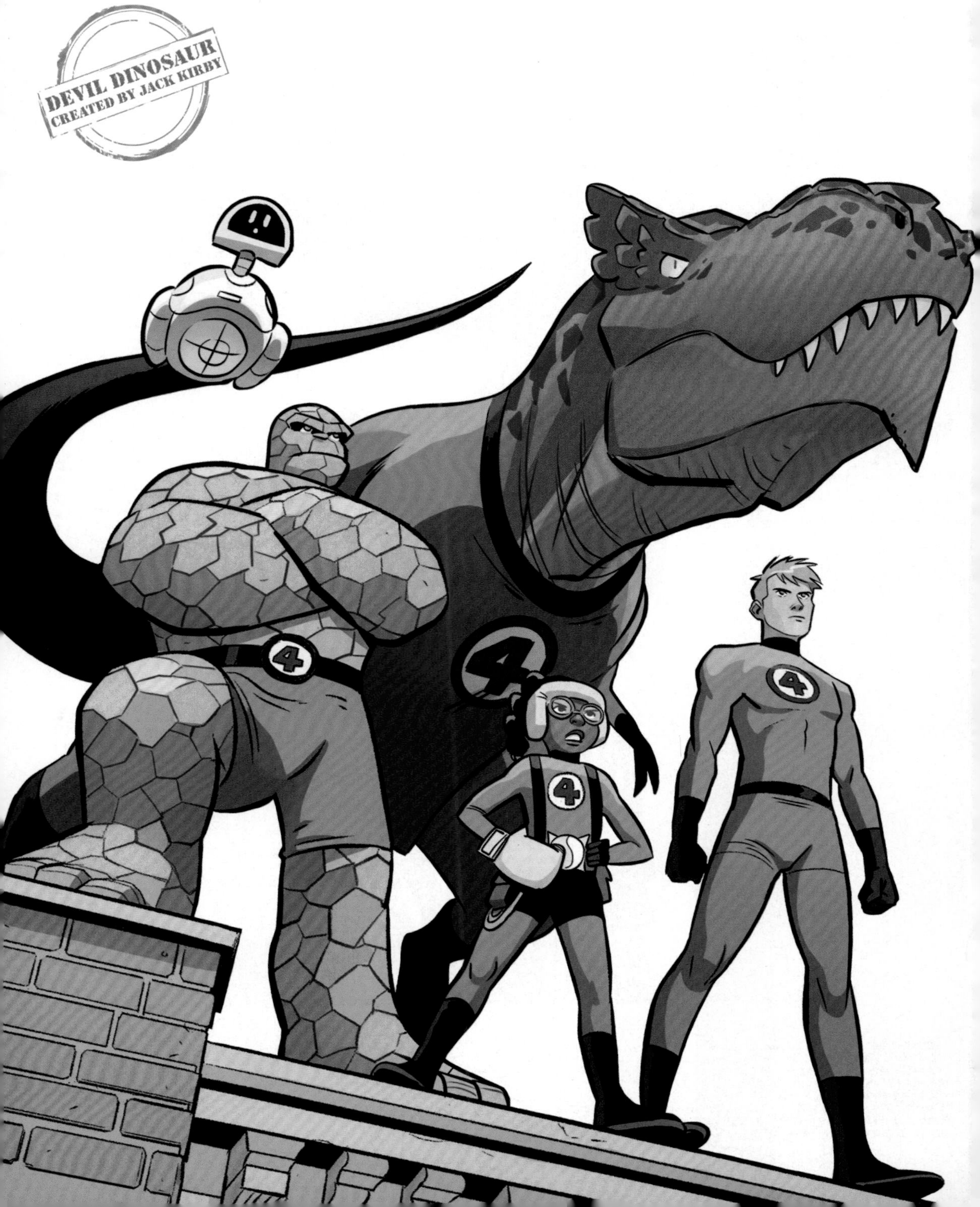
DEVIL DINOSAUR
CREATED BY JACK KIRBY

MOON GIRL AND DEVIL DINOSAUR

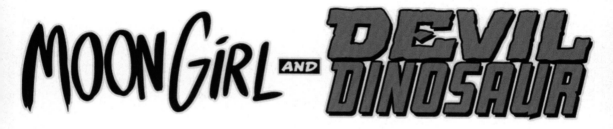

FANTASTIC THREE

Brandon Montclare
WRITER

Natacha Bustos
ARTIST, #25 & #27-30

Alitha E. Martinez
PENCILER, #26

Roberto Poggi with Alitha E. Martinez
INKERS, #26

Tamra Bonvillain
COLOR ARTIST

VC's Travis Lanham
LETTERER

Natacha Bustos
COVER ART

Chris Robinson
ASSISTANT EDITOR

Mark Paniccia
EDITOR

COLLECTION EDITOR: Jennifer Grünwald
ASSISTANT EDITOR: Caitlin O'Connell
ASSOCIATE MANAGING EDITOR: Kateri Woody
EDITOR, SPECIAL PROJECTS: Mark D. Beazley
VP, PRODUCTION & SPECIAL PROJECTS: Jeff Youngquist
SVP PRINT, SALES & MARKETING: David Gabriel
BOOK DESIGNER: Jay Bowen

EDITOR IN CHIEF: C.B. Cebulski
CHIEF CREATIVE OFFICER: Joe Quesada
PRESIDENT: Dan Buckley
EXECUTIVE PRODUCER: Alan Fine

MOON GIRL AND DEVIL DINOSAUR VOL. 5: FANTASTIC THREE. Contains material originally published in magazine form as MOON GIRL AND DEVIL DINOSAUR #25-30. First printing 2018. ISBN 978-1-302-91099-0. Published by MARVEL WORLDWIDE, INC., a subsidiary of MARVEL ENTERTAINMENT, LLC. OFFICE OF PUBLICATION: 135 West 50th Street, New York, NY 10020. **Printed in Canada.** DAN BUCKLEY, President, Marvel Entertainment; JOHN NEE, Publisher; JOE QUESADA, Chief Creative Officer; TOM BREVOORT, SVP of Publishing; DAVID BOGART, SVP of Business Affairs & Operations, Publishing & Partnership; DAVID GABRIEL, SVP of Sales & Marketing, Publishing; JEFF YOUNGQUIST, VP of Production & Special Projects; DAN CARR, Executive Director of Publishing Technology; ALEX MORALES, Director of Publishing Operations; DAN EDINGTON, Managing Editor; SUSAN CRESPI, Production Manager; STAN LEE, Chairman Emeritus. For information regarding advertising in Marvel Comics or on Marvel.com, please contact Vit DeBellis, Custom Solutions & Integrated Advertising Manager, at vdebellis@marvel.com. For Marvel subscription inquiries, please call 888-511-5480. **Manufactured between 5/4/2018 and 6/5/2018 by SOLISCO PRINTERS, SCOTT, QC, CANADA.**

10 9 8 7 6 5 4 3 2 1

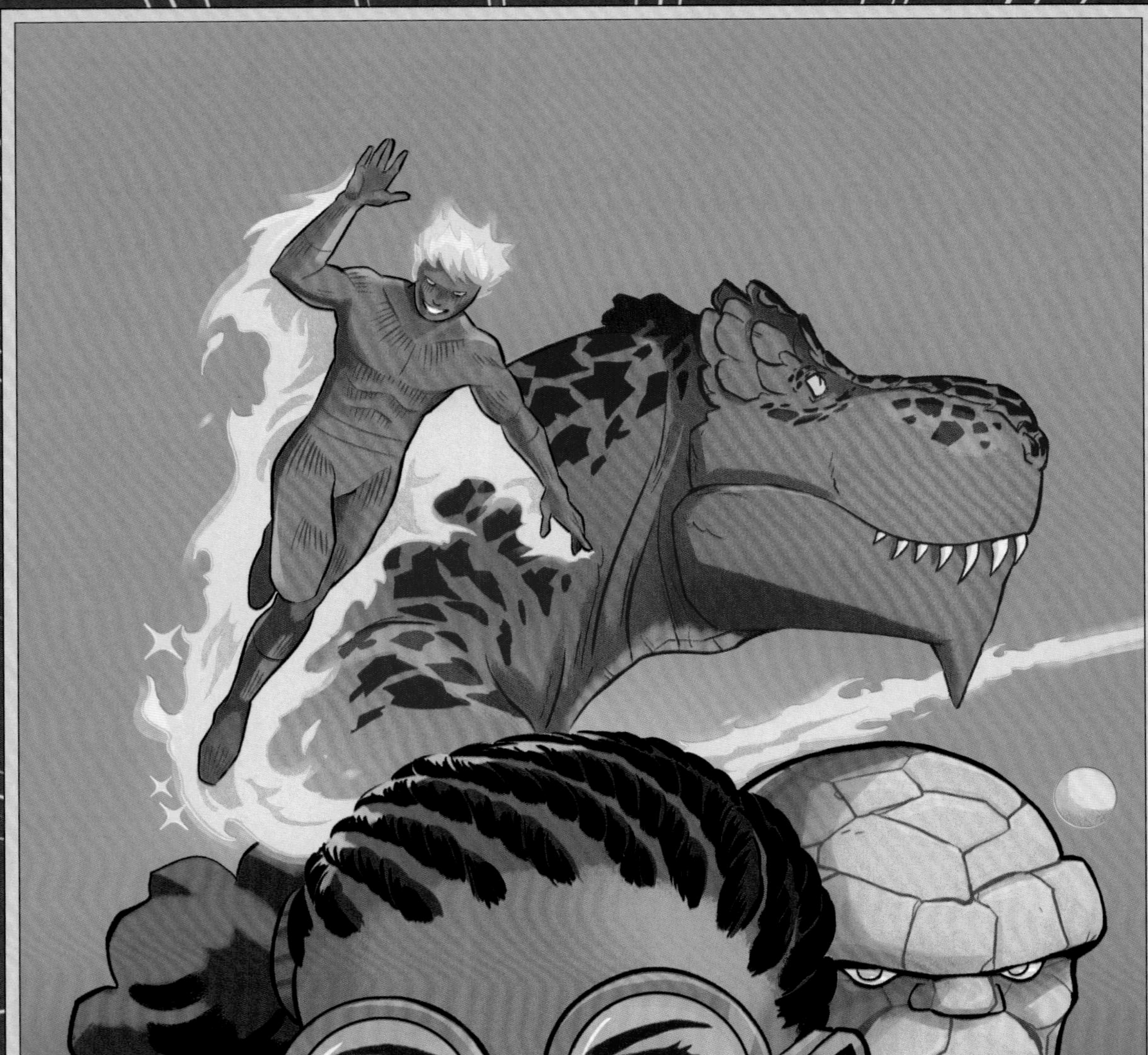
NAT.

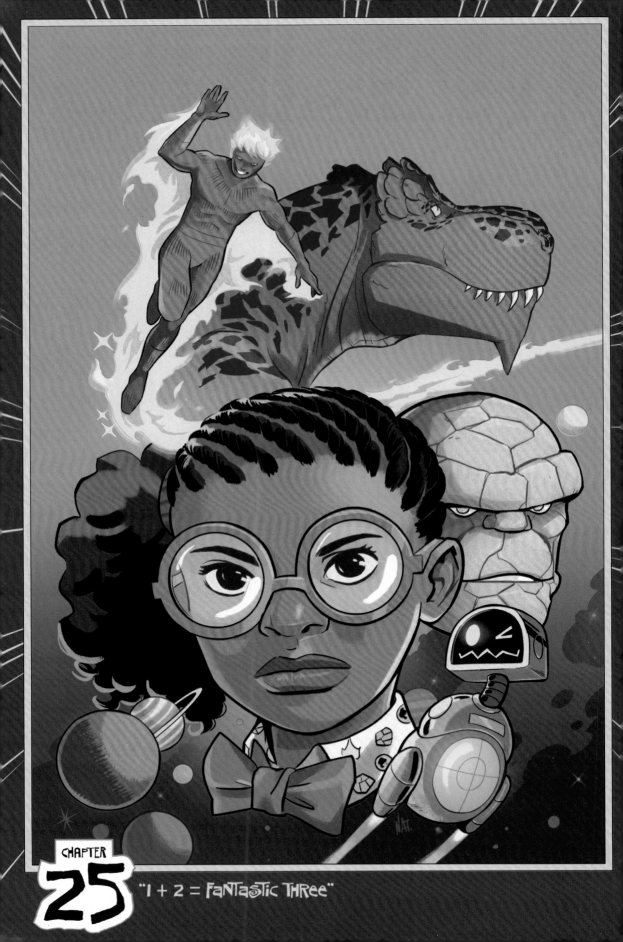

CHAPTER 25

"1 + 2 = FANTASTIC THREE"

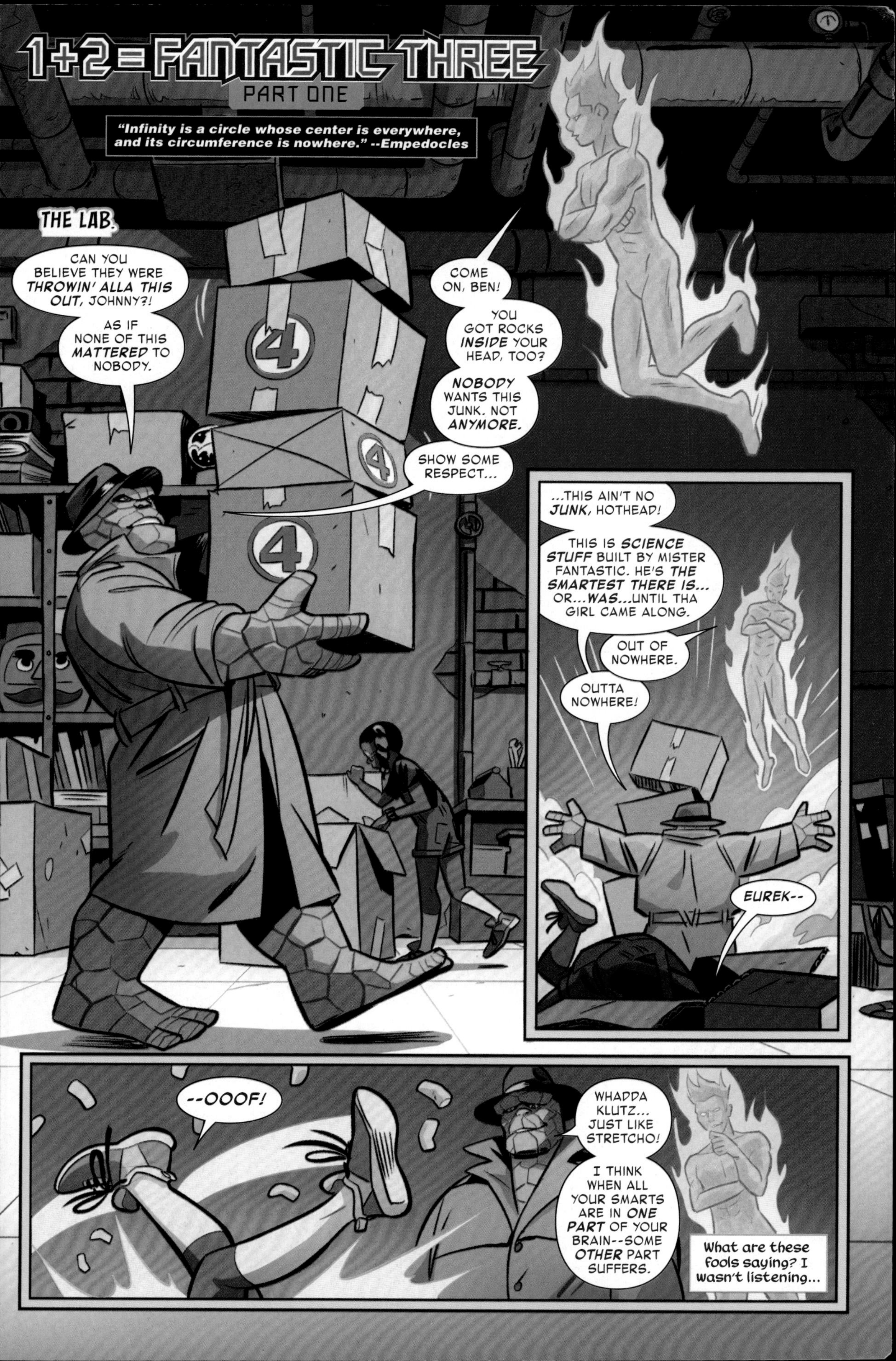
1+2 = FANTASTIC THREE
PART ONE
"Infinity is a circle whose center is everywhere, and its circumference is nowhere." --Empedocles
THE LAB.
CAN YOU BELIEVE THEY WERE THROWIN' ALLA THIS OUT, JOHNNY?!
AS IF NONE OF THIS MATTERED TO NOBODY.
COME ON, BEN!
YOU GOT ROCKS INSIDE YOUR HEAD, TOO?
NOBODY WANTS THIS JUNK. NOT ANYMORE.
SHOW SOME RESPECT...
...THIS AIN'T NO JUNK, HOTHEAD!
THIS IS SCIENCE STUFF BUILT BY MISTER FANTASTIC. HE'S THE SMARTEST THERE IS... OR...WAS...UNTIL THA GIRL CAME ALONG.
OUT OF NOWHERE.
OUTTA NOWHERE!
EUREK--
--OOOF!
WHADDA KLUTZ... JUST LIKE STRETCHO!
I THINK WHEN ALL YOUR SMARTS ARE IN ONE PART OF YOUR BRAIN--SOME OTHER PART SUFFERS.
What are these fools saying? I wasn't listening...

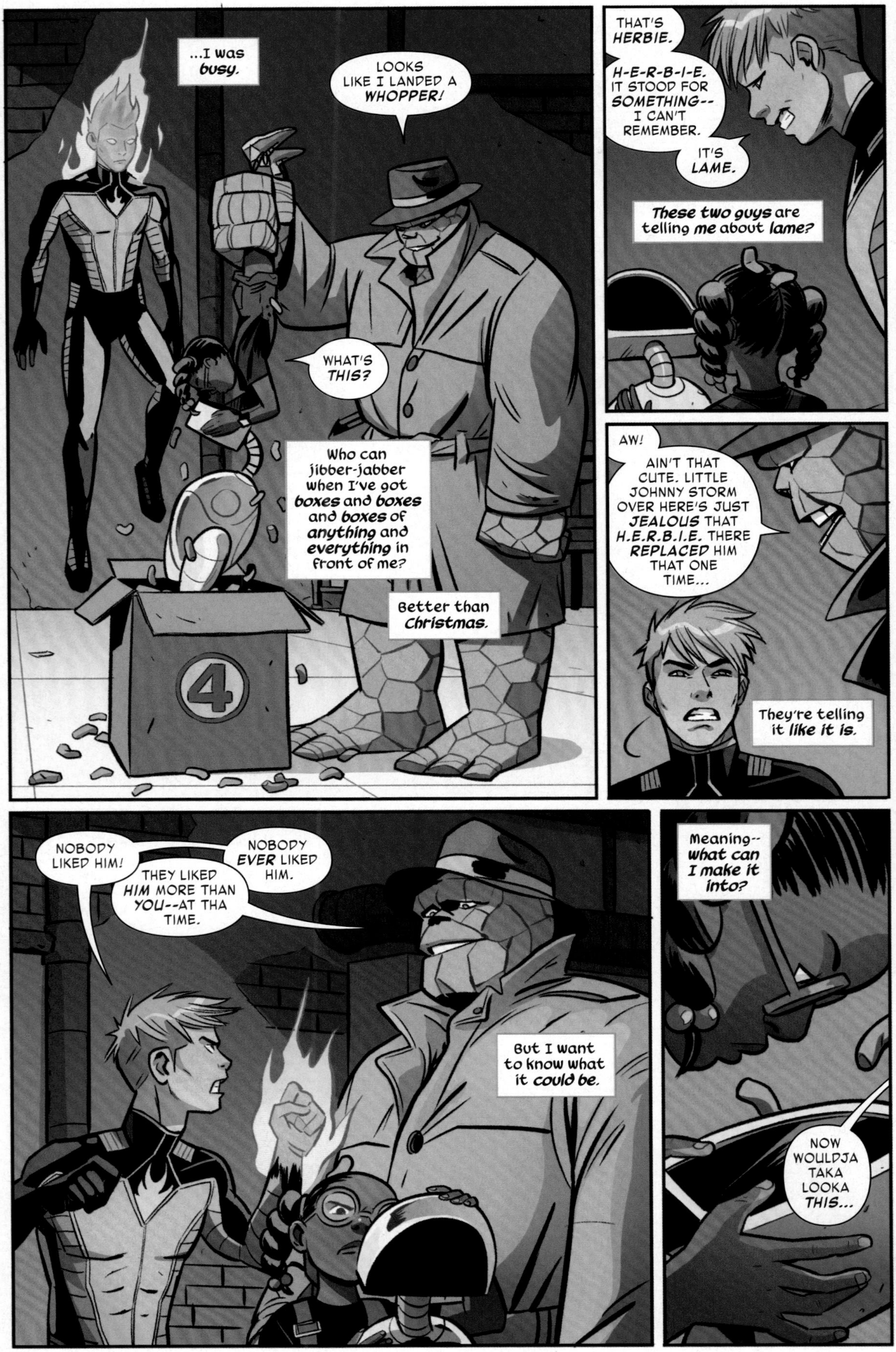
...I was busy.
LOOKS LIKE I LANDED A WHOPPER!
WHAT'S THIS?
Who can jibber-jabber when I've got boxes and boxes and boxes of anything and everything in front of me?
Better than Christmas.
THAT'S HERBIE.
H-E-R-B-I-E. IT STOOD FOR SOMETHING-- I CAN'T REMEMBER.
IT'S LAME.
These two guys are telling me about lame?
AW!
AIN'T THAT CUTE. LITTLE JOHNNY STORM OVER HERE'S JUST JEALOUS THAT H.E.R.B.I.E. THERE REPLACED HIM THAT ONE TIME...
They're telling it like it is.
NOBODY LIKED HIM!
NOBODY EVER LIKED HIM.
THEY LIKED HIM MORE THAN YOU--AT THA TIME.
But I want to know what it could be.
Meaning-- what can I make it into?
NOW WOULDJA TAKA LOOKA THIS...

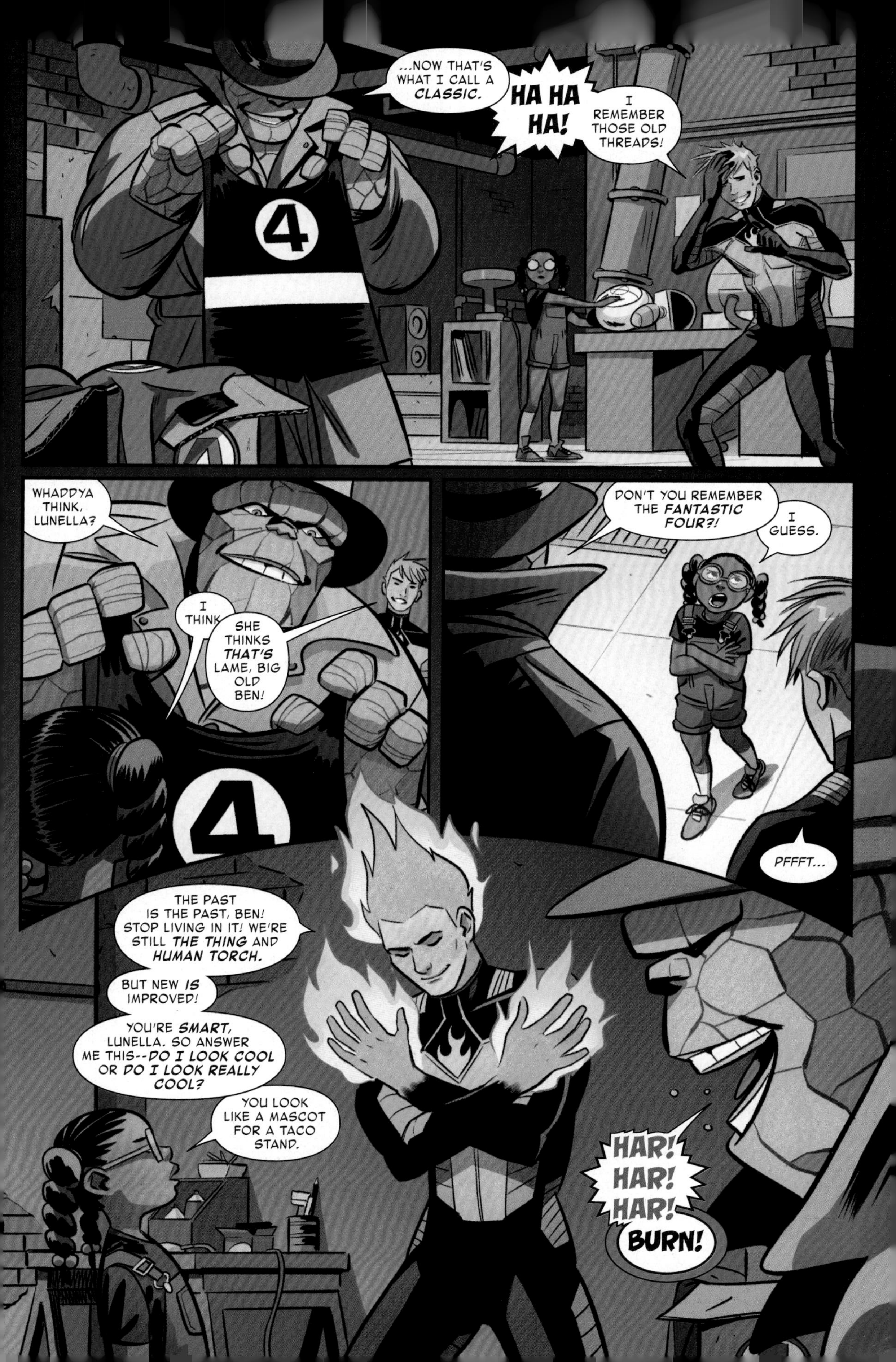
...NOW THAT'S WHAT I CALL A CLASSIC.
HA HA HA!
I REMEMBER THOSE OLD THREADS!
WHADDYA THINK, LUNELLA?
I THINK
SHE THINKS THAT'S LAME, BIG OLD BEN!
DON'T YOU REMEMBER THE FANTASTIC FOUR?!
I GUESS.
PFFFT...
THE PAST IS THE PAST, BEN! STOP LIVING IN IT! WE'RE STILL THE THING AND HUMAN TORCH.
BUT NEW IS IMPROVED!
YOU'RE SMART, LUNELLA. SO ANSWER ME THIS--DO I LOOK COOL OR DO I LOOK REALLY COOL?
YOU LOOK LIKE A MASCOT FOR A TACO STAND.
HAR! HAR! HAR!
BURN!

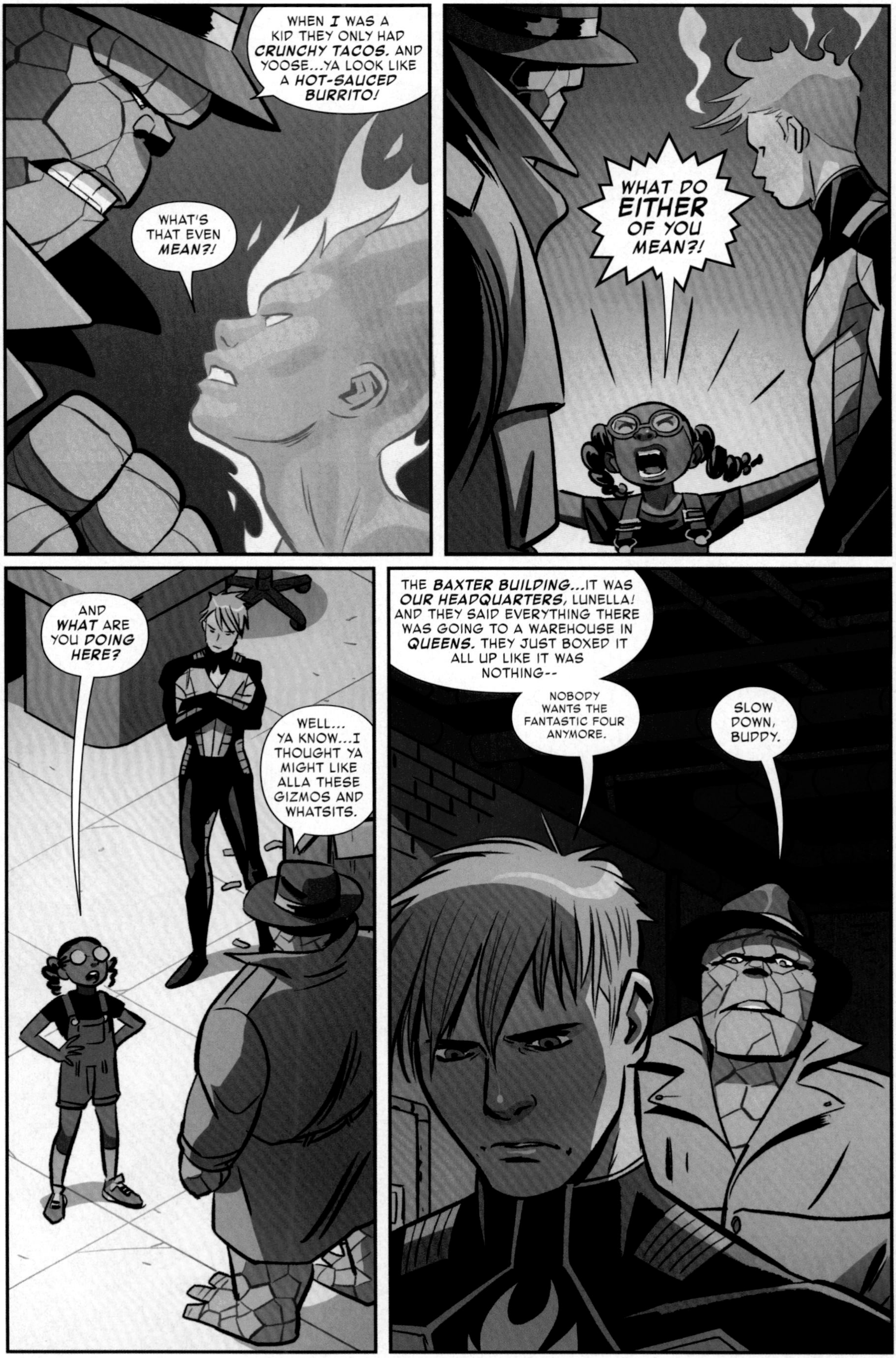

WHEN I WAS A KID THEY ONLY HAD CRUNCHY TACOS. AND YOOSE...YA LOOK LIKE A HOT-SAUCED BURRITO!
WHAT'S THAT EVEN MEAN?!
WHAT DO EITHER OF YOU MEAN?!
AND WHAT ARE YOU DOING HERE?
WELL... YA KNOW...I THOUGHT YA MIGHT LIKE ALLA THESE GIZMOS AND WHATSITS.
THE BAXTER BUILDING...IT WAS OUR HEADQUARTERS, LUNELLA! AND THEY SAID EVERYTHING THERE WAS GOING TO A WAREHOUSE IN QUEENS. THEY JUST BOXED IT ALL UP LIKE IT WAS NOTHING--
NOBODY WANTS THE FANTASTIC FOUR ANYMORE.
SLOW DOWN, BUDDY.

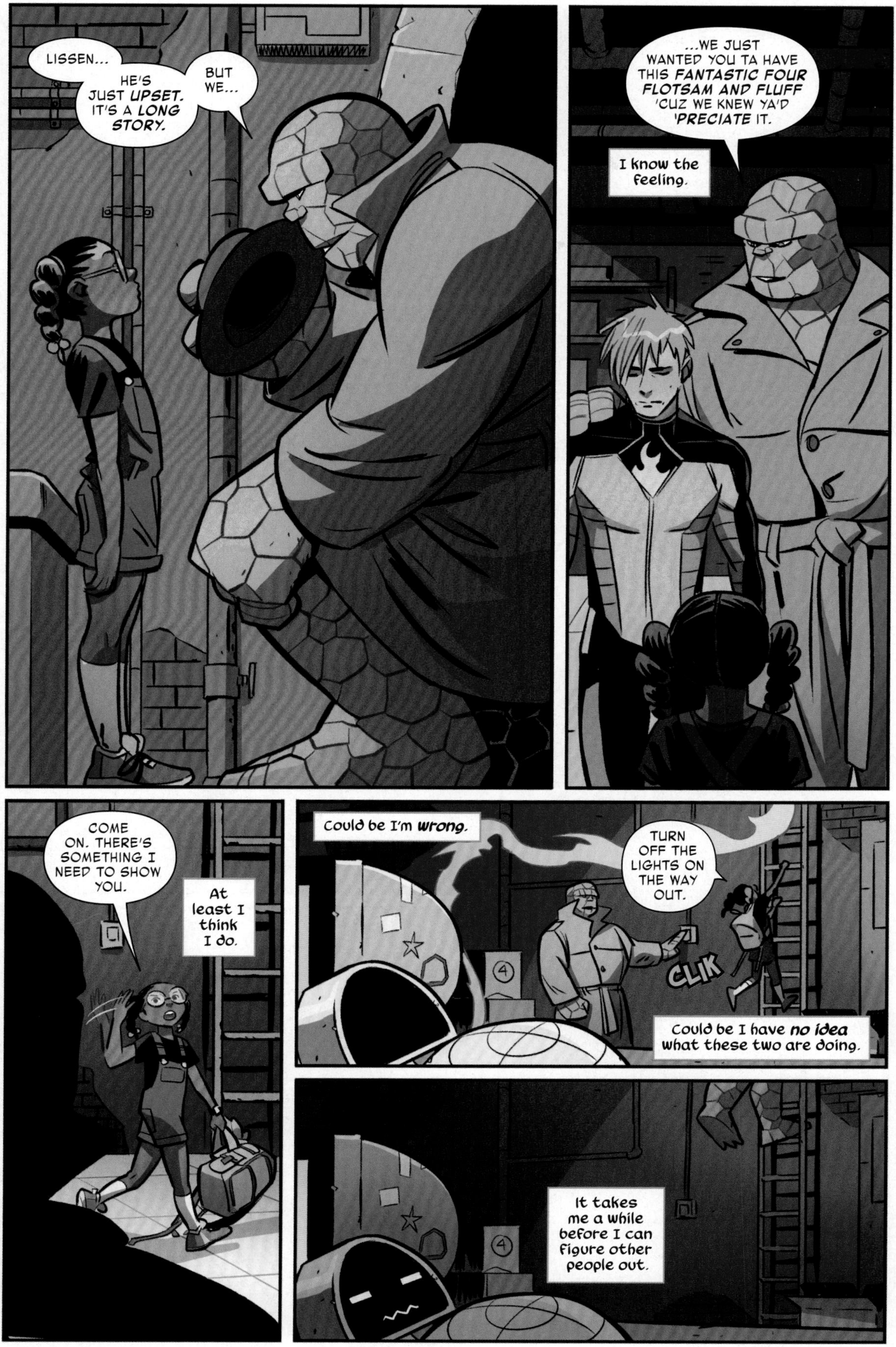

LISSEN...
HE'S JUST UPSET. IT'S A LONG STORY.
BUT WE...
...WE JUST WANTED YOU TA HAVE THIS FANTASTIC FOUR FLOTSAM AND FLUFF 'CUZ WE KNEW YA'D 'PRECIATE IT.
I know the feeling.
COME ON. THERE'S SOMETHING I NEED TO SHOW YOU.
At least I think I do.
Could be I'm wrong.
TURN OFF THE LIGHTS ON THE WAY OUT.
CLIK
Could be I have no idea what these two are doing.
It takes me a while before I can figure other people out.

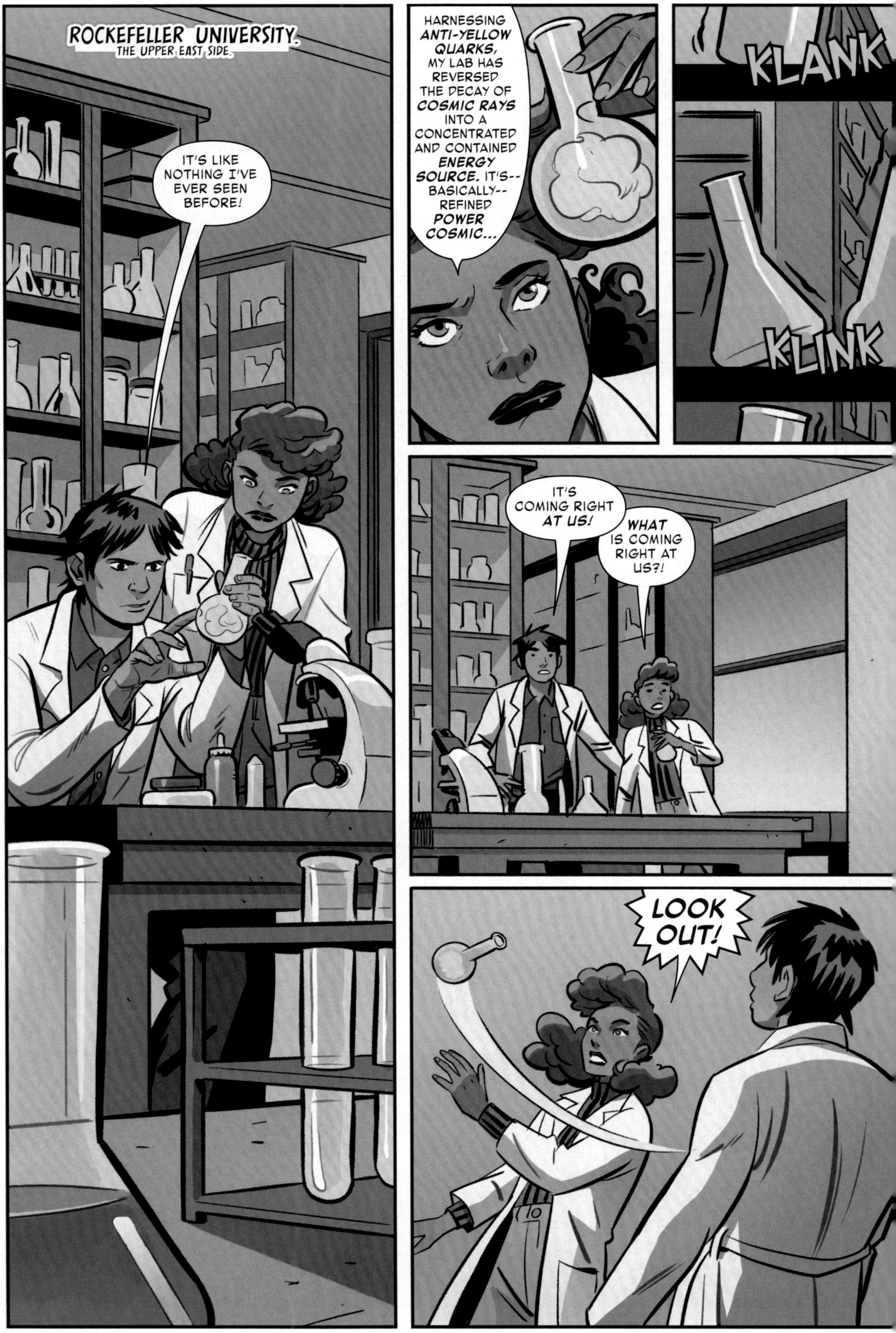
ROCKEFELLER UNIVERSITY.
THE UPPER EAST SIDE.
IT'S LIKE NOTHING I'VE EVER SEEN BEFORE!
HARNESSING ANTI-YELLOW QUARKS, MY LAB HAS REVERSED THE DECAY OF COSMIC RAYS INTO A CONCENTRATED AND CONTAINED ENERGY SOURCE. IT'S--BASICALLY--REFINED POWER COSMIC...
KLANK
KLINK
IT'S COMING RIGHT AT US!
WHAT IS COMING RIGHT AT US?!
LOOK OUT!

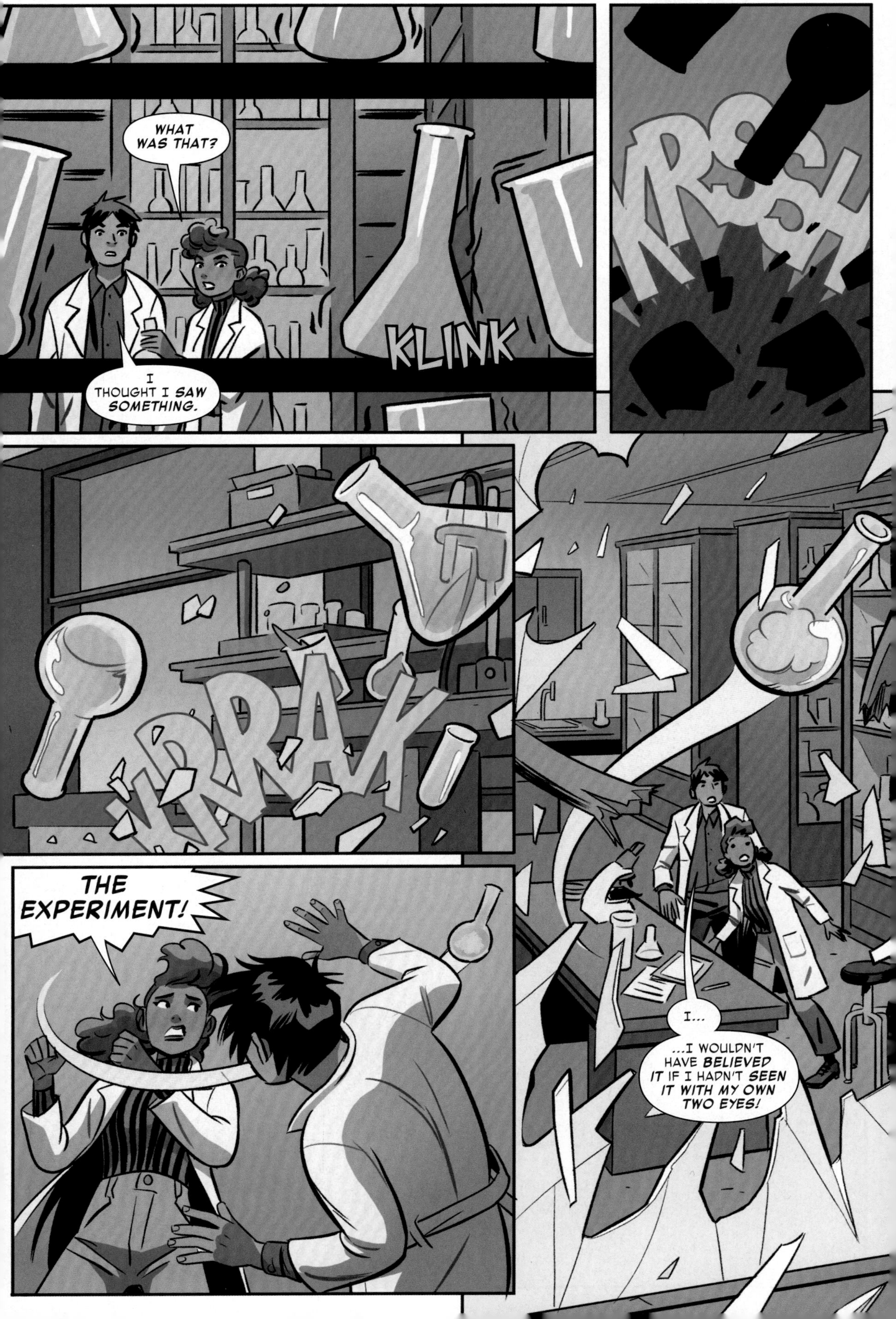
WHAT WAS THAT?
I THOUGHT I SAW SOMETHING.
KLINK
KRRAK
THE EXPERIMENT!
I...
...I WOULDN'T HAVE BELIEVED IT IF I HADN'T SEEN IT WITH MY OWN TWO EYES!

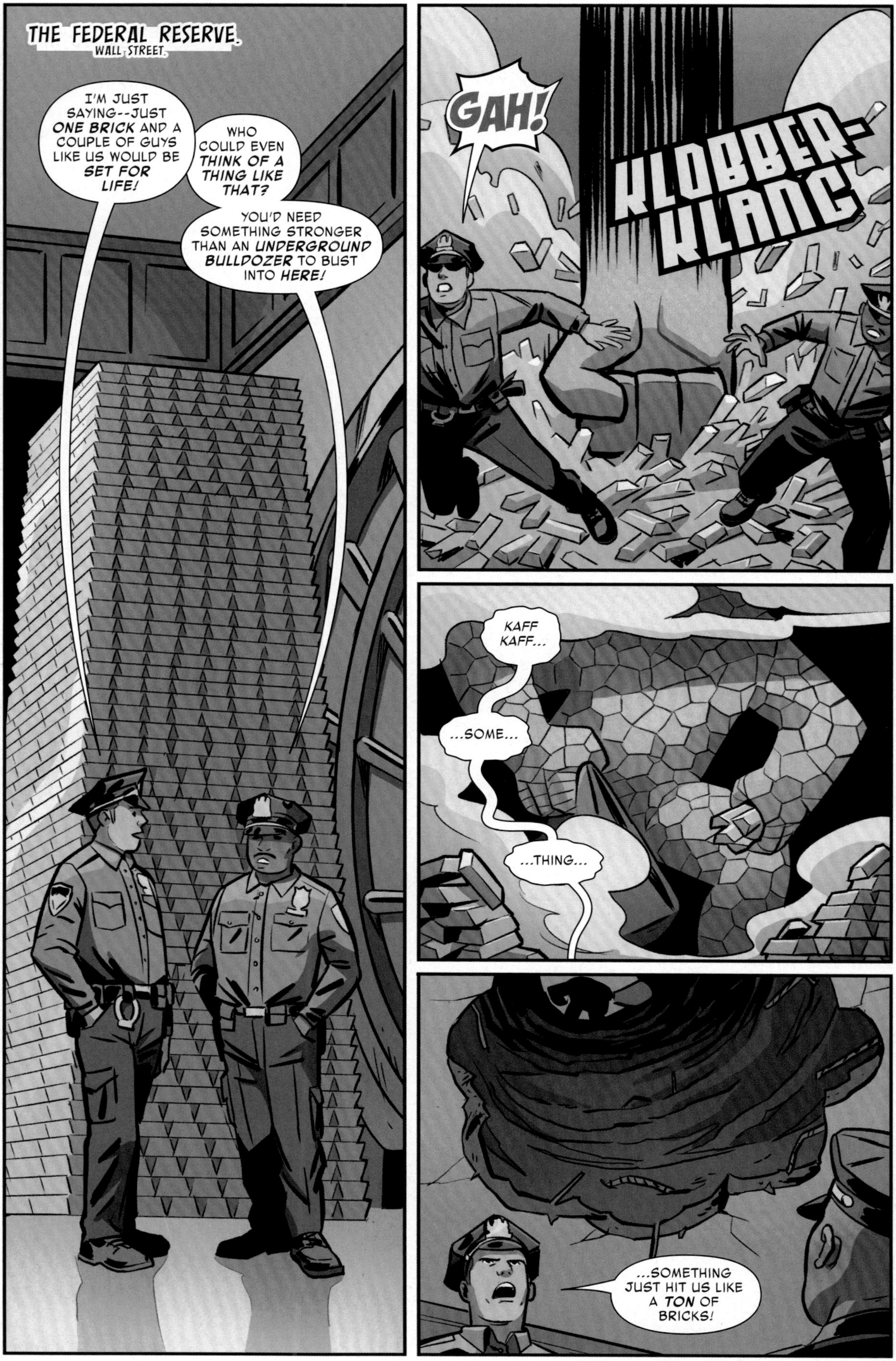
THE FEDERAL RESERVE.
WALL STREET.
I'M JUST SAYING--JUST ONE BRICK AND A COUPLE OF GUYS LIKE US WOULD BE SET FOR LIFE!
WHO COULD EVEN THINK OF A THING LIKE THAT?
YOU'D NEED SOMETHING STRONGER THAN AN UNDERGROUND BULLDOZER TO BUST INTO HERE!
GAH!
KLOBBER-KLANG
KAFF KAFF...
...SOME...
...THING...
...SOMETHING JUST HIT US LIKE A TON OF BRICKS!

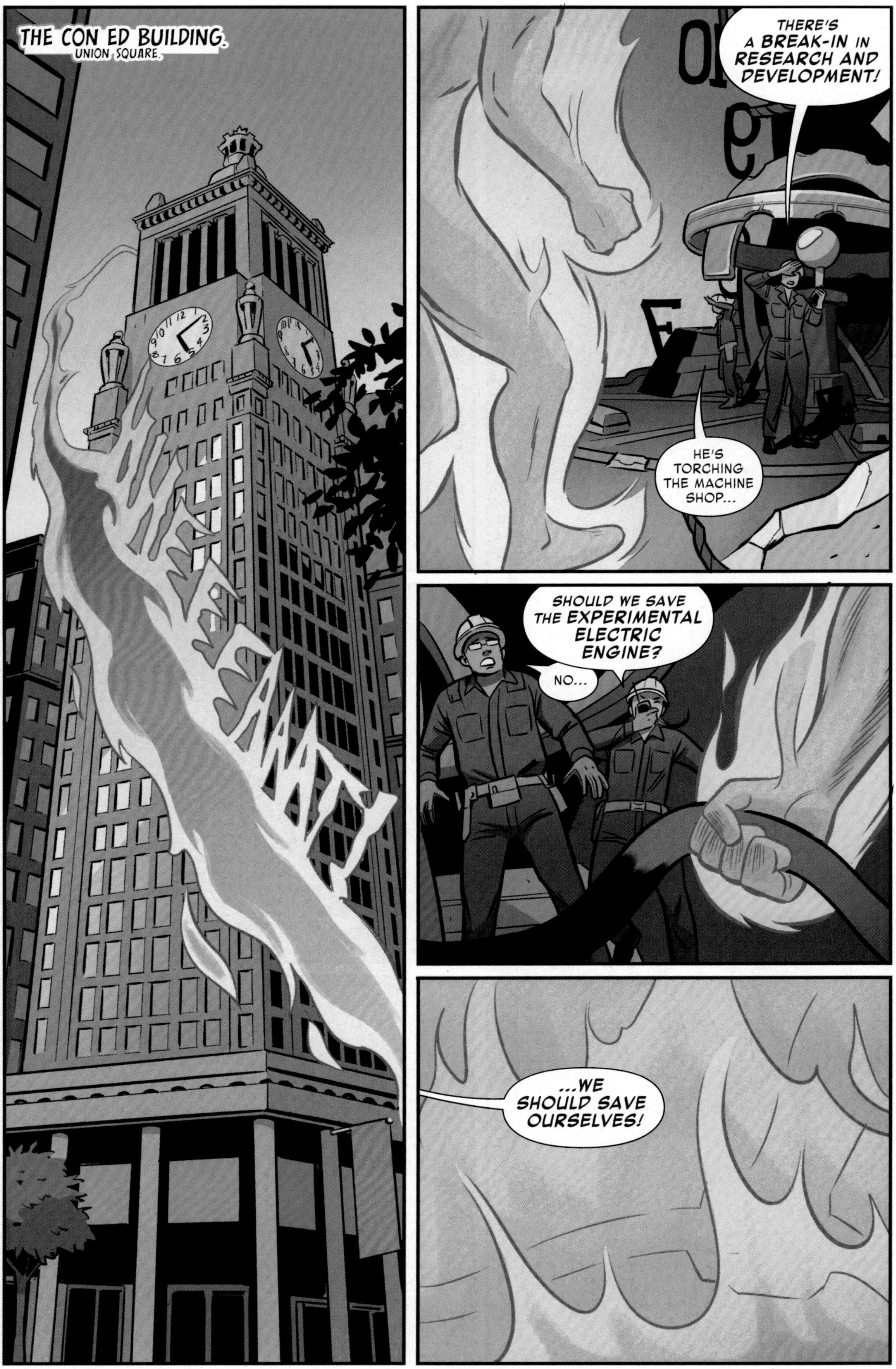
THE CON ED BUILDING.
UNION SQUARE.
THERE'S A BREAK-IN IN RESEARCH AND DEVELOPMENT!
HE'S TORCHING THE MACHINE SHOP...
SHOULD WE SAVE THE EXPERIMENTAL ELECTRIC ENGINE?
NO...
...WE SHOULD SAVE OURSELVES!

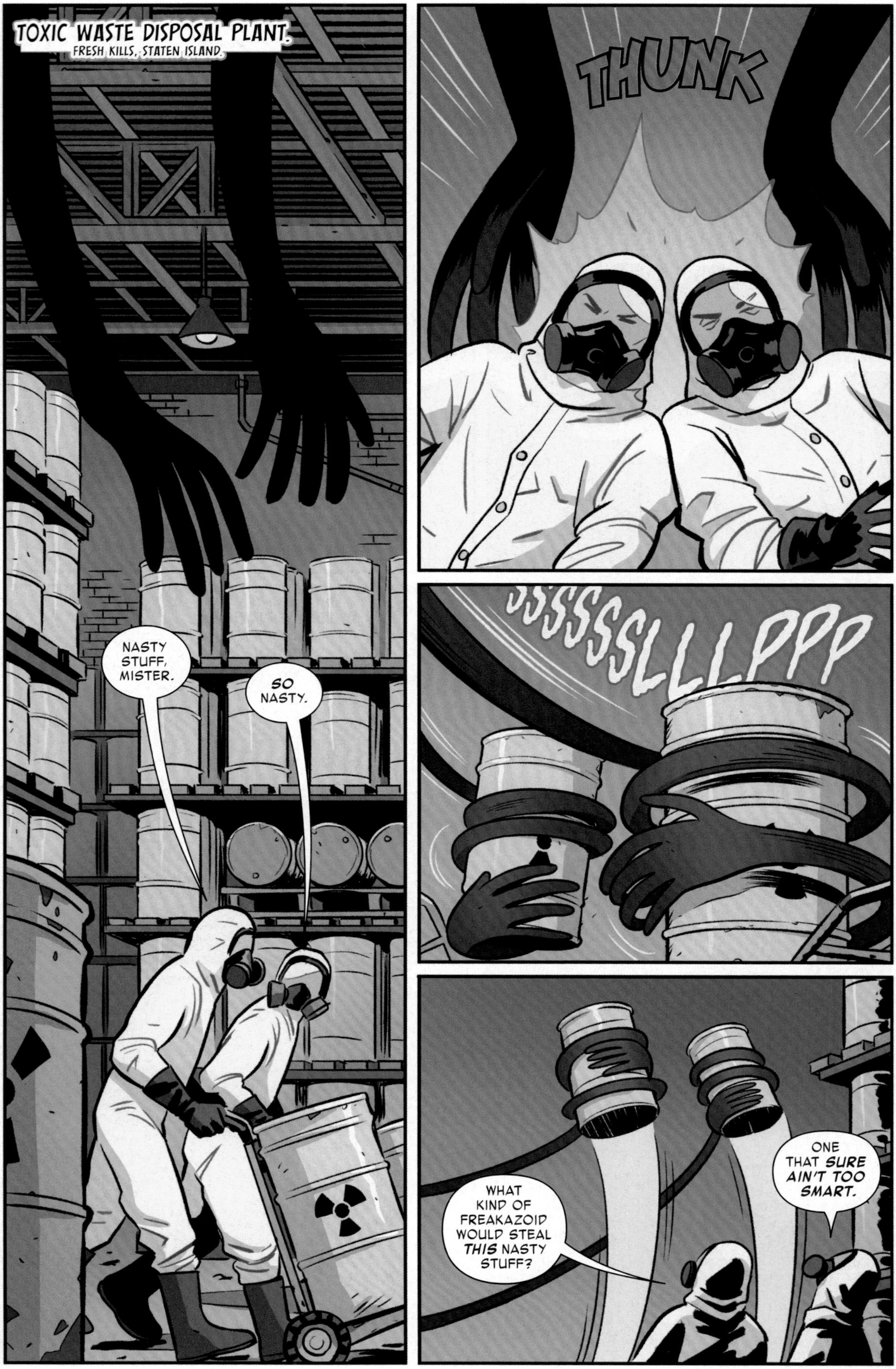
TOXIC WASTE DISPOSAL PLANT.
FRESH KILLS, STATEN ISLAND.
NASTY STUFF, MISTER.
SO NASTY.
THUNK
SSSSSSLLLPPP
WHAT KIND OF FREAKAZOID WOULD STEAL THIS NASTY STUFF?
ONE THAT SURE AIN'T TOO SMART.

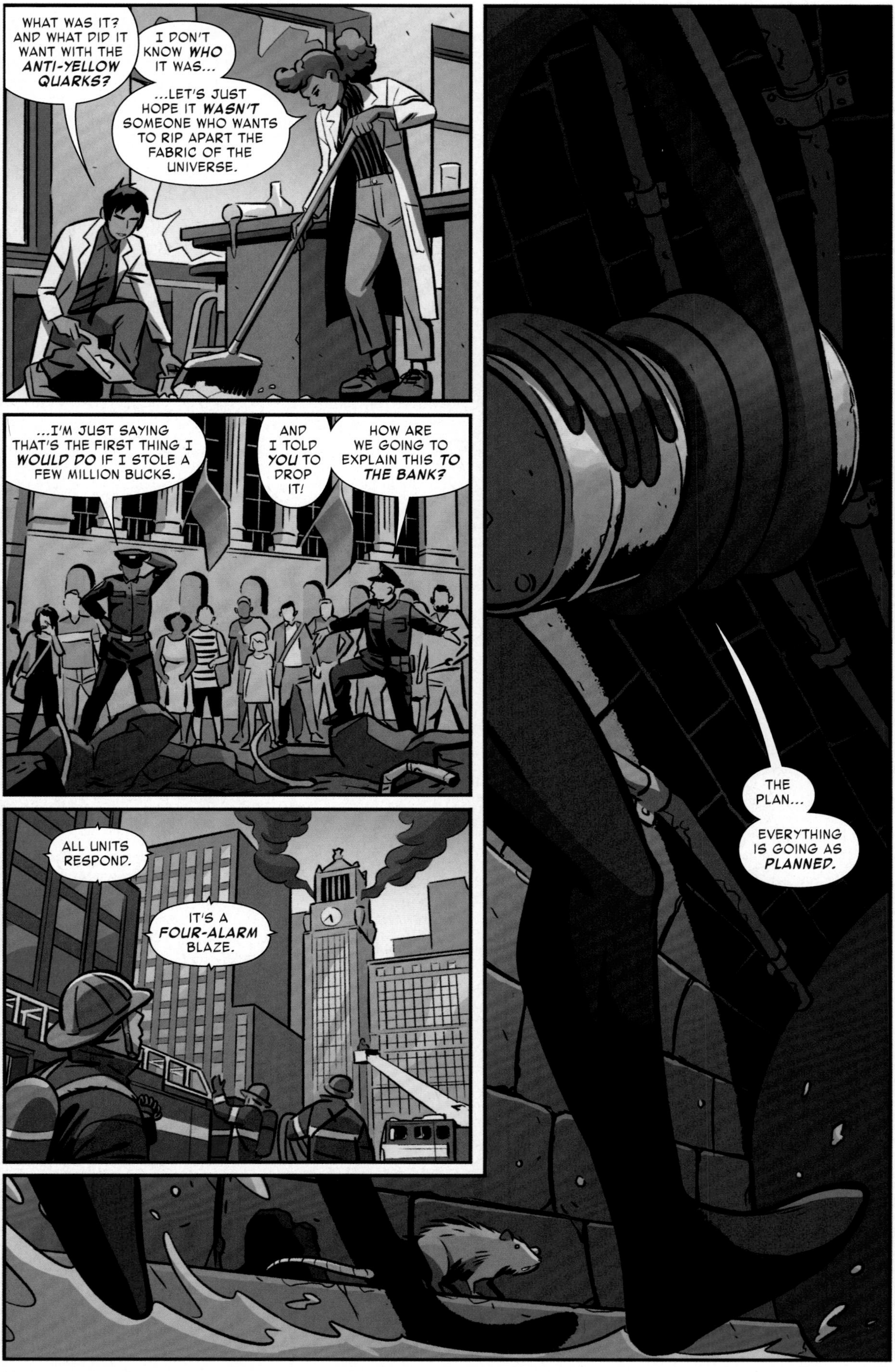
WHAT WAS IT? AND WHAT DID IT WANT WITH THE ANTI-YELLOW QUARKS?
I DON'T KNOW WHO IT WAS...
...LET'S JUST HOPE IT WASN'T SOMEONE WHO WANTS TO RIP APART THE FABRIC OF THE UNIVERSE.
...I'M JUST SAYING THAT'S THE FIRST THING I WOULD DO IF I STOLE A FEW MILLION BUCKS.
AND I TOLD YOU TO DROP IT!
HOW ARE WE GOING TO EXPLAIN THIS TO THE BANK?
ALL UNITS RESPOND.
IT'S A FOUR-ALARM BLAZE.
THE PLAN...
EVERYTHING IS GOING AS PLANNED.

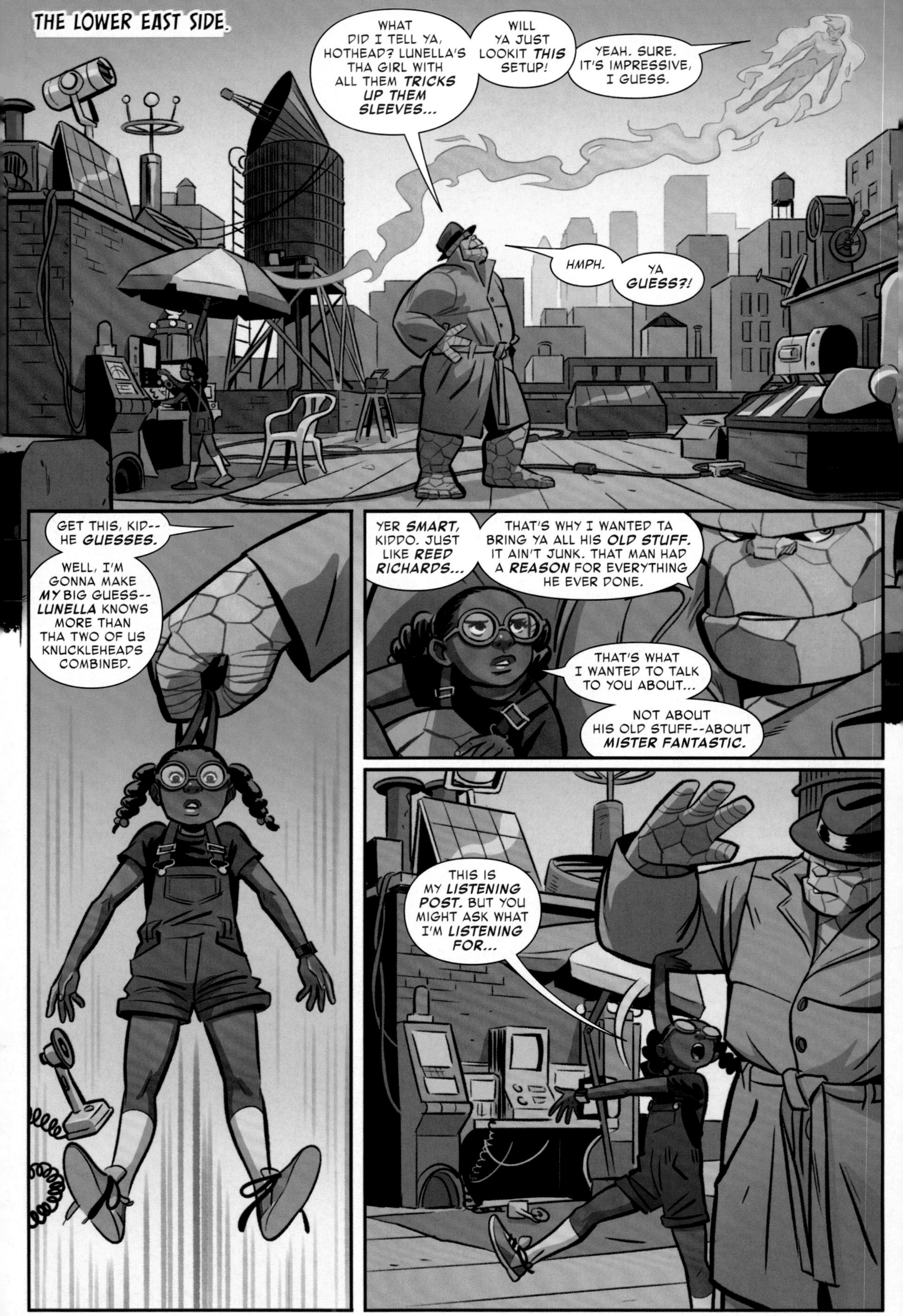
THE LOWER EAST SIDE.
WHAT DID I TELL YA, HOTHEAD? LUNELLA'S THA GIRL WITH ALL THEM TRICKS UP THEM SLEEVES...
WILL YA JUST LOOKIT THIS SETUP!
YEAH. SURE. IT'S IMPRESSIVE, I GUESS.
HMPH.
YA GUESS?!
GET THIS, KID-- HE GUESSES.
WELL, I'M GONNA MAKE MY BIG GUESS-- LUNELLA KNOWS MORE THAN THA TWO OF US KNUCKLEHEADS COMBINED.
YER SMART, KIDDO. JUST LIKE REED RICHARDS...
THAT'S WHY I WANTED TA BRING YA ALL HIS OLD STUFF. IT AIN'T JUNK. THAT MAN HAD A REASON FOR EVERYTHING HE EVER DONE.
THAT'S WHAT I WANTED TO TALK TO YOU ABOUT...
NOT ABOUT HIS OLD STUFF--ABOUT MISTER FANTASTIC.
THIS IS MY LISTENING POST. BUT YOU MIGHT ASK WHAT I'M LISTENING FOR...

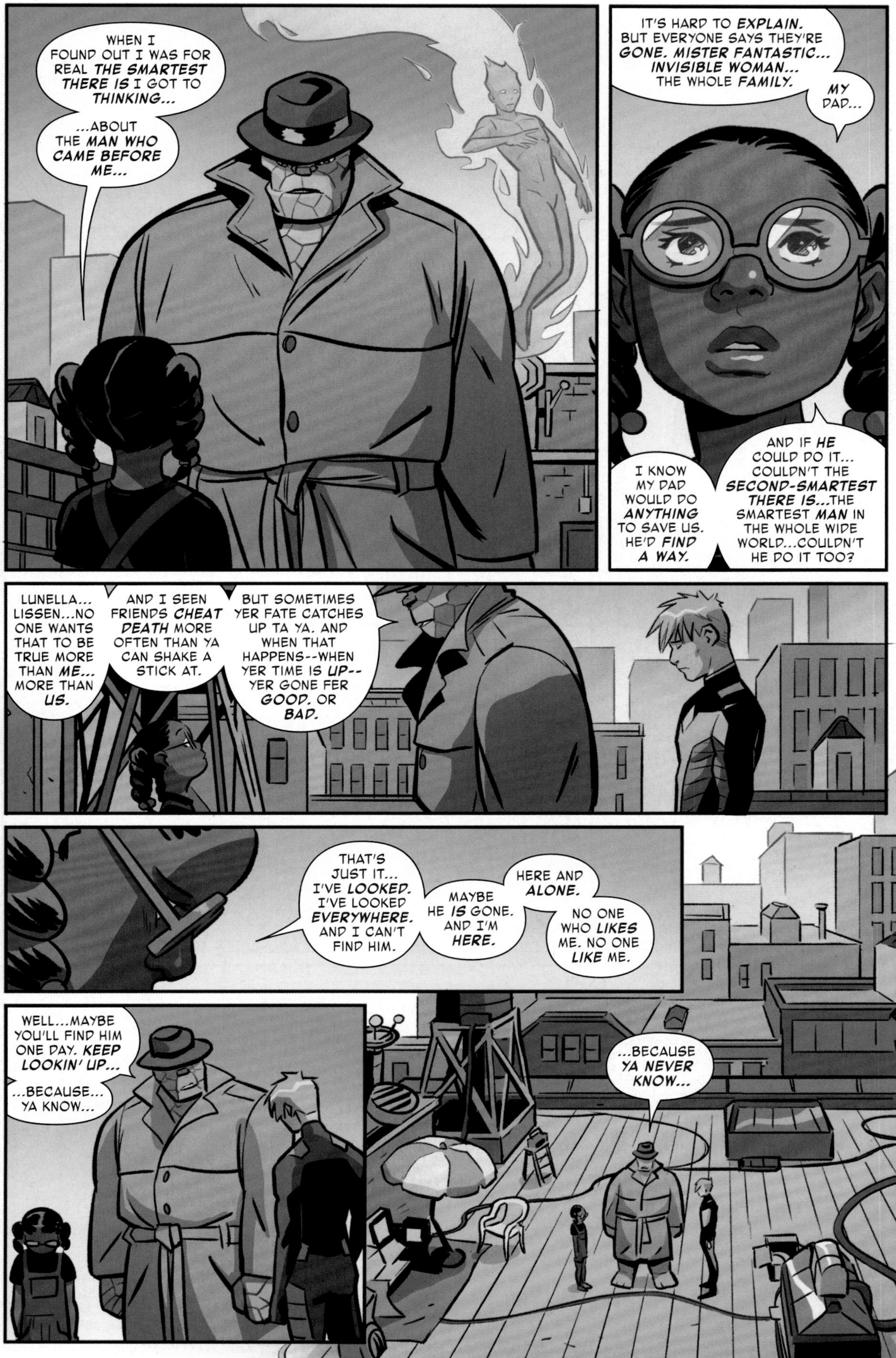

WHEN I FOUND OUT I WAS FOR REAL THE SMARTEST THERE IS I GOT TO THINKING...
...ABOUT THE MAN WHO CAME BEFORE ME...
IT'S HARD TO EXPLAIN. BUT EVERYONE SAYS THEY'RE GONE. MISTER FANTASTIC... INVISIBLE WOMAN... THE WHOLE FAMILY.
MY DAD...
I KNOW MY DAD WOULD DO ANYTHING TO SAVE US. HE'D FIND A WAY.
AND IF HE COULD DO IT... COULDN'T THE SECOND-SMARTEST THERE IS...THE SMARTEST MAN IN THE WHOLE WIDE WORLD...COULDN'T HE DO IT TOO?
LUNELLA... LISSEN...NO ONE WANTS THAT TO BE TRUE MORE THAN ME... MORE THAN US.
AND I SEEN FRIENDS CHEAT DEATH MORE OFTEN THAN YA CAN SHAKE A STICK AT.
BUT SOMETIMES YER FATE CATCHES UP TA YA. AND WHEN THAT HAPPENS--WHEN YER TIME IS UP--YER GONE FER GOOD. OR BAD.
THAT'S JUST IT... I'VE LOOKED. I'VE LOOKED EVERYWHERE. AND I CAN'T FIND HIM.
MAYBE HE IS GONE. AND I'M HERE.
HERE AND ALONE.
NO ONE WHO LIKES ME. NO ONE LIKE ME.
WELL...MAYBE YOU'LL FIND HIM ONE DAY. KEEP LOOKIN' UP...
...BECAUSE... YA KNOW...
...BECAUSE YA NEVER KNOW...

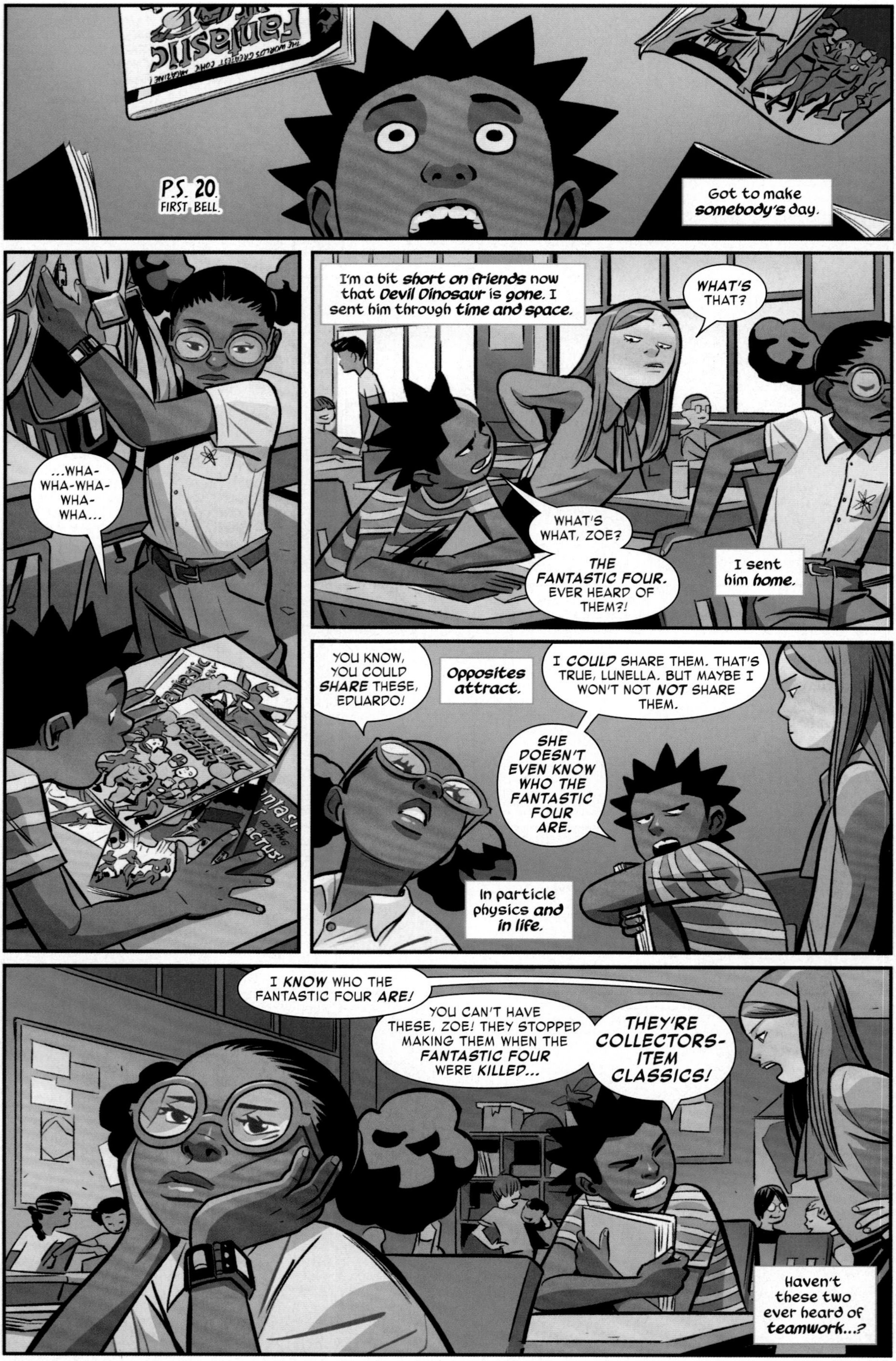
THE FANTASTIC FOUR
THE WORLD'S GREATEST COMIC MAGAZINE!
P.S. 20.
FIRST BELL.
Got to make somebody's day.
...WHA-WHA-WHA-WHA-WHA...
I'm a bit short on friends now that Devil Dinosaur is gone. I sent him through time and space.
WHAT'S THAT?
WHAT'S WHAT, ZOE?
THE FANTASTIC FOUR. EVER HEARD OF THEM?!
I sent him home.
YOU KNOW, YOU COULD SHARE THESE, EDUARDO!
Opposites attract.
I COULD SHARE THEM. THAT'S TRUE, LUNELLA. BUT MAYBE I WON'T NOT NOT SHARE THEM.
SHE DOESN'T EVEN KNOW WHO THE FANTASTIC FOUR ARE.
In particle physics and in life.
I KNOW WHO THE FANTASTIC FOUR ARE!
YOU CAN'T HAVE THESE, ZOE! THEY STOPPED MAKING THEM WHEN THE FANTASTIC FOUR WERE KILLED...
THEY'RE COLLECTORS-ITEM CLASSICS!
Haven't these two ever heard of teamwork...?

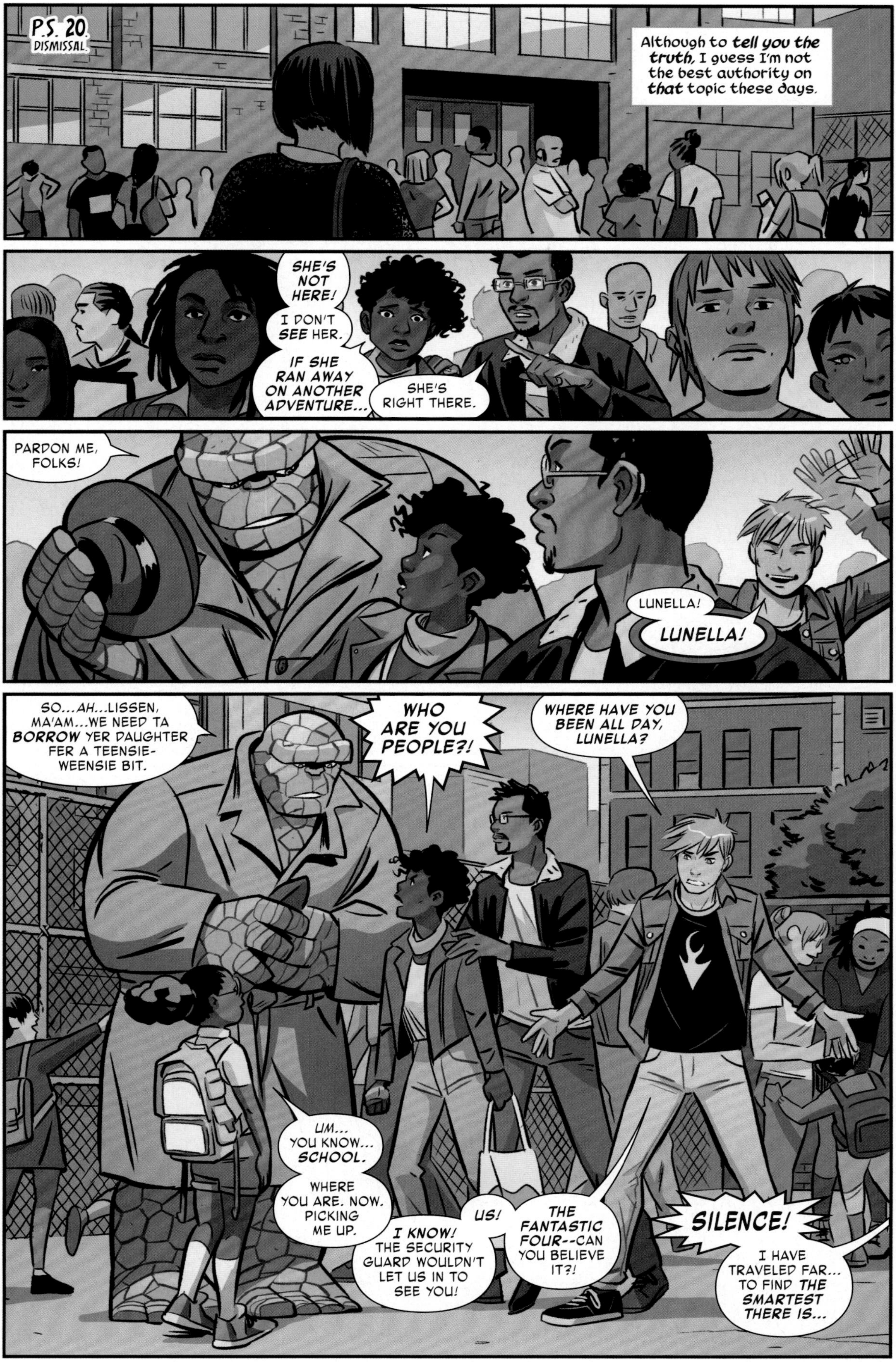
P.S. 20. DISMISSAL.
Although to tell you the truth, I guess I'm not the best authority on that topic these days.
SHE'S NOT HERE!
I DON'T SEE HER.
IF SHE RAN AWAY ON ANOTHER ADVENTURE...
SHE'S RIGHT THERE.
PARDON ME, FOLKS!
LUNELLA!
LUNELLA!
SO...AH...LISSEN, MA'AM...WE NEED TA BORROW YER DAUGHTER FER A TEENSIE-WEENSIE BIT.
WHO ARE YOU PEOPLE?!
WHERE HAVE YOU BEEN ALL DAY, LUNELLA?
UM... YOU KNOW... SCHOOL.
WHERE YOU ARE. NOW. PICKING ME UP.
I KNOW! THE SECURITY GUARD WOULDN'T LET US IN TO SEE YOU!
US!
THE FANTASTIC FOUR--CAN YOU BELIEVE IT?!
SILENCE!
I HAVE TRAVELED FAR... TO FIND THE SMARTEST THERE IS...

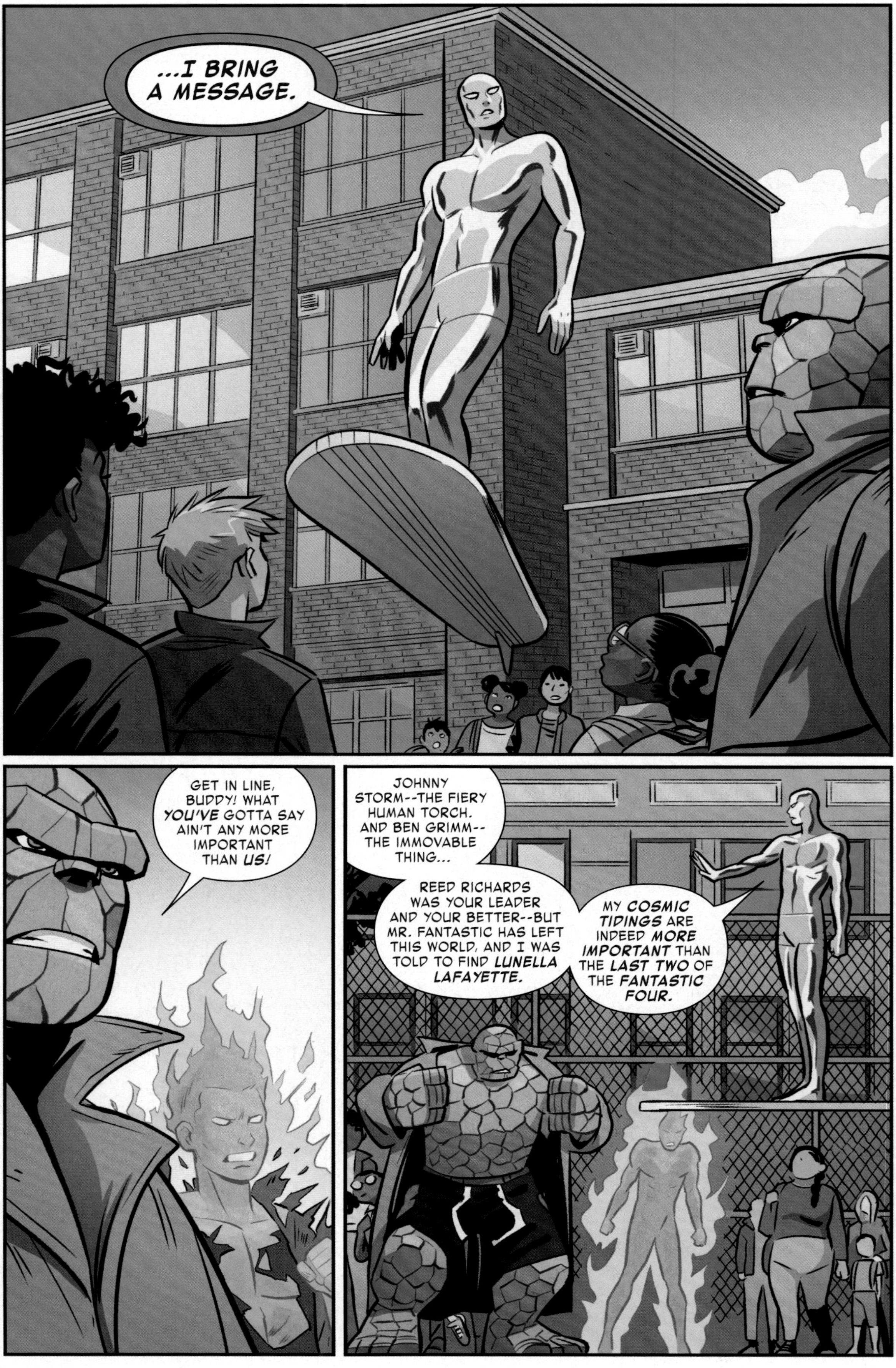
...I BRING A MESSAGE.
GET IN LINE, BUDDY! WHAT *YOU'VE* GOTTA SAY AIN'T ANY MORE IMPORTANT THAN *US!*
JOHNNY STORM--THE FIERY HUMAN TORCH. AND BEN GRIMM--THE IMMOVABLE THING...
REED RICHARDS WAS YOUR LEADER AND YOUR BETTER--BUT MR. FANTASTIC HAS LEFT THIS WORLD, AND I WAS TOLD TO FIND *LUNELLA LAFAYETTE.*
MY *COSMIC TIDINGS* ARE INDEED *MORE IMPORTANT* THAN THE *LAST TWO* OF THE *FANTASTIC FOUR.*

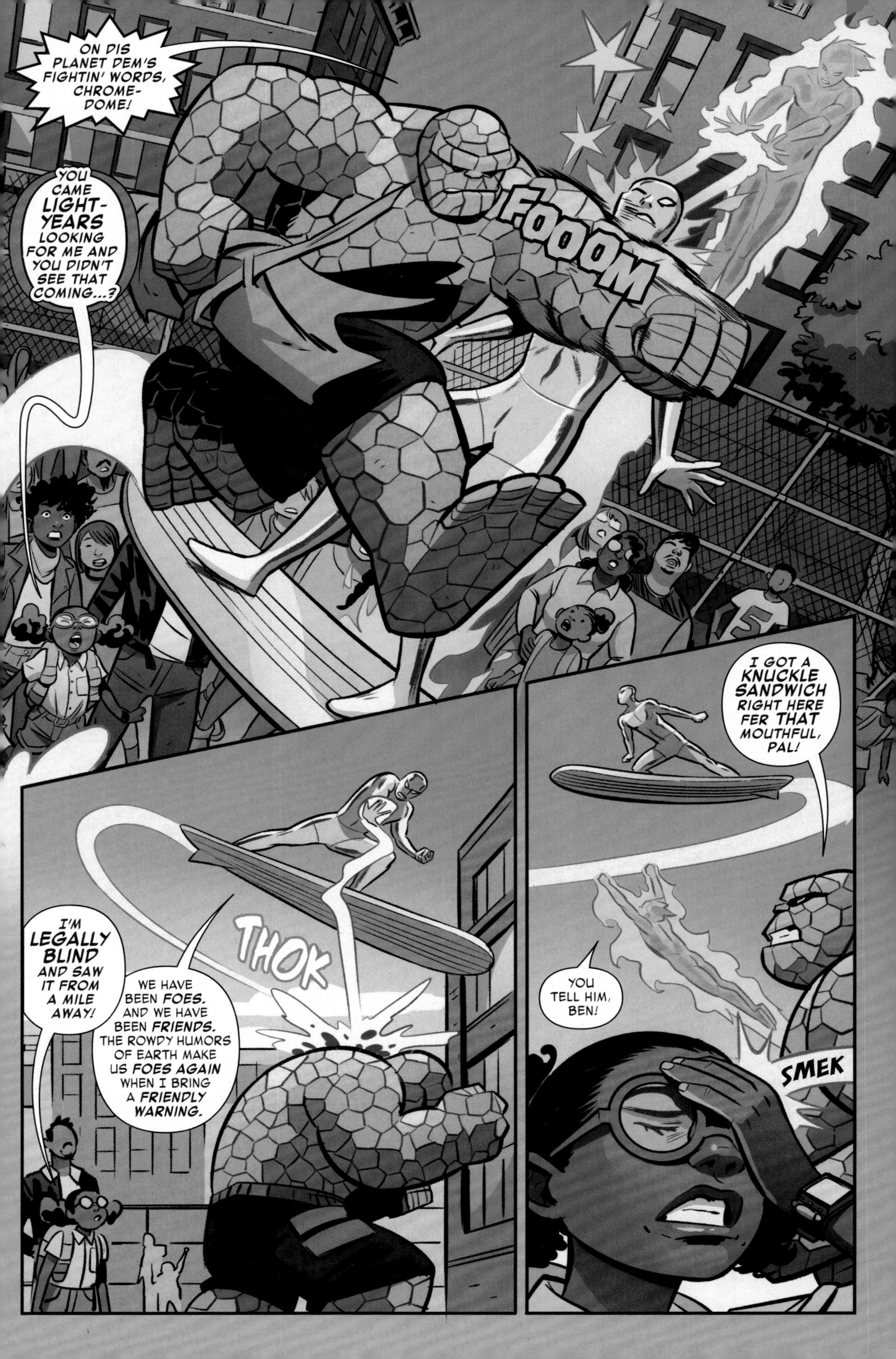
ON DIS PLANET DEM'S FIGHTIN' WORDS, CHROME-DOME!
YOU CAME LIGHT-YEARS LOOKING FOR ME AND YOU DIDN'T SEE THAT COMING...?
FOOOM
I'M LEGALLY BLIND AND SAW IT FROM A MILE AWAY!
WE HAVE BEEN FOES. AND WE HAVE BEEN FRIENDS. THE ROWDY HUMORS OF EARTH MAKE US FOES AGAIN WHEN I BRING A FRIENDLY WARNING.
THOK
I GOT A KNUCKLE SANDWICH RIGHT HERE FER THAT MOUTHFUL, PAL!
YOU TELL HIM, BEN!
SMEK

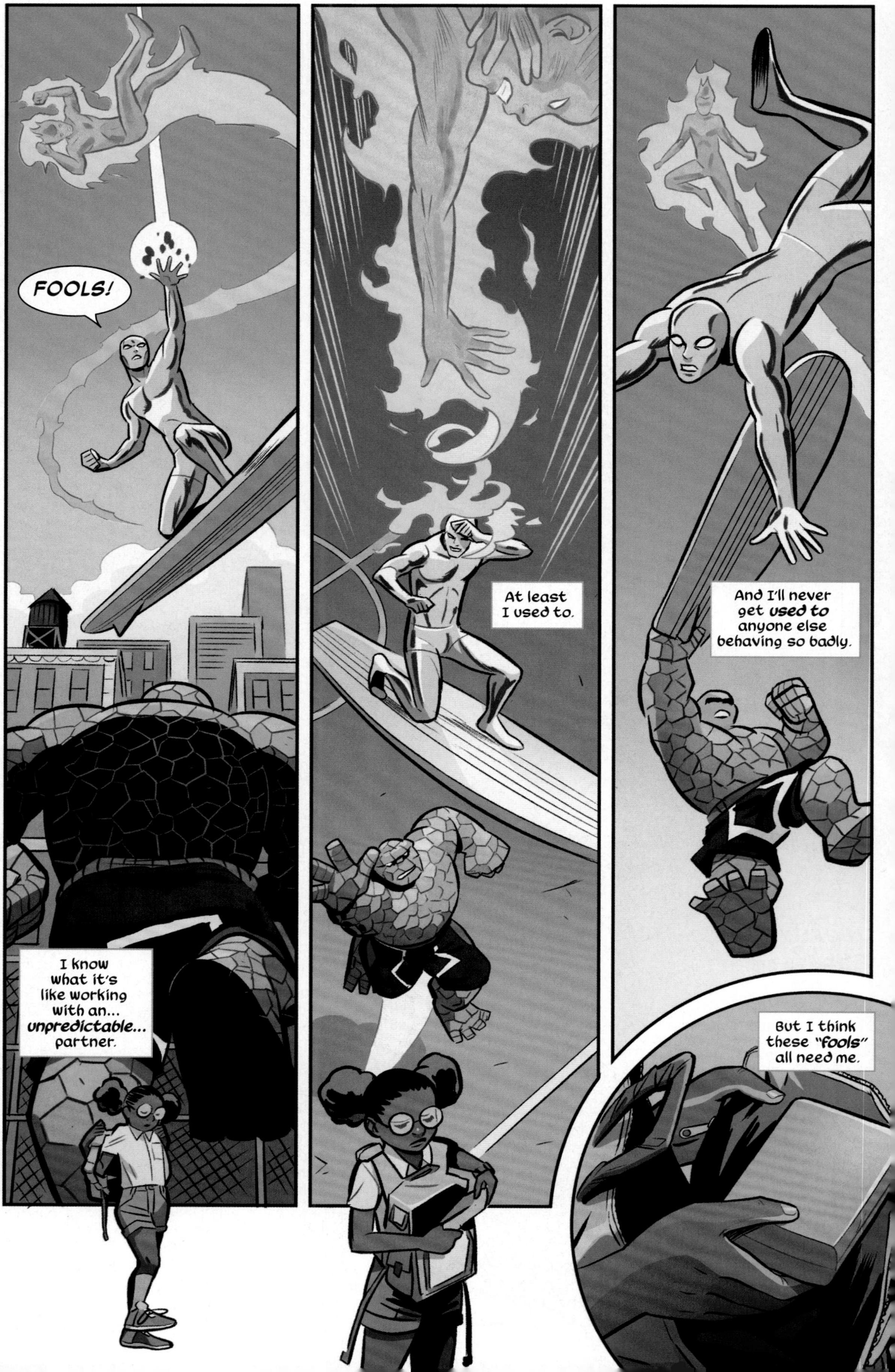
FOOLS!
I know what it's like working with an... *unpredictable...* partner.
At least I used to.
And I'll never get *used to* anyone else behaving so badly.
But I think these *"fools"* all need me.

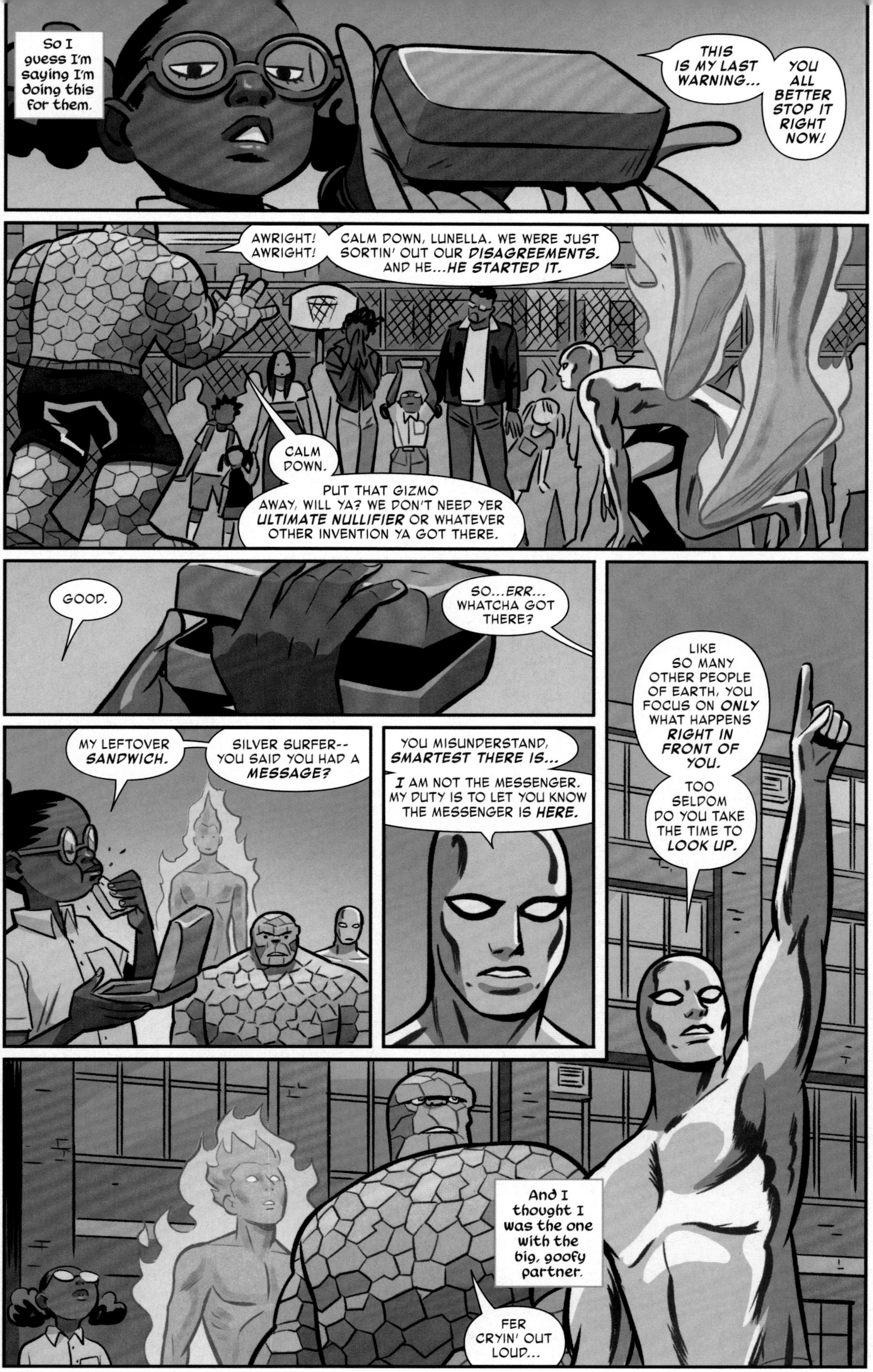

So I guess I'm saying I'm doing this for them.
THIS IS MY LAST WARNING...
YOU ALL BETTER STOP IT RIGHT NOW!
AWRIGHT! AWRIGHT!
CALM DOWN, LUNELLA. WE WERE JUST SORTIN' OUT OUR DISAGREEMENTS. AND HE...HE STARTED IT.
CALM DOWN.
PUT THAT GIZMO AWAY, WILL YA? WE DON'T NEED YER ULTIMATE NULLIFIER OR WHATEVER OTHER INVENTION YA GOT THERE.
GOOD.
SO...ERR... WHATCHA GOT THERE?
MY LEFTOVER SANDWICH.
SILVER SURFER-- YOU SAID YOU HAD A MESSAGE?
YOU MISUNDERSTAND, SMARTEST THERE IS...
I AM NOT THE MESSENGER. MY DUTY IS TO LET YOU KNOW THE MESSENGER IS HERE.
LIKE SO MANY OTHER PEOPLE OF EARTH, YOU FOCUS ON ONLY WHAT HAPPENS RIGHT IN FRONT OF YOU.
TOO SELDOM DO YOU TAKE THE TIME TO LOOK UP.
And I thought I was the one with the big, goofy partner.
FER CRYIN' OUT LOUD...

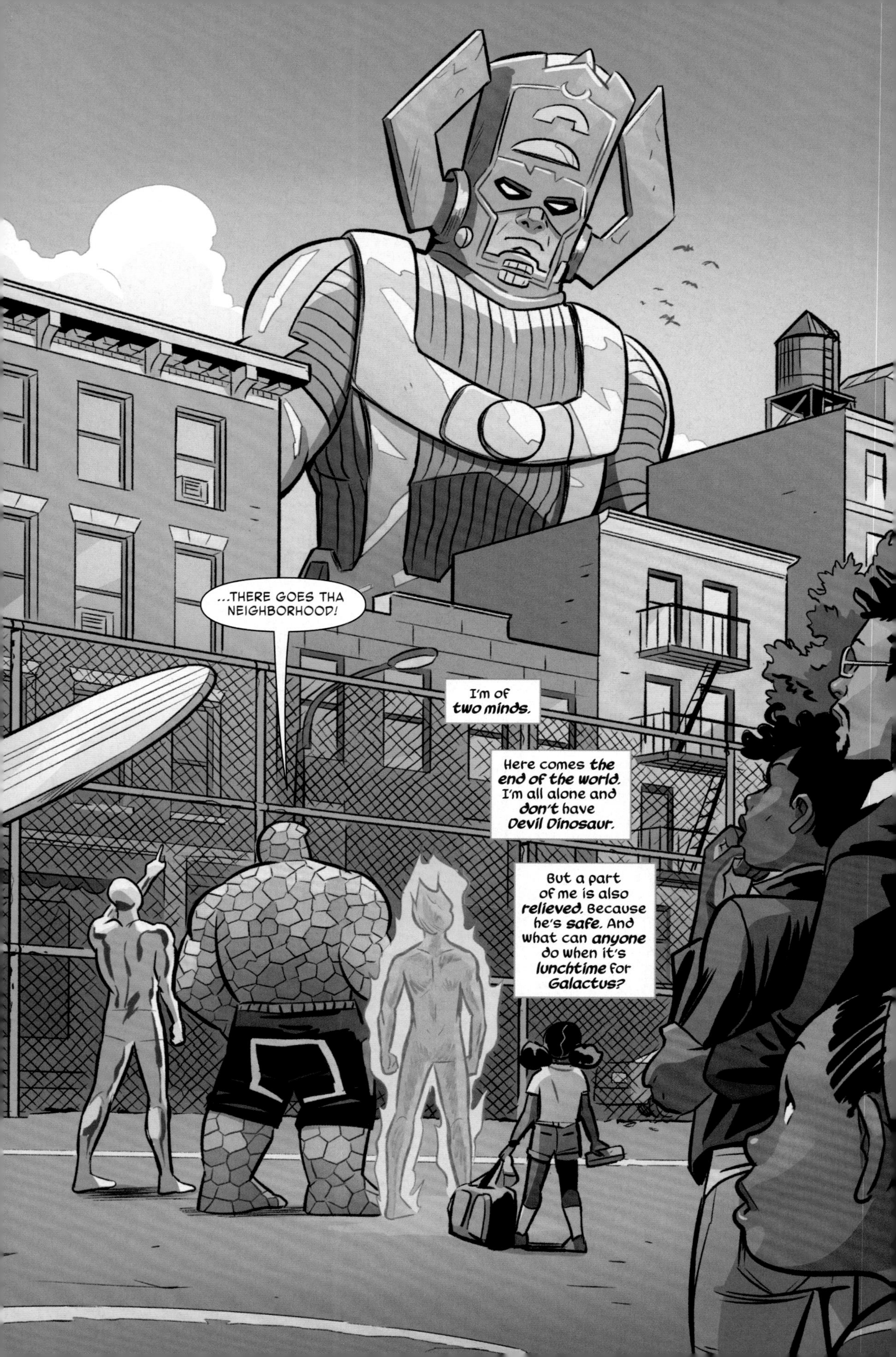
...THERE GOES THA NEIGHBORHOOD!
I'm of two minds.
Here comes the end of the world. I'm all alone and don't have Devil Dinosaur.
But a part of me is also relieved. Because he's safe. And what can anyone do when it's lunchtime for Galactus?

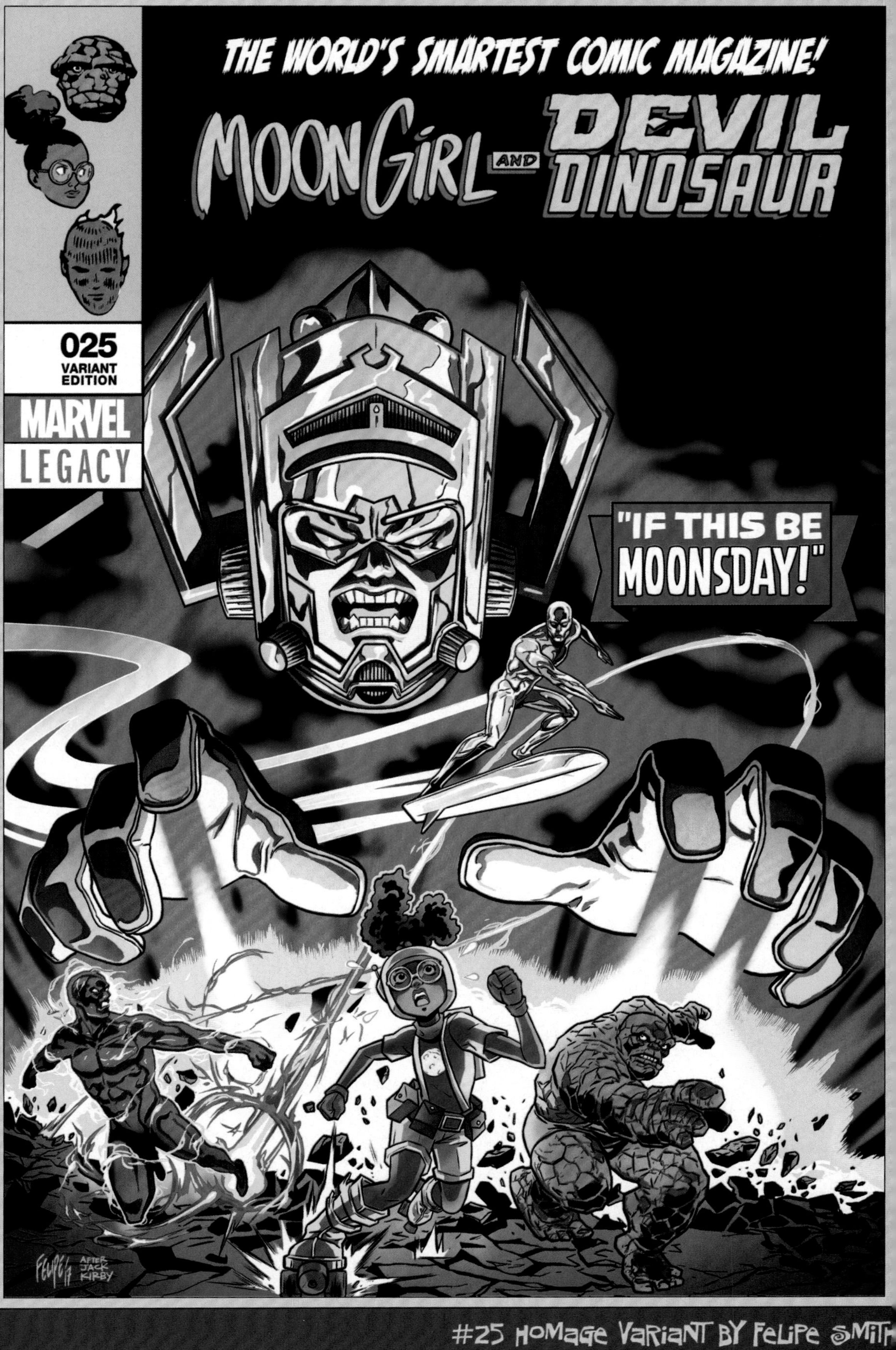
THE WORLD'S SMARTEST COMIC MAGAZINE!
MOON GIRL AND DEVIL DINOSAUR
025
VARIANT EDITION
MARVEL
LEGACY
"IF THIS BE MOONSDAY!"
FELIPE '17 AFTER JACK KIRBY

#25 HOMAGE VARIANT BY FELIPE SMITH

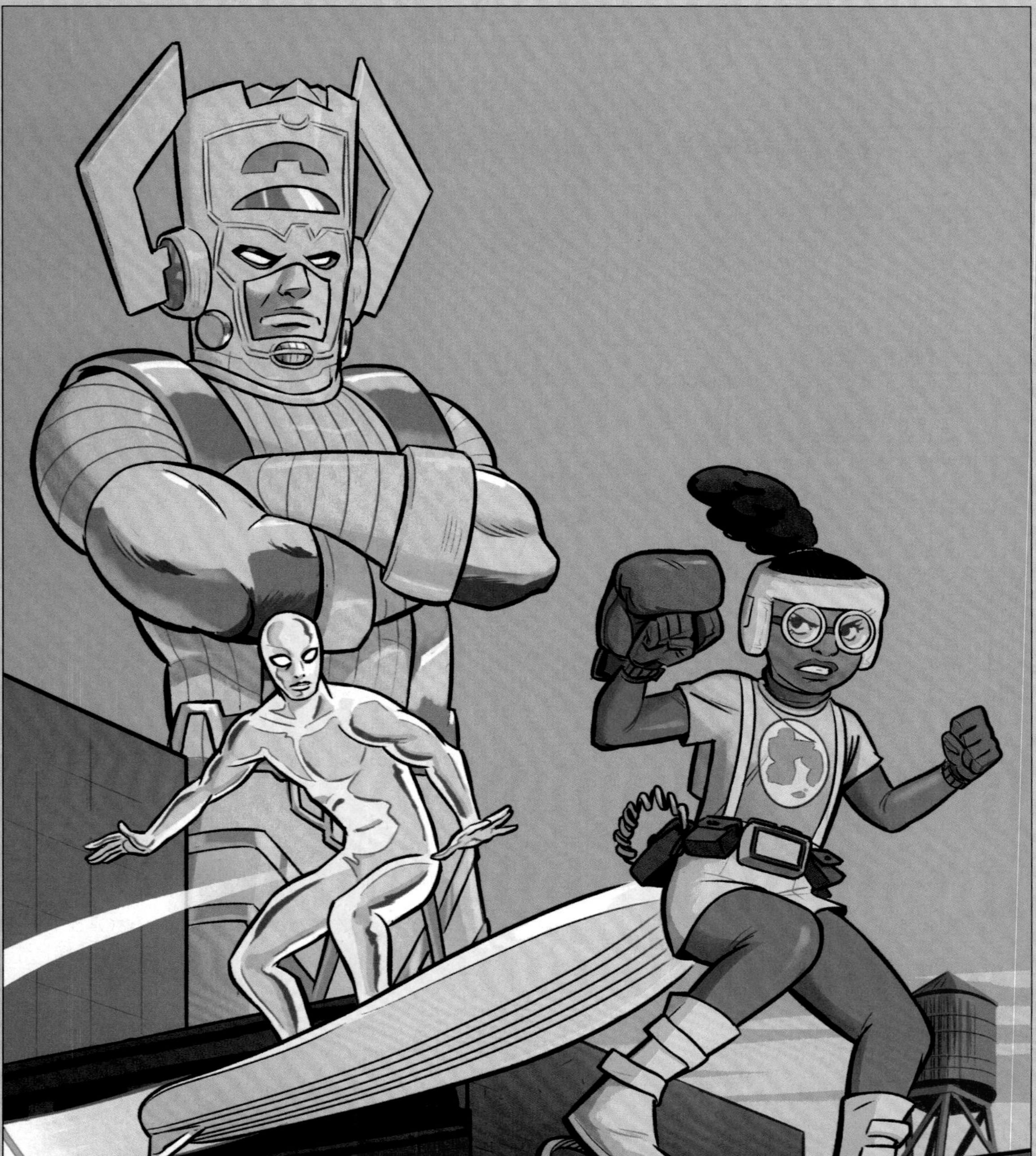

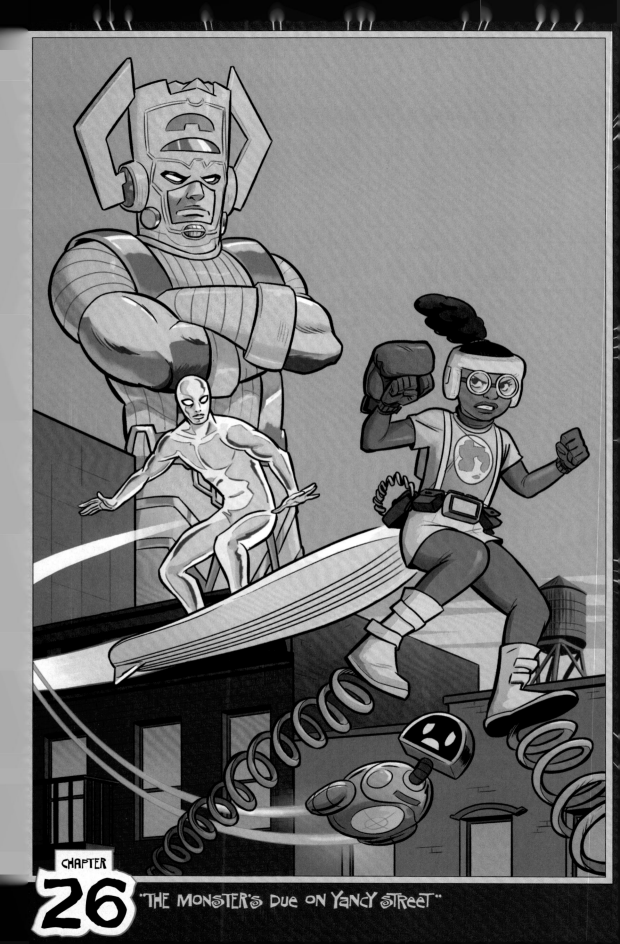

CHAPTER 26

"THE MONSTER'S DUE ON YANCY STREET"

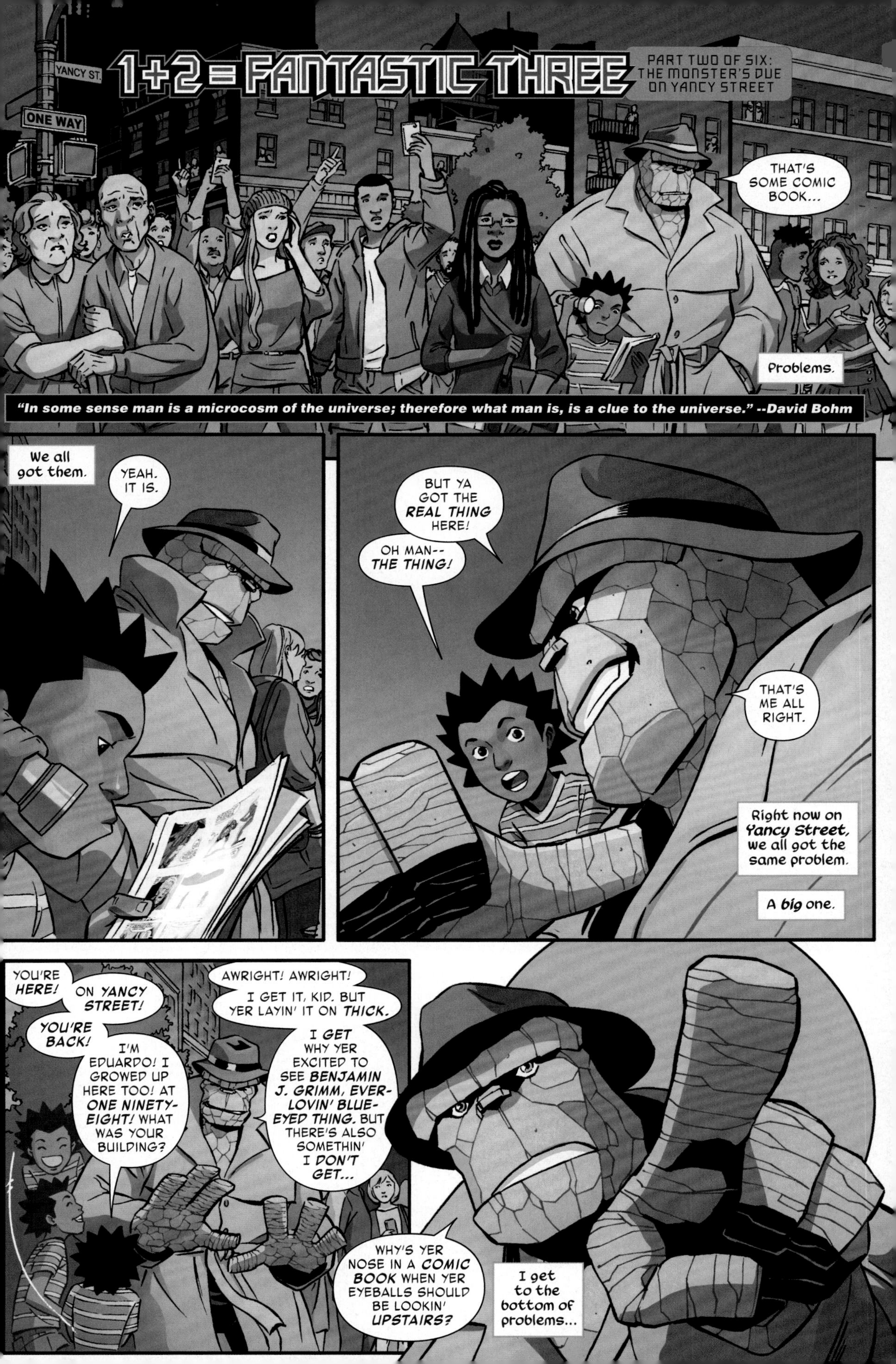
1+2 = FANTASTIC THREE
PART TWO OF SIX: THE MONSTER'S DUE ON YANCY STREET
YANCY ST.
ONE WAY
THAT'S SOME COMIC BOOK...
Problems.
"In some sense man is a microcosm of the universe; therefore what man is, is a clue to the universe." --David Bohm
We all got them.
YEAH. IT IS.
BUT YA GOT THE REAL THING HERE!
OH MAN-- THE THING!
THAT'S ME ALL RIGHT.
Right now on Yancy Street, we all got the same problem.
A big one.
YOU'RE HERE!
ON YANCY STREET!
YOU'RE BACK!
I'M EDUARDO! I GROWED UP HERE TOO! AT ONE NINETY-EIGHT! WHAT WAS YOUR BUILDING?
AWRIGHT! AWRIGHT!
I GET IT, KID. BUT YER LAYIN' IT ON THICK.
I GET WHY YER EXCITED TO SEE BENJAMIN J. GRIMM, EVER-LOVIN' BLUE-EYED THING. BUT THERE'S ALSO SOMETHIN' I DON'T GET...
WHY'S YER NOSE IN A COMIC BOOK WHEN YER EYEBALLS SHOULD BE LOOKIN' UPSTAIRS?
I get to the bottom of problems...

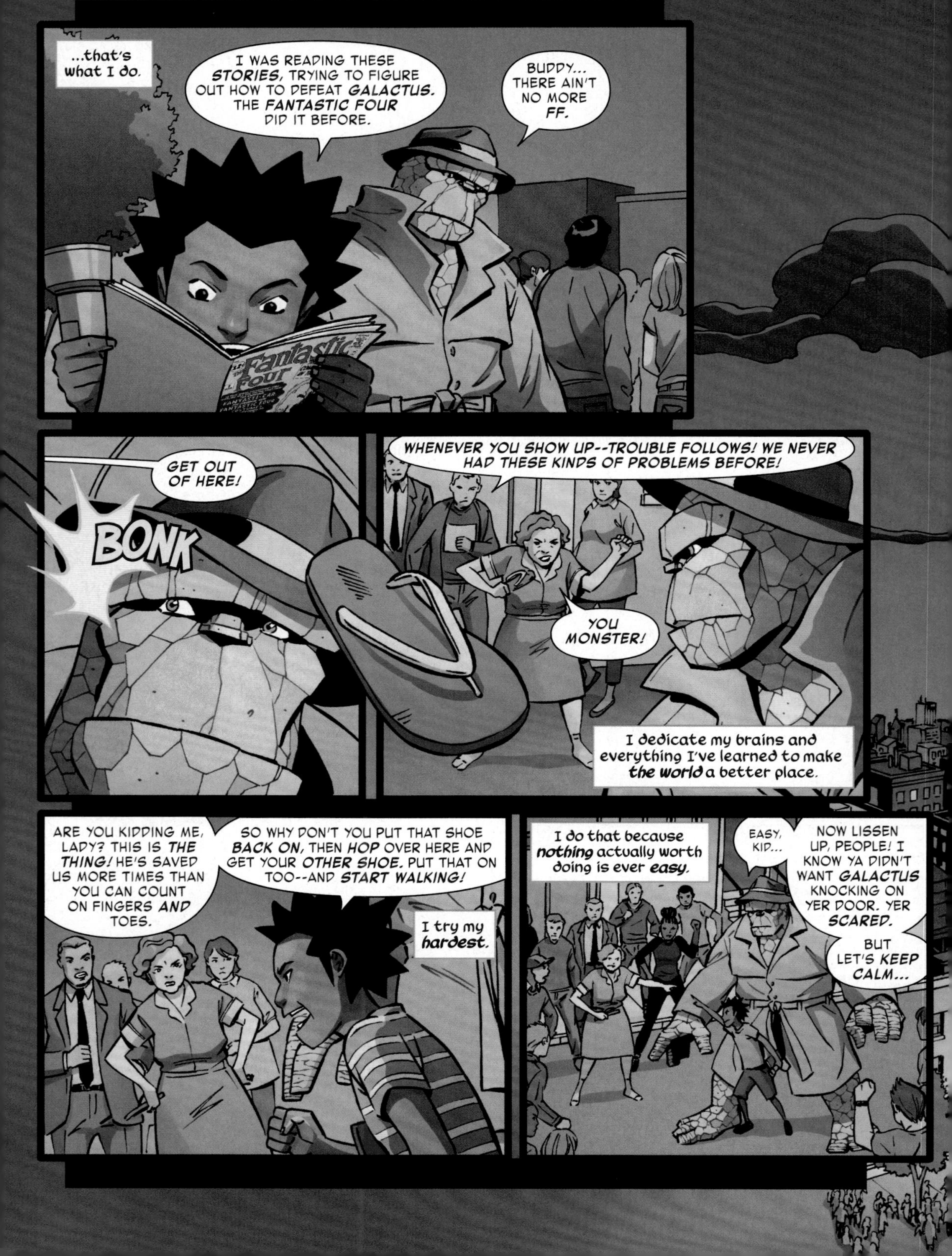

...that's what I do.
I WAS READING THESE STORIES, TRYING TO FIGURE OUT HOW TO DEFEAT GALACTUS. THE FANTASTIC FOUR DID IT BEFORE.
BUDDY... THERE AIN'T NO MORE FF.
Fantastic Four
GET OUT OF HERE!
BONK
WHENEVER YOU SHOW UP--TROUBLE FOLLOWS! WE NEVER HAD THESE KINDS OF PROBLEMS BEFORE!
YOU MONSTER!
I dedicate my brains and everything I've learned to make the world a better place.
ARE YOU KIDDING ME, LADY? THIS IS THE THING! HE'S SAVED US MORE TIMES THAN YOU CAN COUNT ON FINGERS AND TOES.
SO WHY DON'T YOU PUT THAT SHOE BACK ON, THEN HOP OVER HERE AND GET YOUR OTHER SHOE. PUT THAT ON TOO--AND START WALKING!
I try my hardest.
I do that because nothing actually worth doing is ever easy.
EASY, KID...
NOW LISSEN UP, PEOPLE! I KNOW YA DIDN'T WANT GALACTUS KNOCKING ON YER DOOR. YER SCARED.
BUT LET'S KEEP CALM...

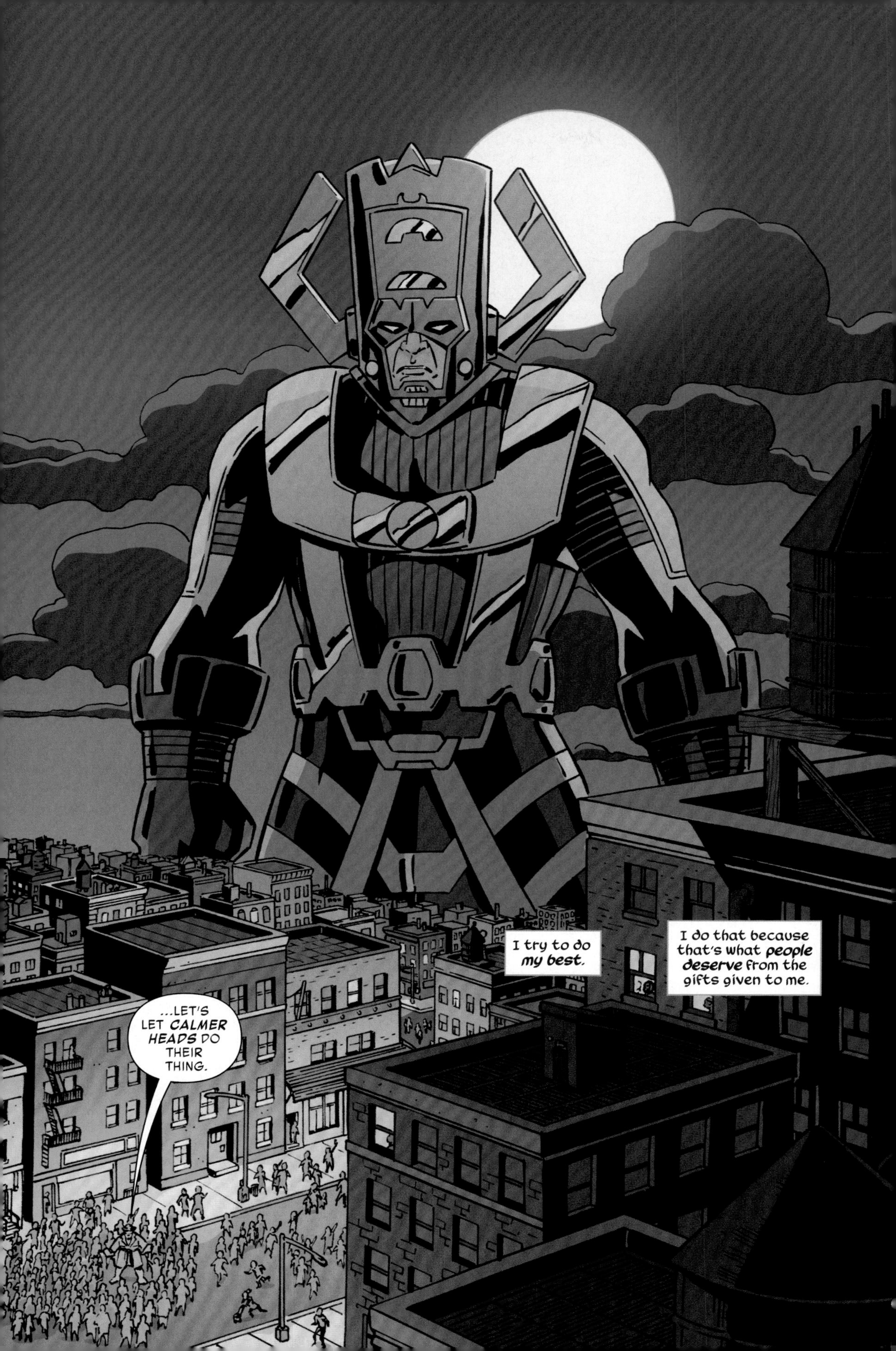
...LET'S LET CALMER HEADS DO THEIR THING.
I try to do my best.
I do that because that's what people deserve from the gifts given to me.

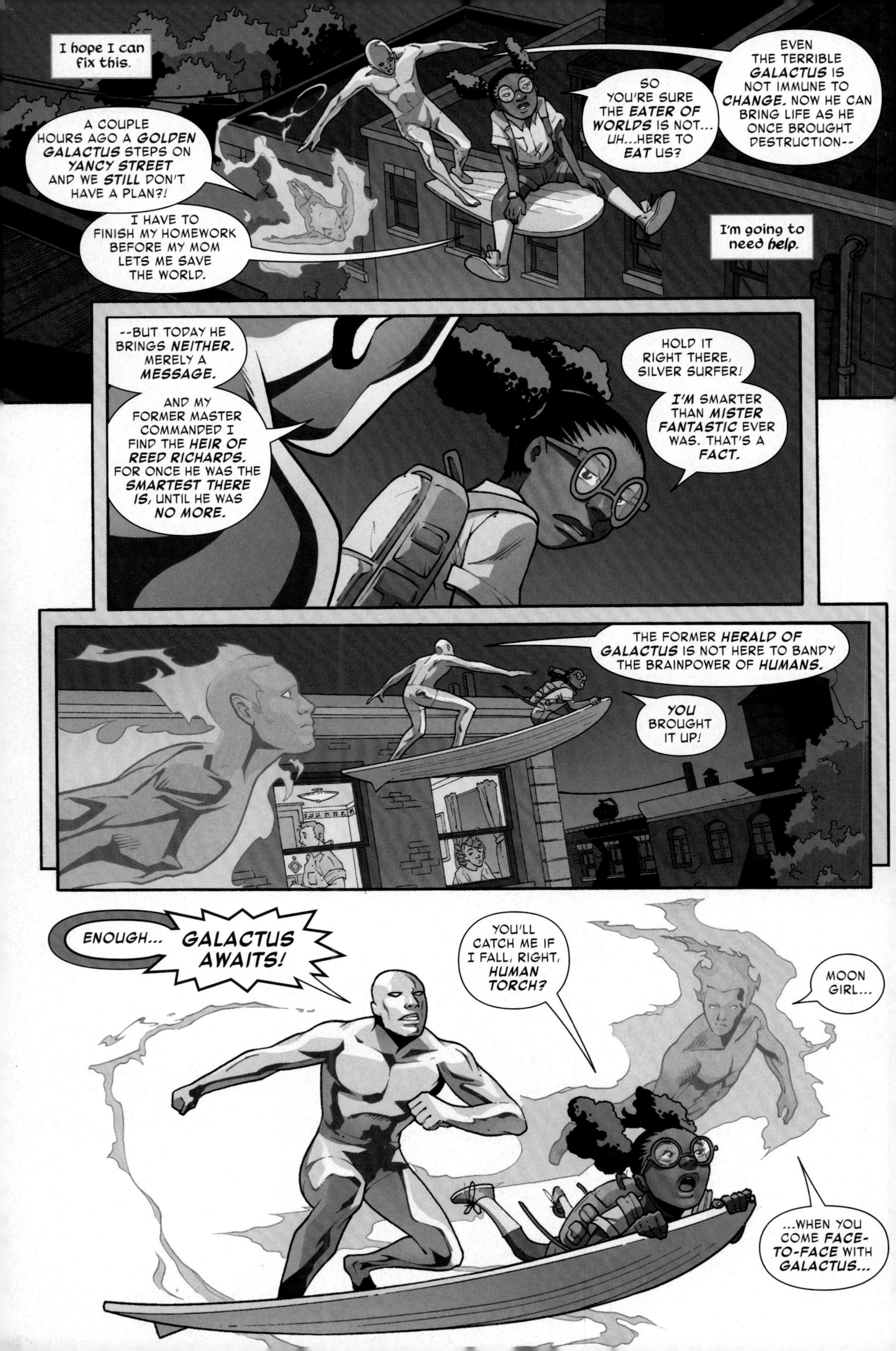
I hope I can fix this.
A COUPLE HOURS AGO A GOLDEN GALACTUS STEPS ON YANCY STREET AND WE STILL DON'T HAVE A PLAN?!
I HAVE TO FINISH MY HOMEWORK BEFORE MY MOM LETS ME SAVE THE WORLD.
SO YOU'RE SURE THE EATER OF WORLDS IS NOT... UH...HERE TO EAT US?
EVEN THE TERRIBLE GALACTUS IS NOT IMMUNE TO CHANGE. NOW HE CAN BRING LIFE AS HE ONCE BROUGHT DESTRUCTION--
I'm going to need help.
--BUT TODAY HE BRINGS NEITHER. MERELY A MESSAGE.
AND MY FORMER MASTER COMMANDED I FIND THE HEIR OF REED RICHARDS. FOR ONCE HE WAS THE SMARTEST THERE IS, UNTIL HE WAS NO MORE.
HOLD IT RIGHT THERE, SILVER SURFER!
I'M SMARTER THAN MISTER FANTASTIC EVER WAS. THAT'S A FACT.
THE FORMER HERALD OF GALACTUS IS NOT HERE TO BANDY THE BRAINPOWER OF HUMANS.
YOU BROUGHT IT UP!
ENOUGH...
GALACTUS AWAITS!
YOU'LL CATCH ME IF I FALL, RIGHT, HUMAN TORCH?
MOON GIRL...
...WHEN YOU COME FACE-TO-FACE WITH GALACTUS...

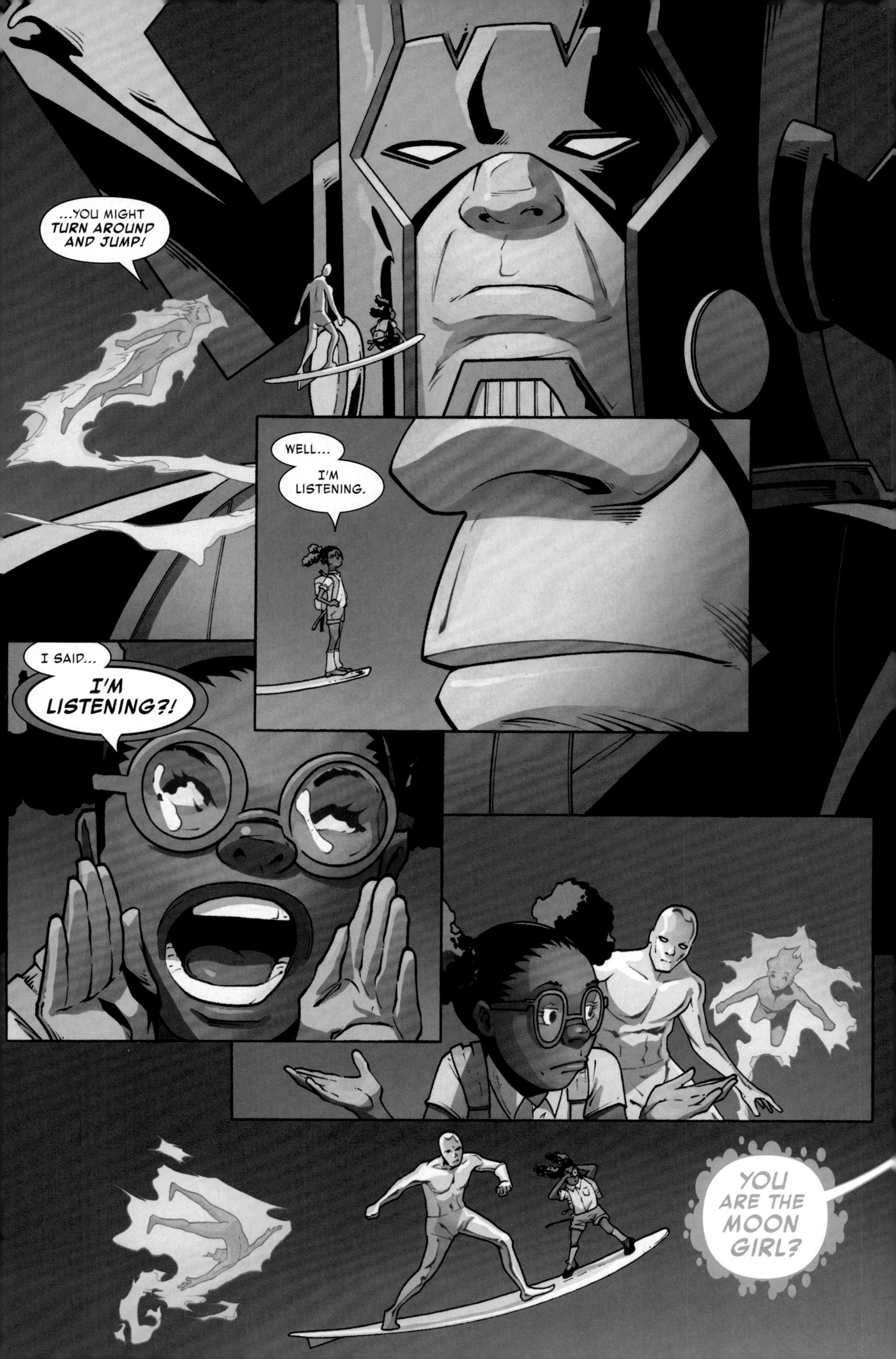
...YOU MIGHT TURN AROUND AND JUMP!
WELL...
I'M LISTENING.
I SAID...
I'M LISTENING?!
YOU ARE THE MOON GIRL?

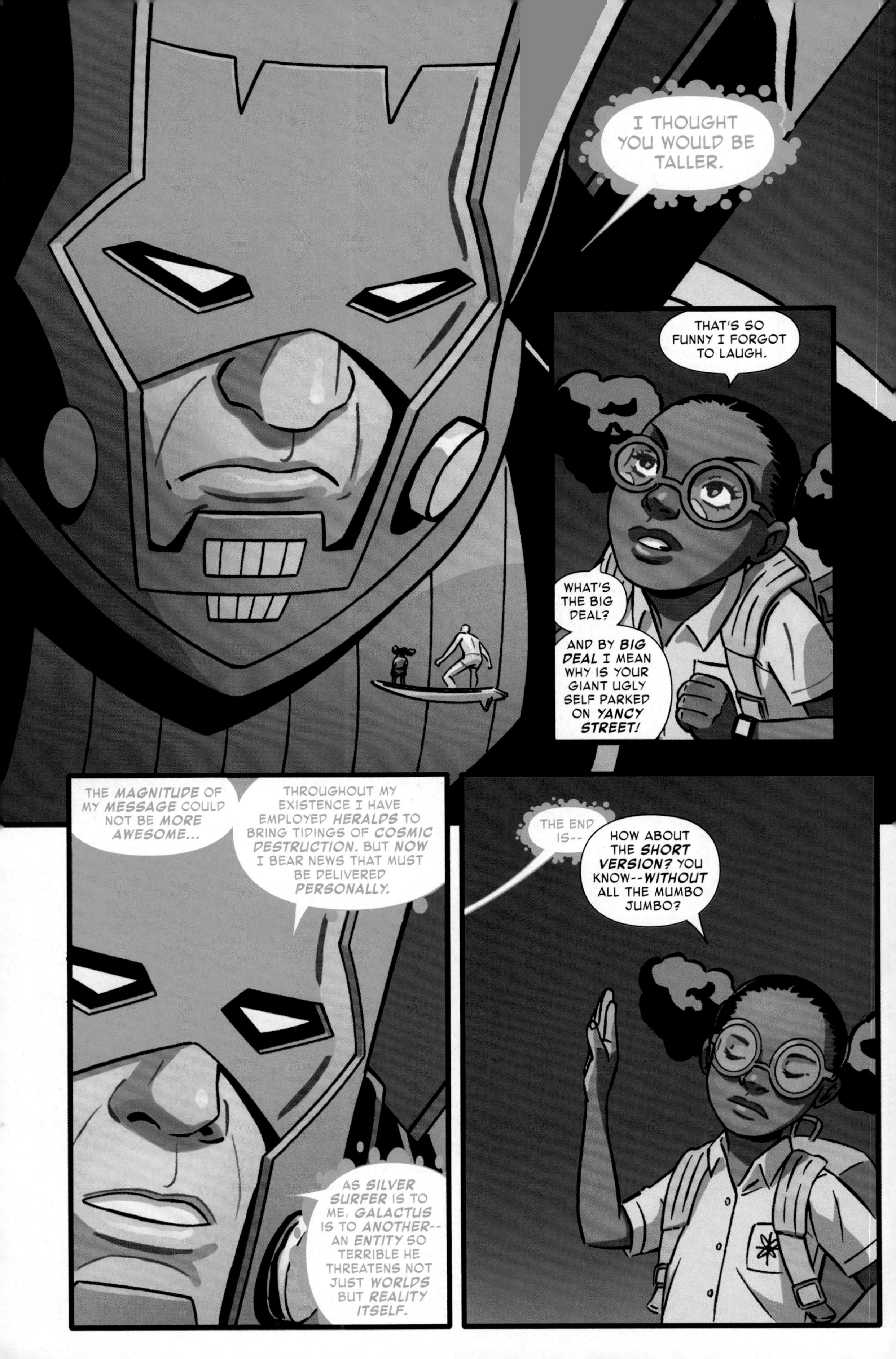

I THOUGHT YOU WOULD BE TALLER.
THAT'S SO FUNNY I FORGOT TO LAUGH.
WHAT'S THE BIG DEAL?
AND BY BIG DEAL I MEAN WHY IS YOUR GIANT UGLY SELF PARKED ON YANCY STREET!
THE MAGNITUDE OF MY MESSAGE COULD NOT BE MORE AWESOME...
THROUGHOUT MY EXISTENCE I HAVE EMPLOYED HERALDS TO BRING TIDINGS OF COSMIC DESTRUCTION. BUT NOW I BEAR NEWS THAT MUST BE DELIVERED PERSONALLY.
AS SILVER SURFER IS TO ME, GALACTUS IS TO ANOTHER--AN ENTITY SO TERRIBLE HE THREATENS NOT JUST WORLDS BUT REALITY ITSELF.
THE END IS--
HOW ABOUT THE SHORT VERSION? YOU KNOW--WITHOUT ALL THE MUMBO JUMBO?

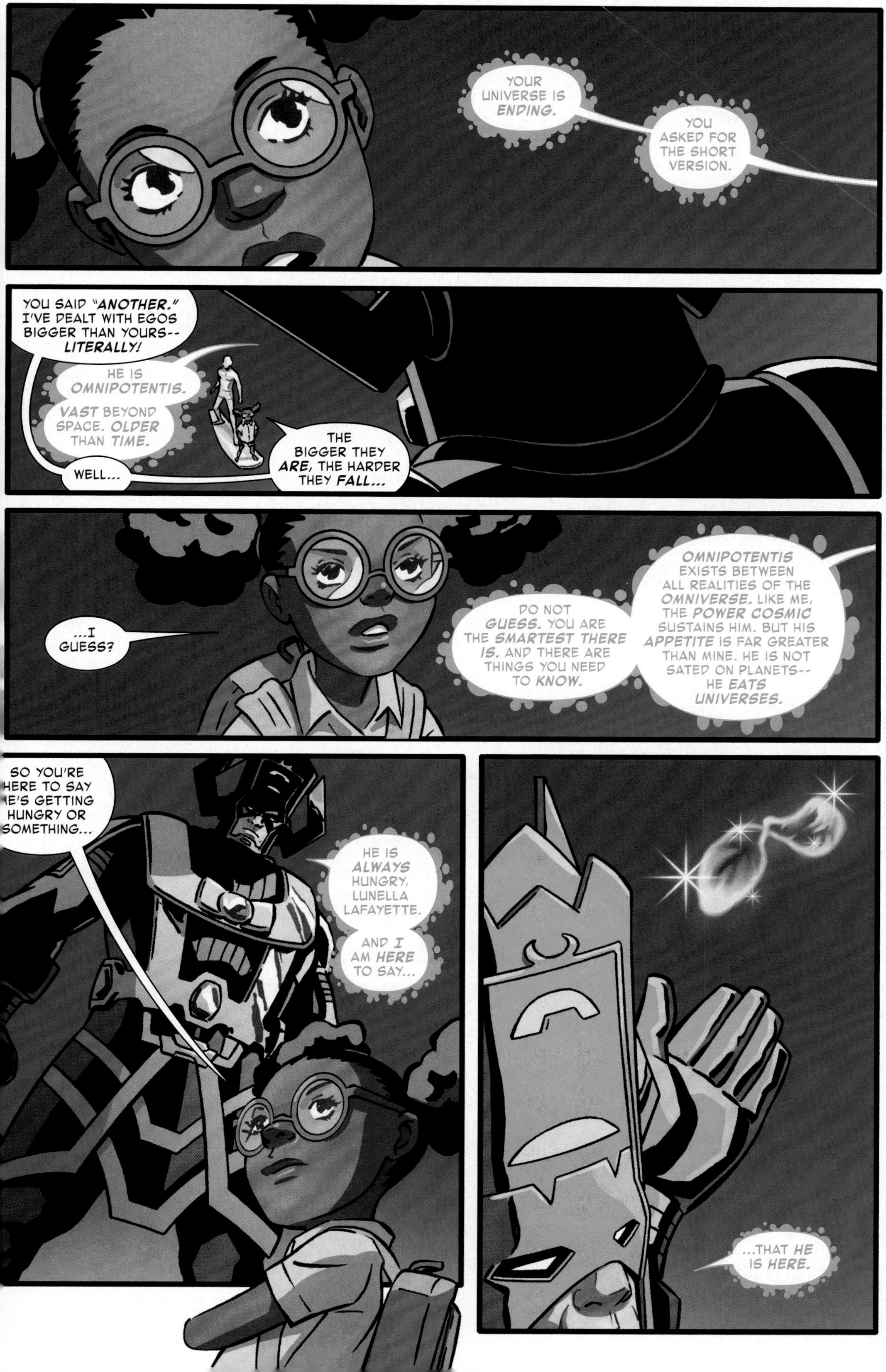
YOUR UNIVERSE IS ENDING.
YOU ASKED FOR THE SHORT VERSION.
YOU SAID "ANOTHER." I'VE DEALT WITH EGOS BIGGER THAN YOURS-- LITERALLY!
HE IS OMNIPOTENTIS.
VAST BEYOND SPACE. OLDER THAN TIME.
WELL...
THE BIGGER THEY ARE, THE HARDER THEY FALL...
...I GUESS?
DO NOT GUESS. YOU ARE THE SMARTEST THERE IS. AND THERE ARE THINGS YOU NEED TO KNOW.
OMNIPOTENTIS EXISTS BETWEEN ALL REALITIES OF THE OMNIVERSE. LIKE ME, THE POWER COSMIC SUSTAINS HIM. BUT HIS APPETITE IS FAR GREATER THAN MINE. HE IS NOT SATED ON PLANETS-- HE EATS UNIVERSES.
SO YOU'RE HERE TO SAY HE'S GETTING HUNGRY OR SOMETHING...
HE IS ALWAYS HUNGRY, LUNELLA LAFAYETTE.
AND I AM HERE TO SAY...
...THAT HE IS HERE.

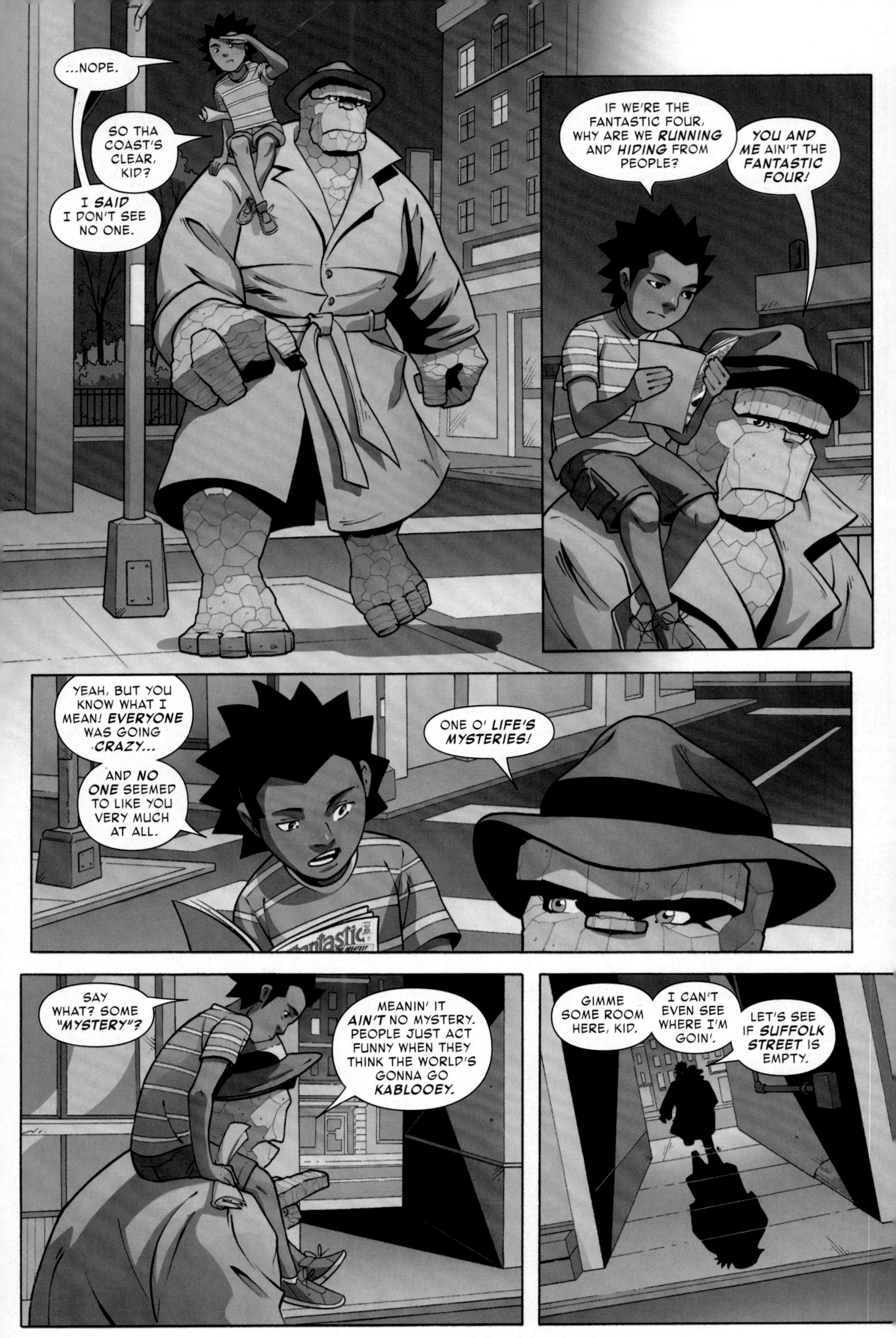
...NOPE.
SO THA COAST'S CLEAR, KID?
I SAID I DON'T SEE NO ONE.
IF WE'RE THE FANTASTIC FOUR, WHY ARE WE RUNNING AND HIDING FROM PEOPLE?
YOU AND ME AIN'T THE FANTASTIC FOUR!
YEAH, BUT YOU KNOW WHAT I MEAN! EVERYONE WAS GOING CRAZY...
AND NO ONE SEEMED TO LIKE YOU VERY MUCH AT ALL.
ONE O' LIFE'S MYSTERIES!
SAY WHAT? SOME "MYSTERY"?
MEANIN' IT AIN'T NO MYSTERY. PEOPLE JUST ACT FUNNY WHEN THEY THINK THE WORLD'S GONNA GO KABLOOEY.
GIMME SOME ROOM HERE, KID.
I CAN'T EVEN SEE WHERE I'M GOIN'.
LET'S SEE IF SUFFOLK STREET IS EMPTY.

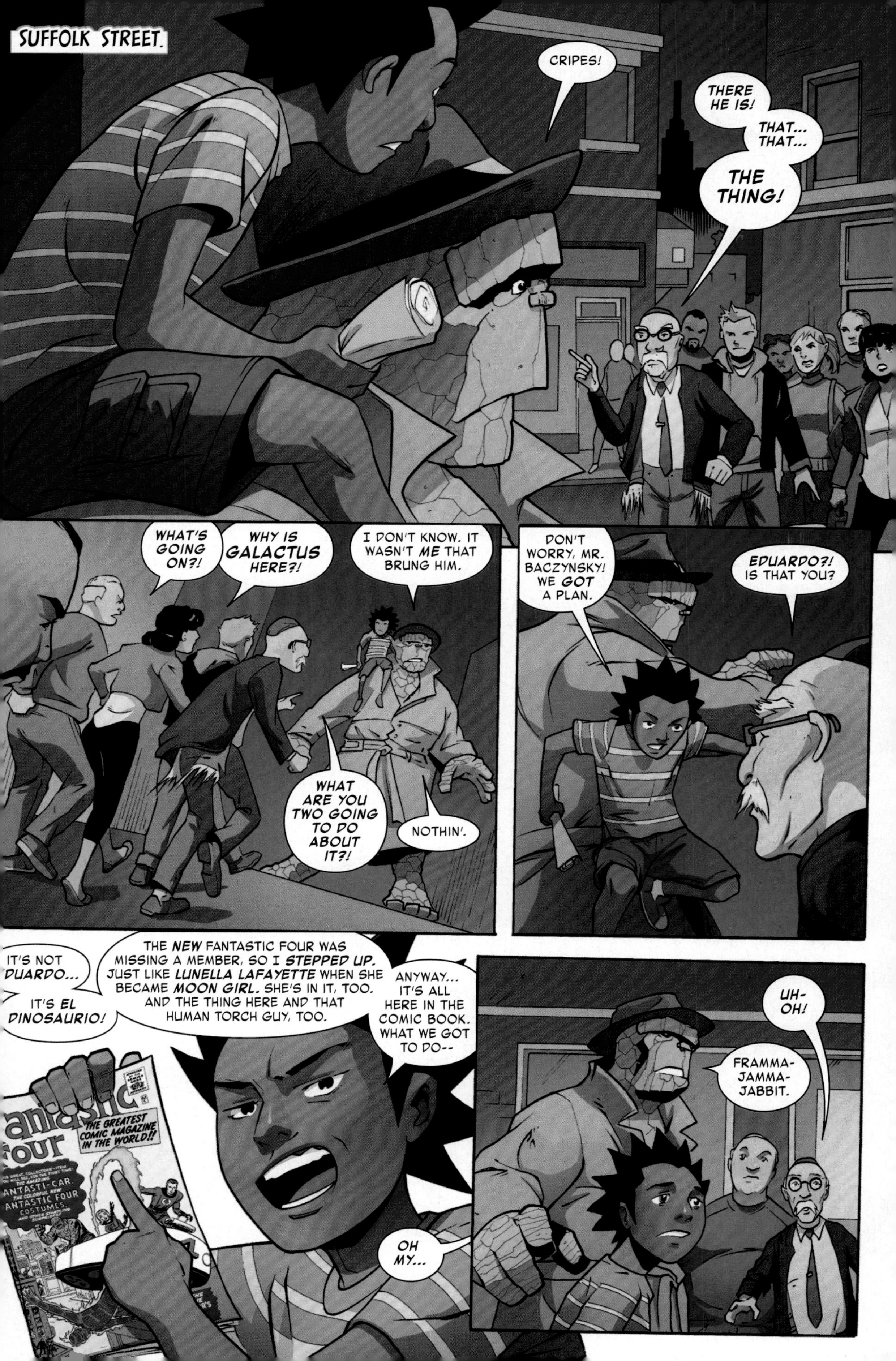
SUFFOLK STREET.
CRIPES!
THERE HE IS!
THAT... THAT...
THE THING!
WHAT'S GOING ON?!
WHY IS GALACTUS HERE?!
I DON'T KNOW. IT WASN'T ME THAT BRUNG HIM.
WHAT ARE YOU TWO GOING TO DO ABOUT IT?!
NOTHIN'.
DON'T WORRY, MR. BACZYNSKY! WE GOT A PLAN.
EDUARDO?! IS THAT YOU?
IT'S NOT 'DUARDO...
IT'S EL DINOSAURIO!
THE NEW FANTASTIC FOUR WAS MISSING A MEMBER, SO I STEPPED UP. JUST LIKE LUNELLA LAFAYETTE WHEN SHE BECAME MOON GIRL. SHE'S IN IT, TOO. AND THE THING HERE AND THAT HUMAN TORCH GUY, TOO.
ANYWAY... IT'S ALL HERE IN THE COMIC BOOK. WHAT WE GOT TO DO--
THE GREATEST COMIC MAGAZINE IN THE WORLD!
OH MY...
UH-OH!
FRAMMA-JAMMA-JABBIT.

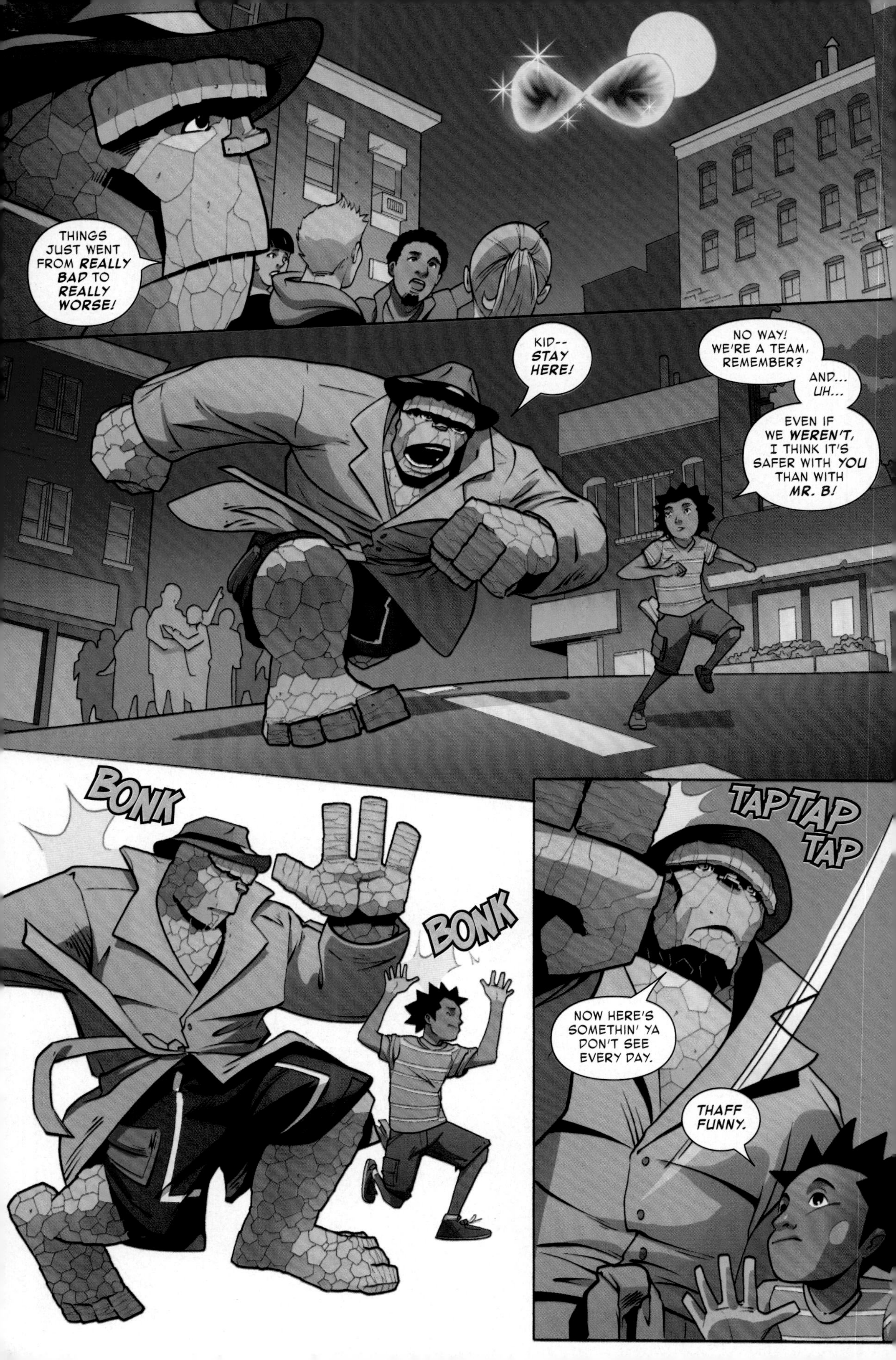
THINGS JUST WENT FROM REALLY BAD TO REALLY WORSE!
KID-- STAY HERE!
NO WAY! WE'RE A TEAM, REMEMBER?
AND... UH...
EVEN IF WE WEREN'T, I THINK IT'S SAFER WITH YOU THAN WITH MR. B!
BONK
BONK
TAP TAP TAP
NOW HERE'S SOMETHIN' YA DON'T SEE EVERY DAY.
THAFF FUNNY.

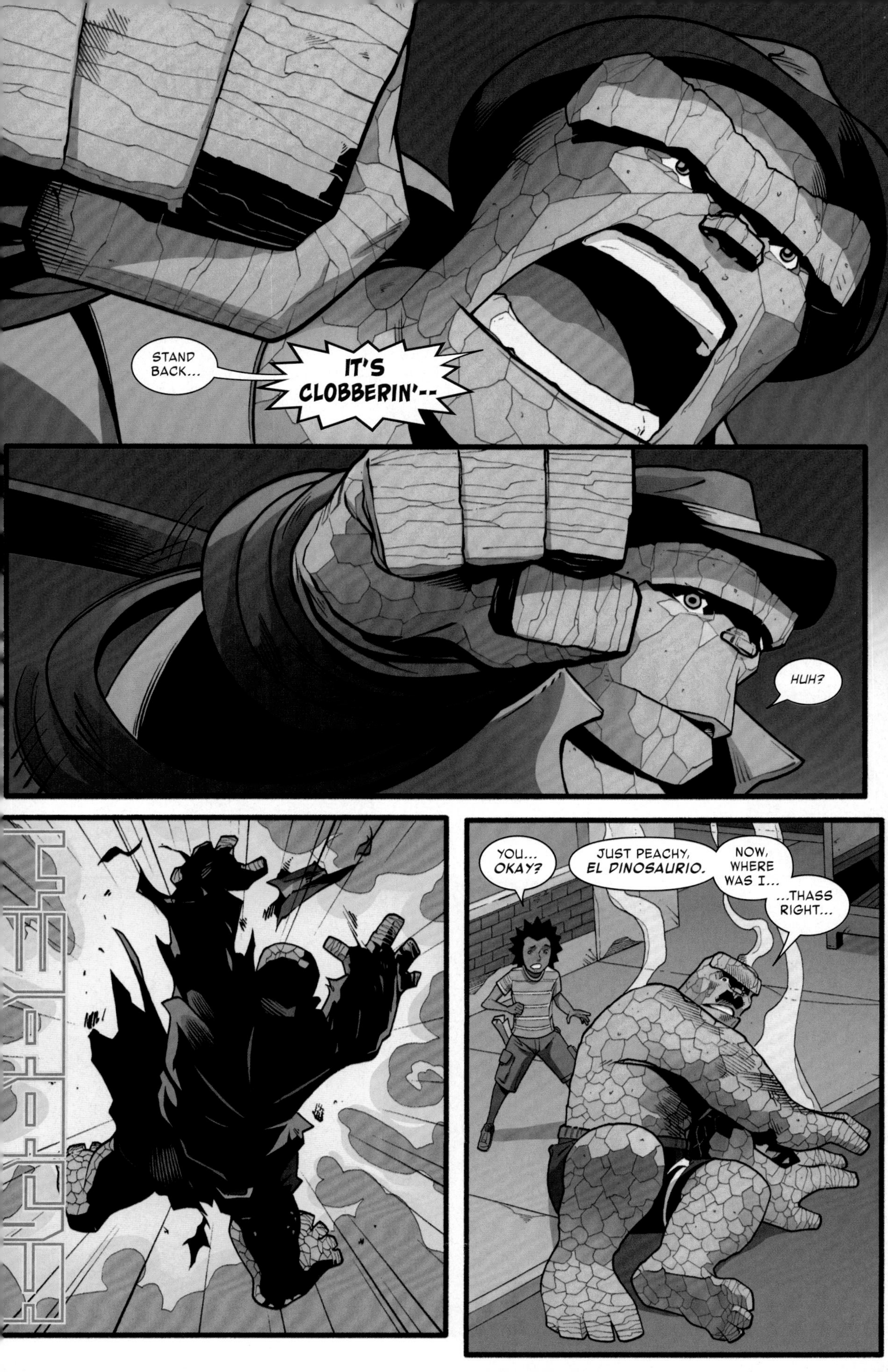
STAND BACK...
IT'S CLOBBERIN'--
HUH?
YOU... OKAY?
JUST PEACHY, EL DINOSAURIO.
NOW, WHERE WAS I...
...THASS RIGHT...

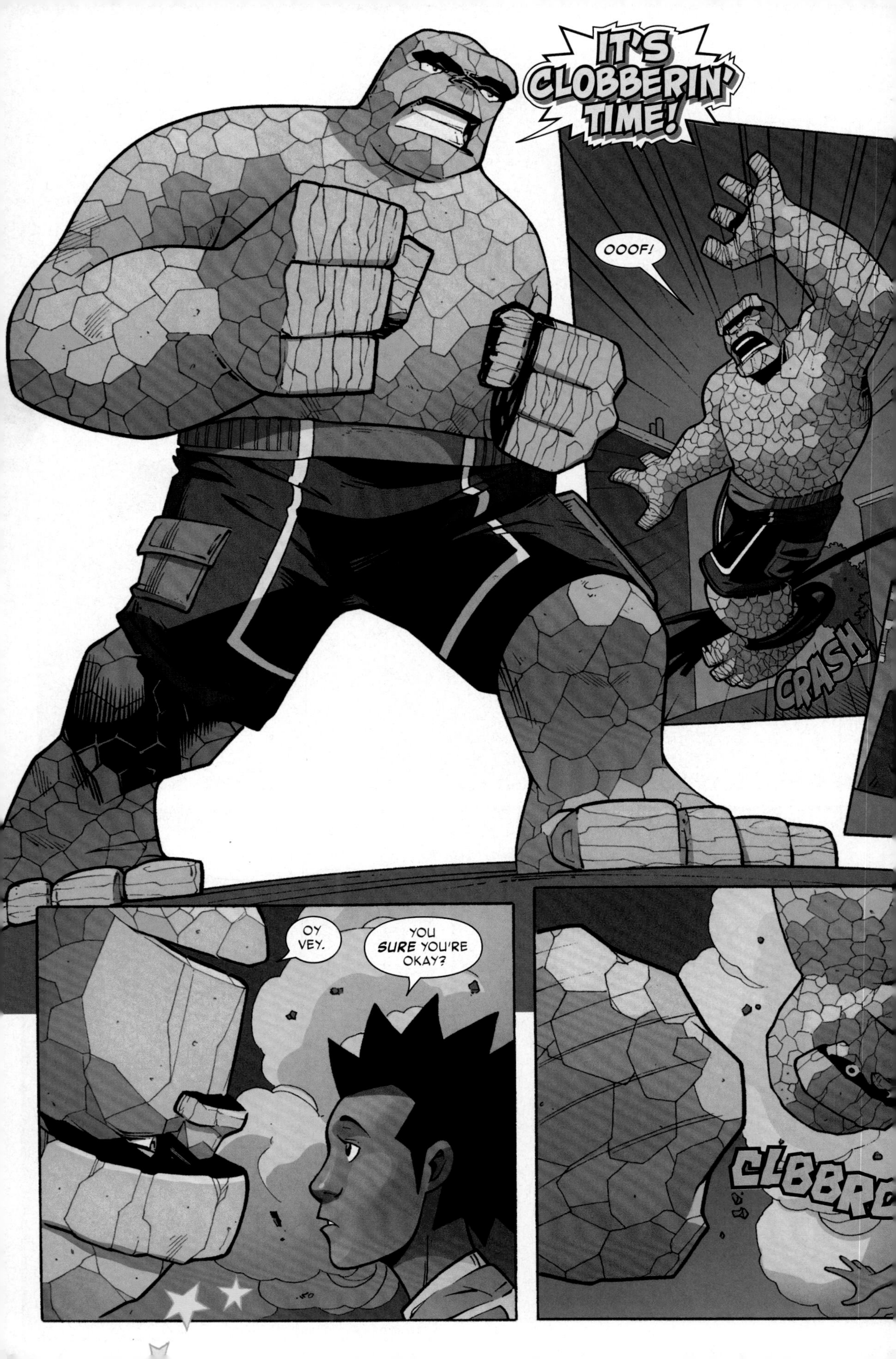
IT'S CLOBBERIN' TIME!
OOOF!
CRASH
OY VEY.
YOU SURE YOU'RE OKAY?
CLBBRO

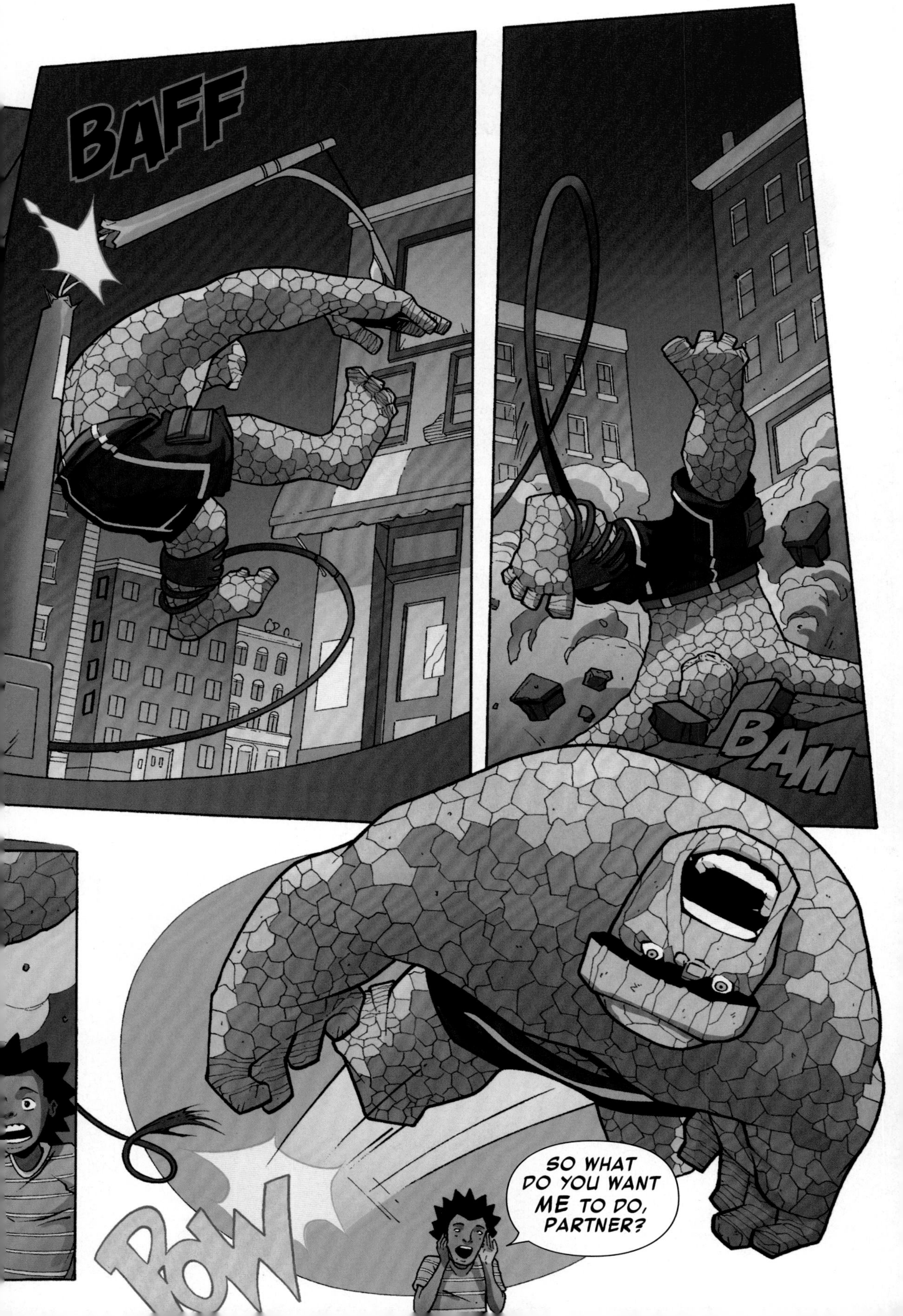
BAFF
BAM
POW
SO WHAT DO YOU WANT ME TO DO, PARTNER?

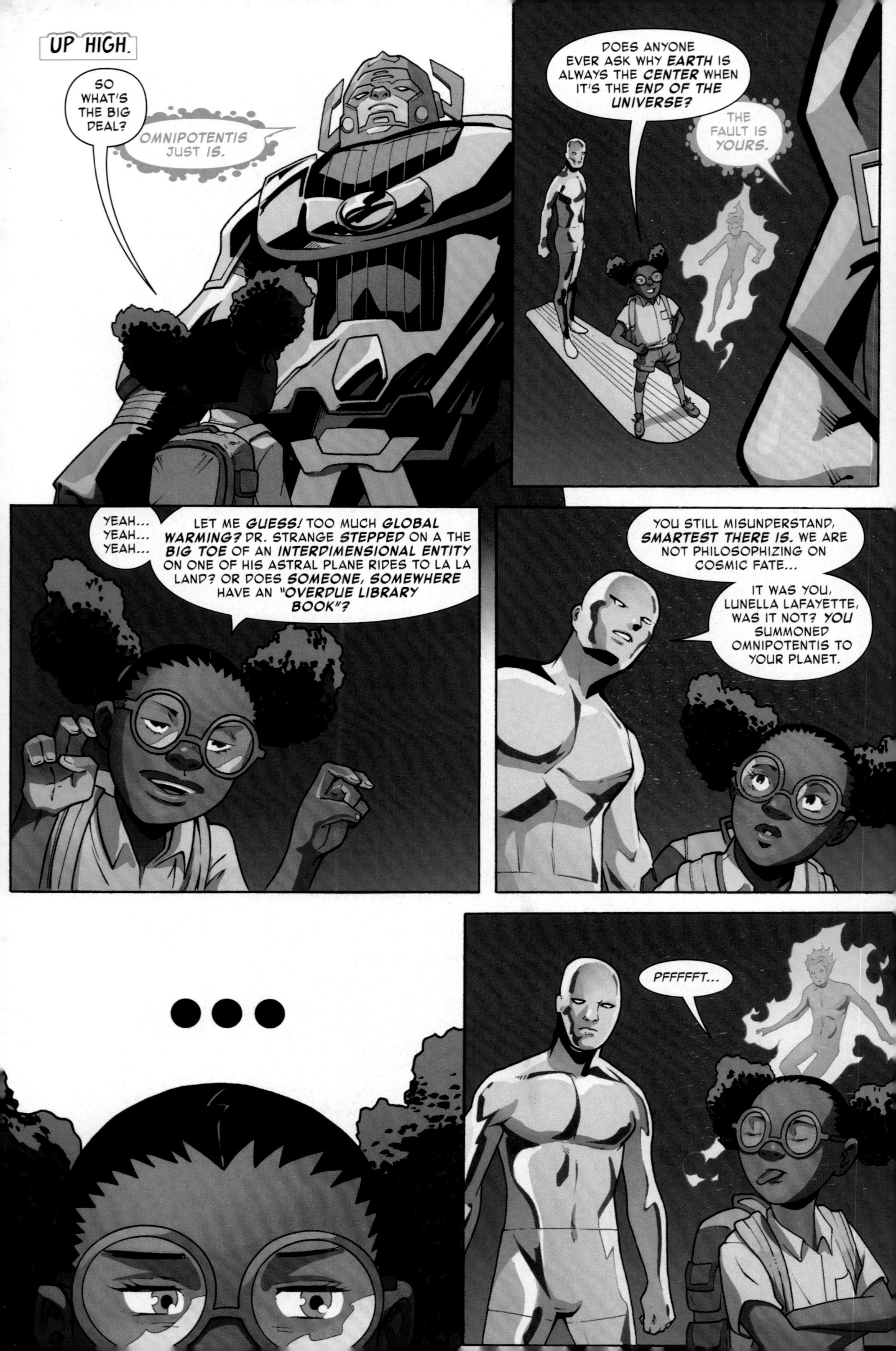
UP HIGH.
SO WHAT'S THE BIG DEAL?
OMNIPOTENTIS JUST IS.
DOES ANYONE EVER ASK WHY EARTH IS ALWAYS THE CENTER WHEN IT'S THE END OF THE UNIVERSE?
THE FAULT IS YOURS.
YEAH... YEAH... YEAH...
LET ME GUESS! TOO MUCH GLOBAL WARMING? DR. STRANGE STEPPED ON A THE BIG TOE OF AN INTERDIMENSIONAL ENTITY ON ONE OF HIS ASTRAL PLANE RIDES TO LA LA LAND? OR DOES SOMEONE, SOMEWHERE HAVE AN "OVERDUE LIBRARY BOOK"?
YOU STILL MISUNDERSTAND, SMARTEST THERE IS. WE ARE NOT PHILOSOPHIZING ON COSMIC FATE...
IT WAS YOU, LUNELLA LAFAYETTE, WAS IT NOT? YOU SUMMONED OMNIPOTENTIS TO YOUR PLANET.
PFFFFFT...

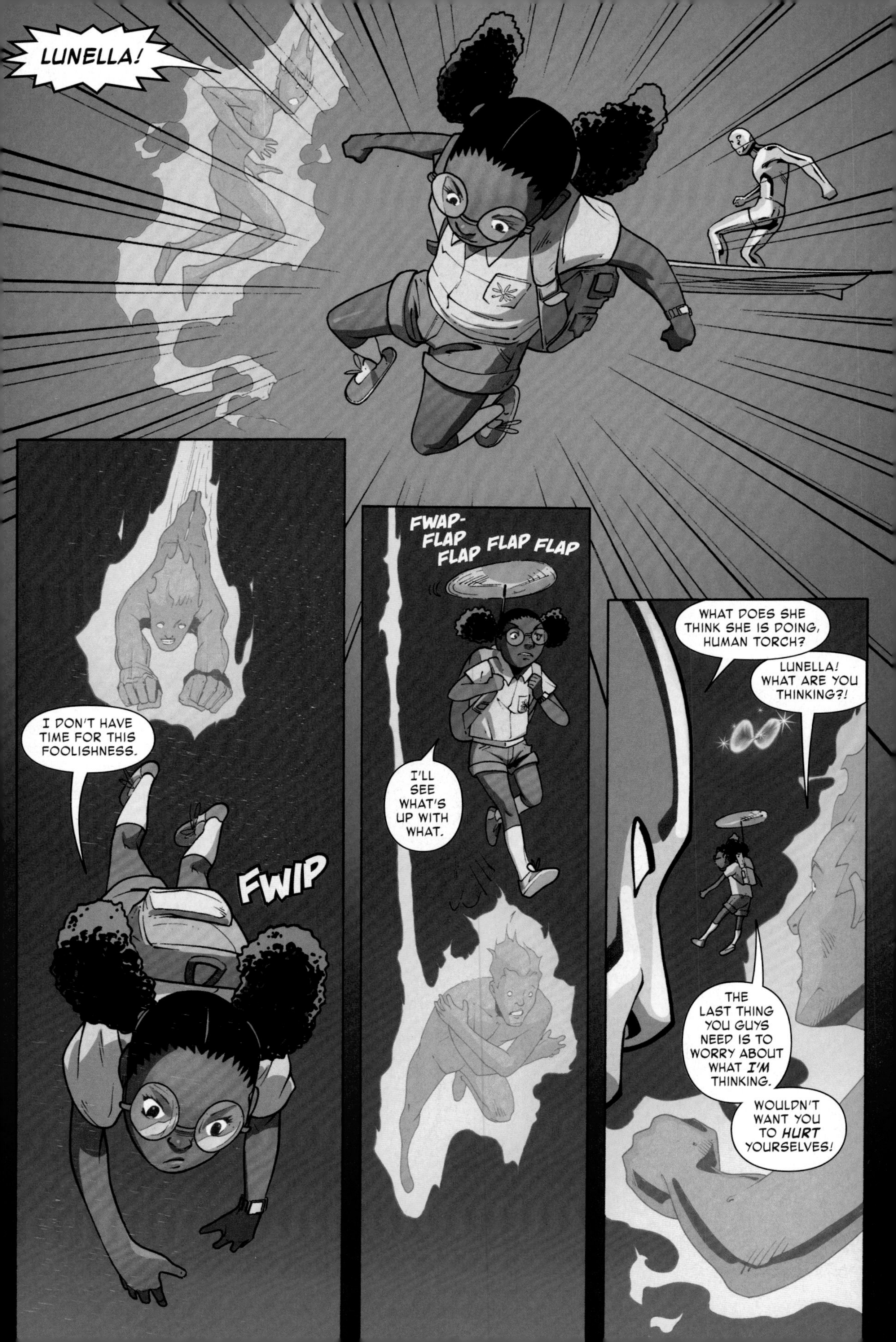
LUNELLA!
I DON'T HAVE TIME FOR THIS FOOLISHNESS.
FWIP
FWAP-FLAP FLAP FLAP FLAP
I'LL SEE WHAT'S UP WITH WHAT.
WHAT DOES SHE THINK SHE IS DOING, HUMAN TORCH?
LUNELLA! WHAT ARE YOU THINKING?!
THE LAST THING YOU GUYS NEED IS TO WORRY ABOUT WHAT *I'M* THINKING.
WOULDN'T WANT YOU TO *HURT* YOURSELVES!

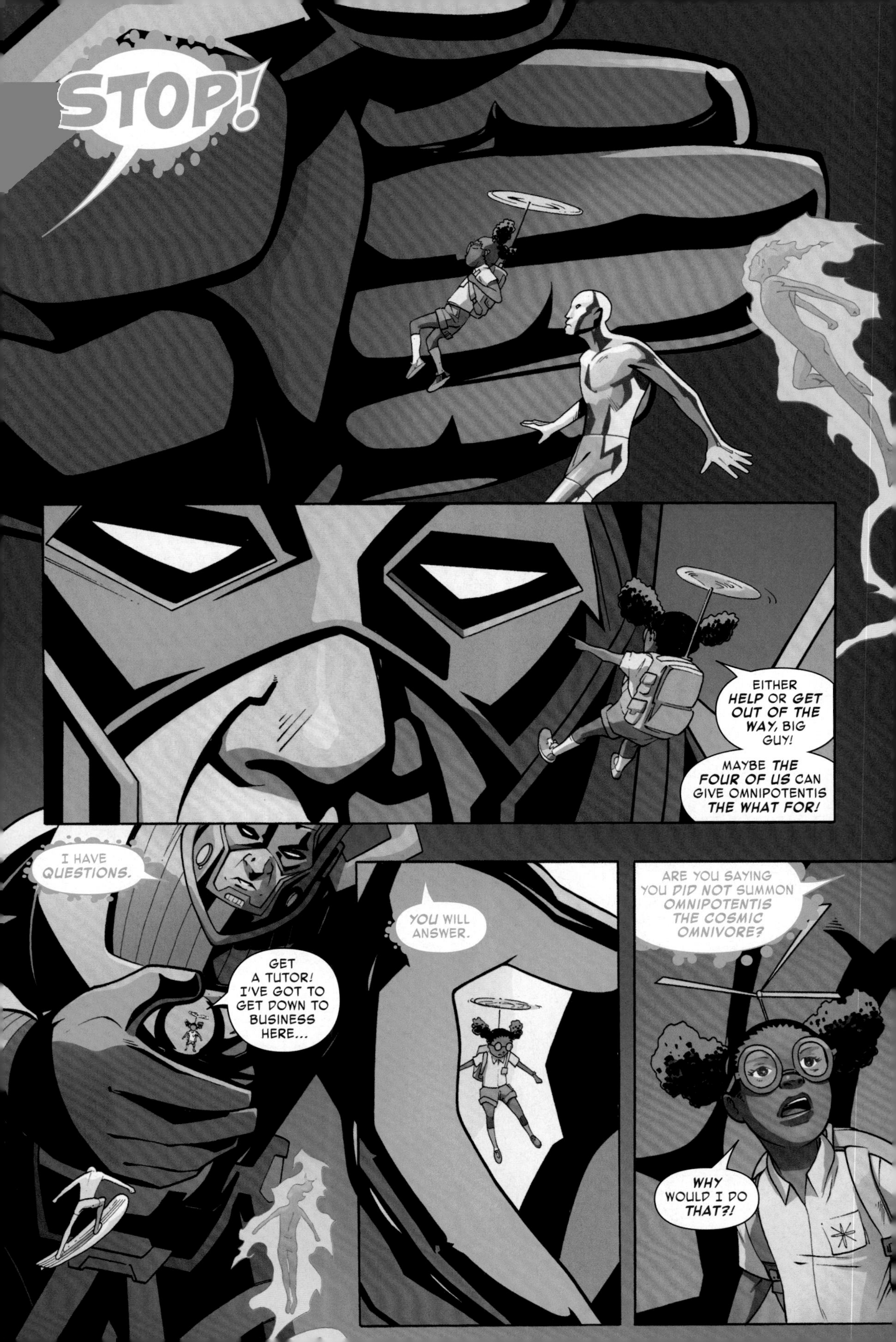
STOP!
EITHER HELP OR GET OUT OF THE WAY, BIG GUY!
MAYBE THE FOUR OF US CAN GIVE OMNIPOTENTIS THE WHAT FOR!
I HAVE QUESTIONS.
GET A TUTOR! I'VE GOT TO GET DOWN TO BUSINESS HERE...
YOU WILL ANSWER.
ARE YOU SAYING YOU DID NOT SUMMON OMNIPOTENTIS THE COSMIC OMNIVORE?
WHY WOULD I DO THAT?!

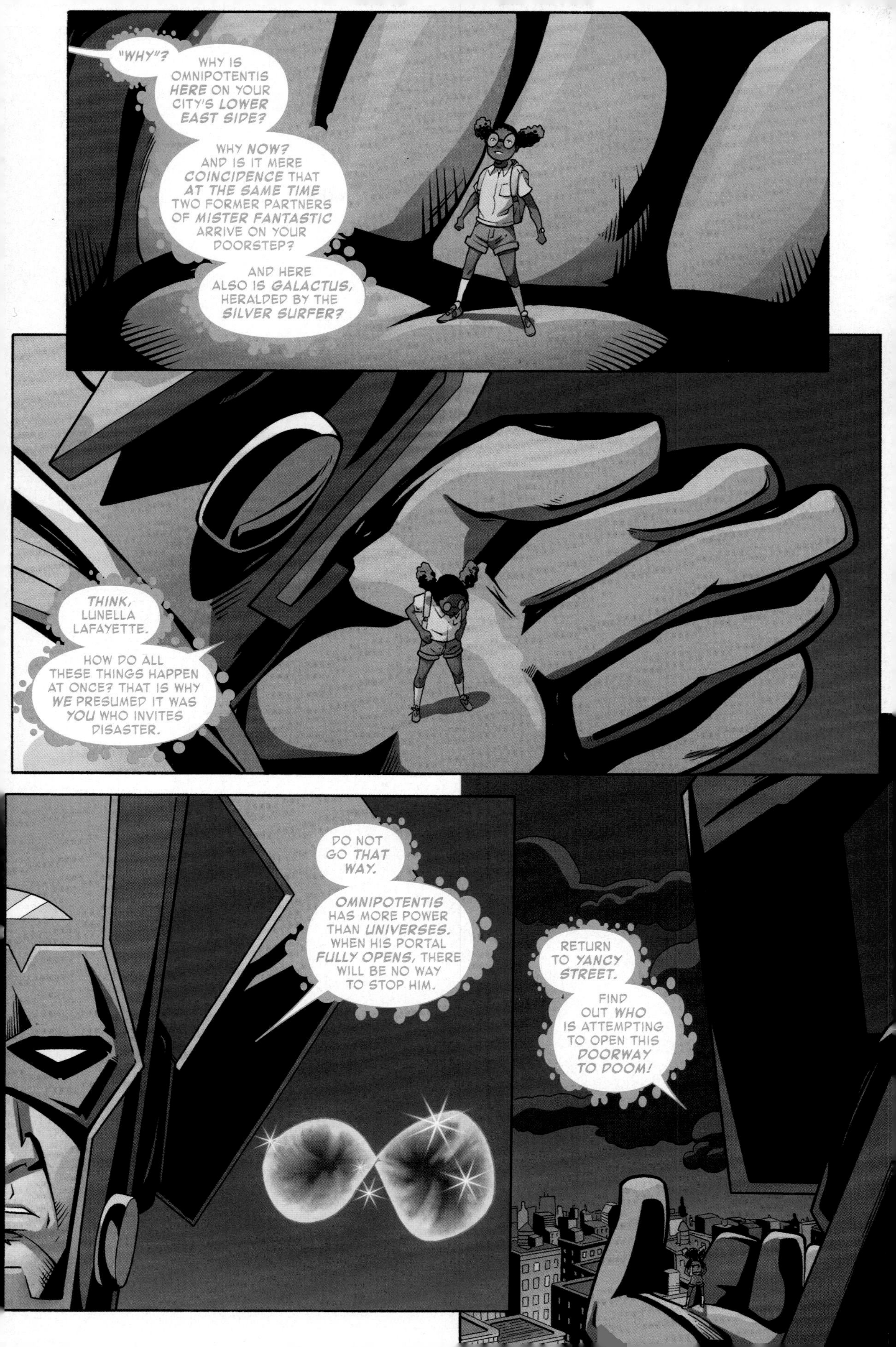
"WHY"? WHY IS OMNIPOTENTIS HERE ON YOUR CITY'S LOWER EAST SIDE?
WHY NOW? AND IS IT MERE COINCIDENCE THAT AT THE SAME TIME TWO FORMER PARTNERS OF MISTER FANTASTIC ARRIVE ON YOUR DOORSTEP?
AND HERE ALSO IS GALACTUS, HERALDED BY THE SILVER SURFER?
THINK, LUNELLA LAFAYETTE.
HOW DO ALL THESE THINGS HAPPEN AT ONCE? THAT IS WHY WE PRESUMED IT WAS YOU WHO INVITES DISASTER.
DO NOT GO THAT WAY.
OMNIPOTENTIS HAS MORE POWER THAN UNIVERSES. WHEN HIS PORTAL FULLY OPENS, THERE WILL BE NO WAY TO STOP HIM.
RETURN TO YANCY STREET.
FIND OUT WHO IS ATTEMPTING TO OPEN THIS DOORWAY TO DOOM!

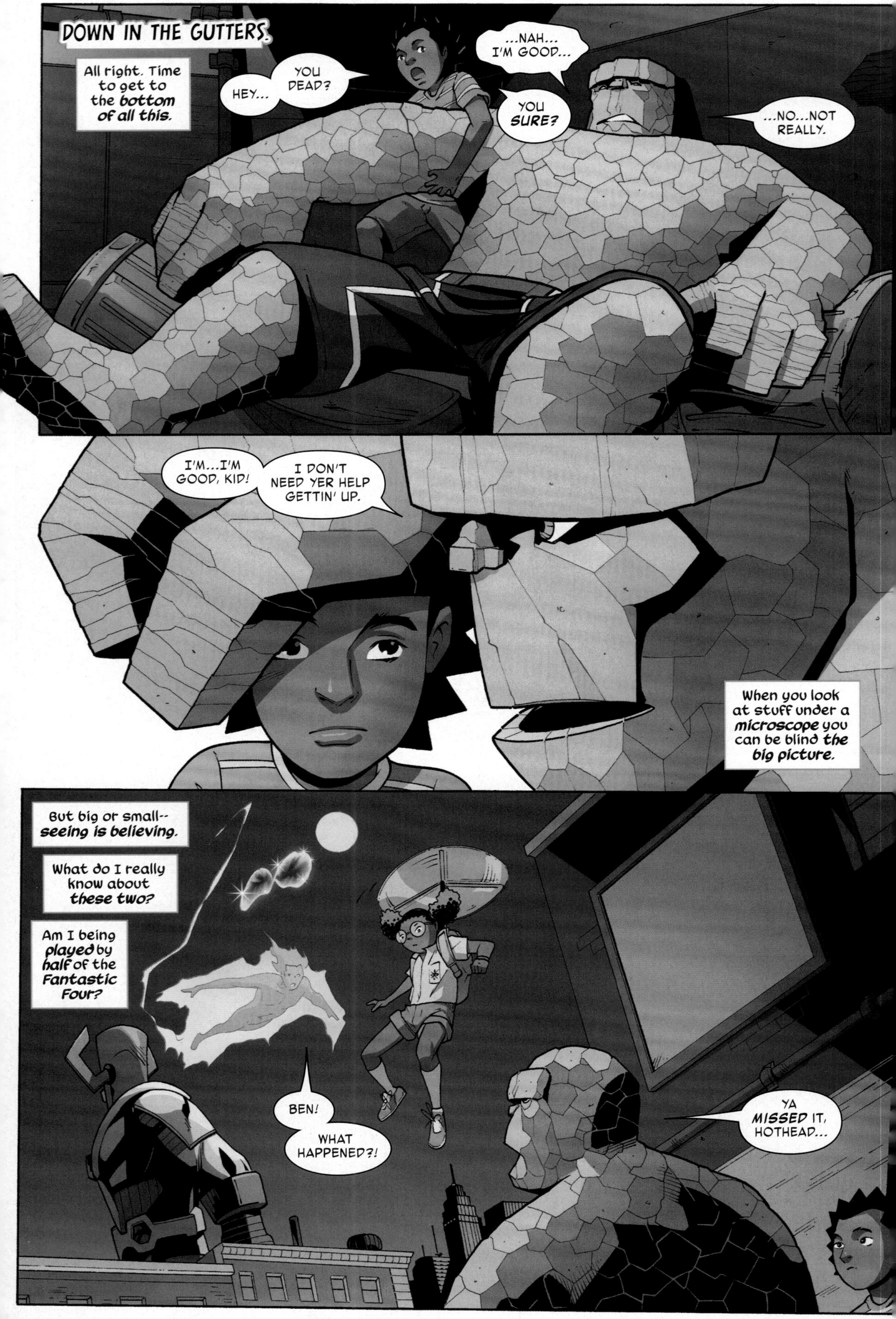
DOWN IN THE GUTTERS.
All right. Time to get to the bottom of all this.
HEY...
YOU DEAD?
...NAH... I'M GOOD...
YOU SURE?
...NO...NOT REALLY.
I'M...I'M GOOD, KID!
I DON'T NEED YER HELP GETTIN' UP.
When you look at stuff under a microscope you can be blind the big picture.
But big or small-- seeing is believing.
What do I really know about these two?
Am I being played by half of the Fantastic Four?
BEN!
WHAT HAPPENED?!
YA MISSED IT, HOTHEAD...

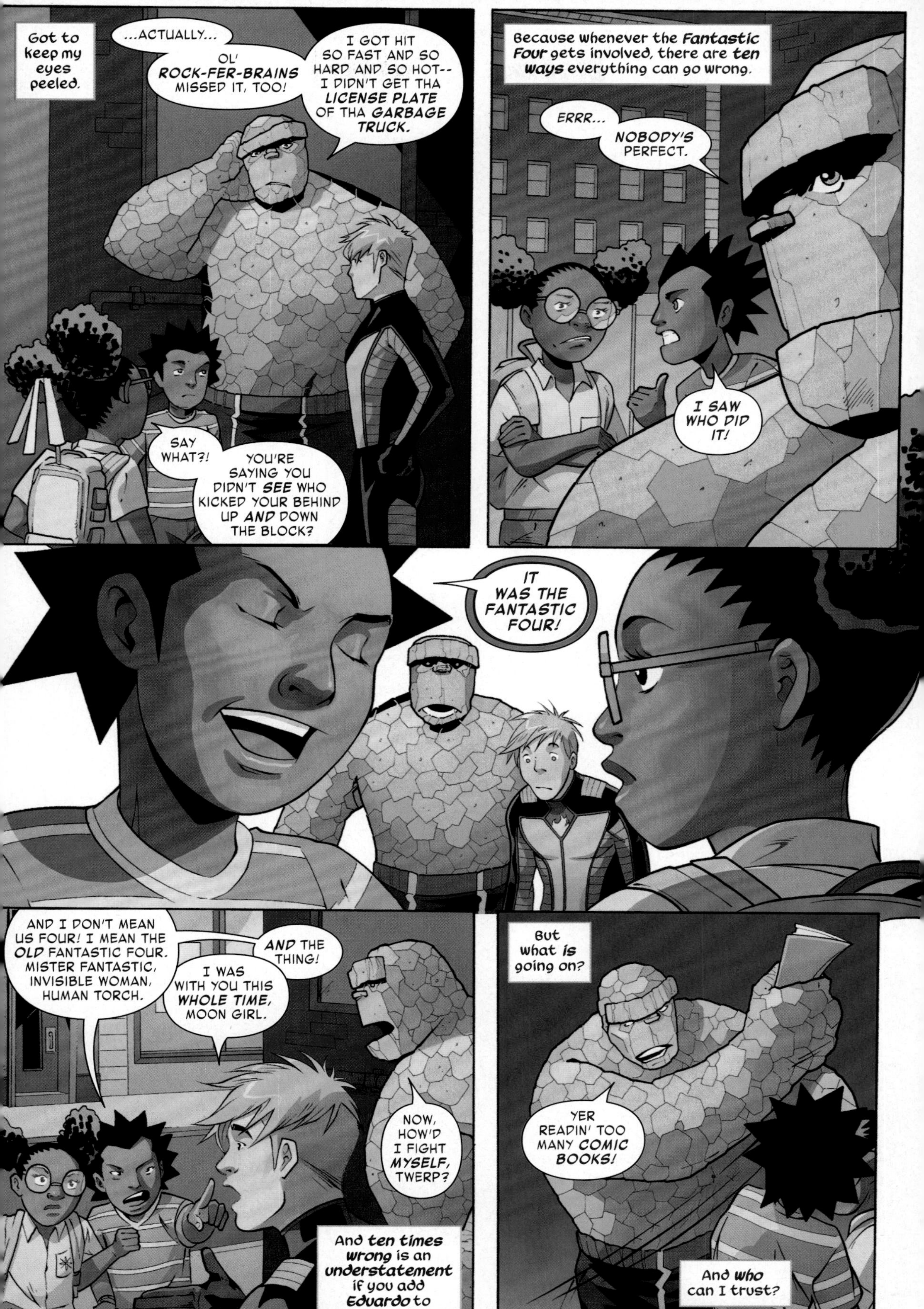
Got to keep my eyes peeled.
...ACTUALLY...
OL' ROCK-FER-BRAINS MISSED IT, TOO!
I GOT HIT SO FAST AND SO HARD AND SO HOT-- I DIDN'T GET THA LICENSE PLATE OF THA GARBAGE TRUCK.
SAY WHAT?!
YOU'RE SAYING YOU DIDN'T SEE WHO KICKED YOUR BEHIND UP AND DOWN THE BLOCK?
Because whenever the Fantastic Four gets involved, there are ten ways everything can go wrong.
ERRR...
NOBODY'S PERFECT.
I SAW WHO DID IT!
IT WAS THE FANTASTIC FOUR!
AND I DON'T MEAN US FOUR! I MEAN THE OLD FANTASTIC FOUR. MISTER FANTASTIC, INVISIBLE WOMAN, HUMAN TORCH.
AND THE THING!
I WAS WITH YOU THIS WHOLE TIME, MOON GIRL.
NOW, HOW'D I FIGHT MYSELF, TWERP?
And ten times wrong is an understatement if you add Eduardo to the equation.
But what is going on?
YER READIN' TOO MANY COMIC BOOKS!
And who can I trust?

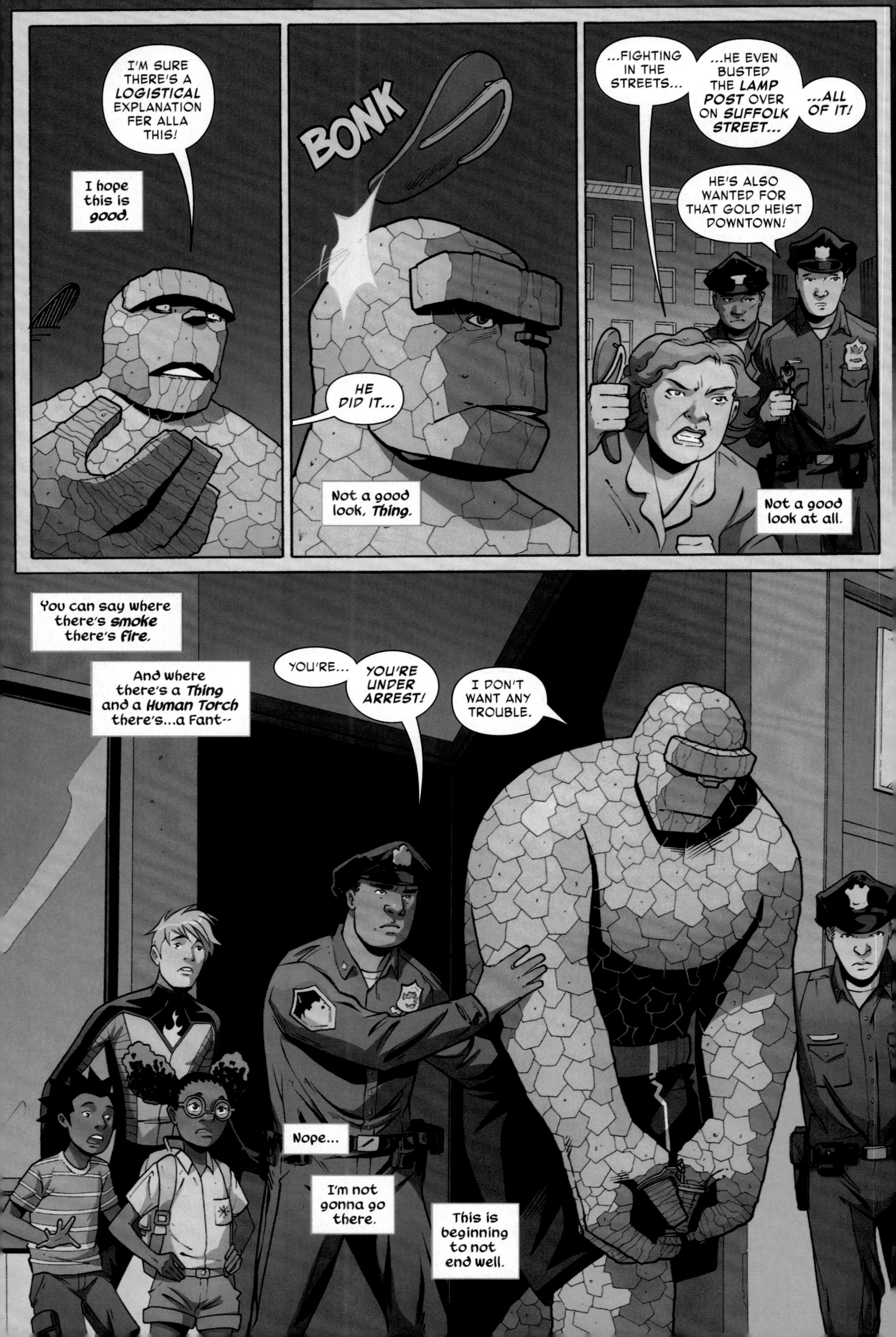
I'M SURE THERE'S A LOGISTICAL EXPLANATION FER ALLA THIS!
I hope this is good.
BONK
HE DID IT...
Not a good look, Thing.
...FIGHTING IN THE STREETS...
...HE EVEN BUSTED THE LAMP POST OVER ON SUFFOLK STREET...
...ALL OF IT!
HE'S ALSO WANTED FOR THAT GOLD HEIST DOWNTOWN!
Not a good look at all.
You can say where there's smoke there's fire.
And where there's a Thing and a Human Torch there's...a Fant--
YOU'RE...
YOU'RE UNDER ARREST!
I DON'T WANT ANY TROUBLE.
Nope...
I'm not gonna go there.
This is beginning to not end well.

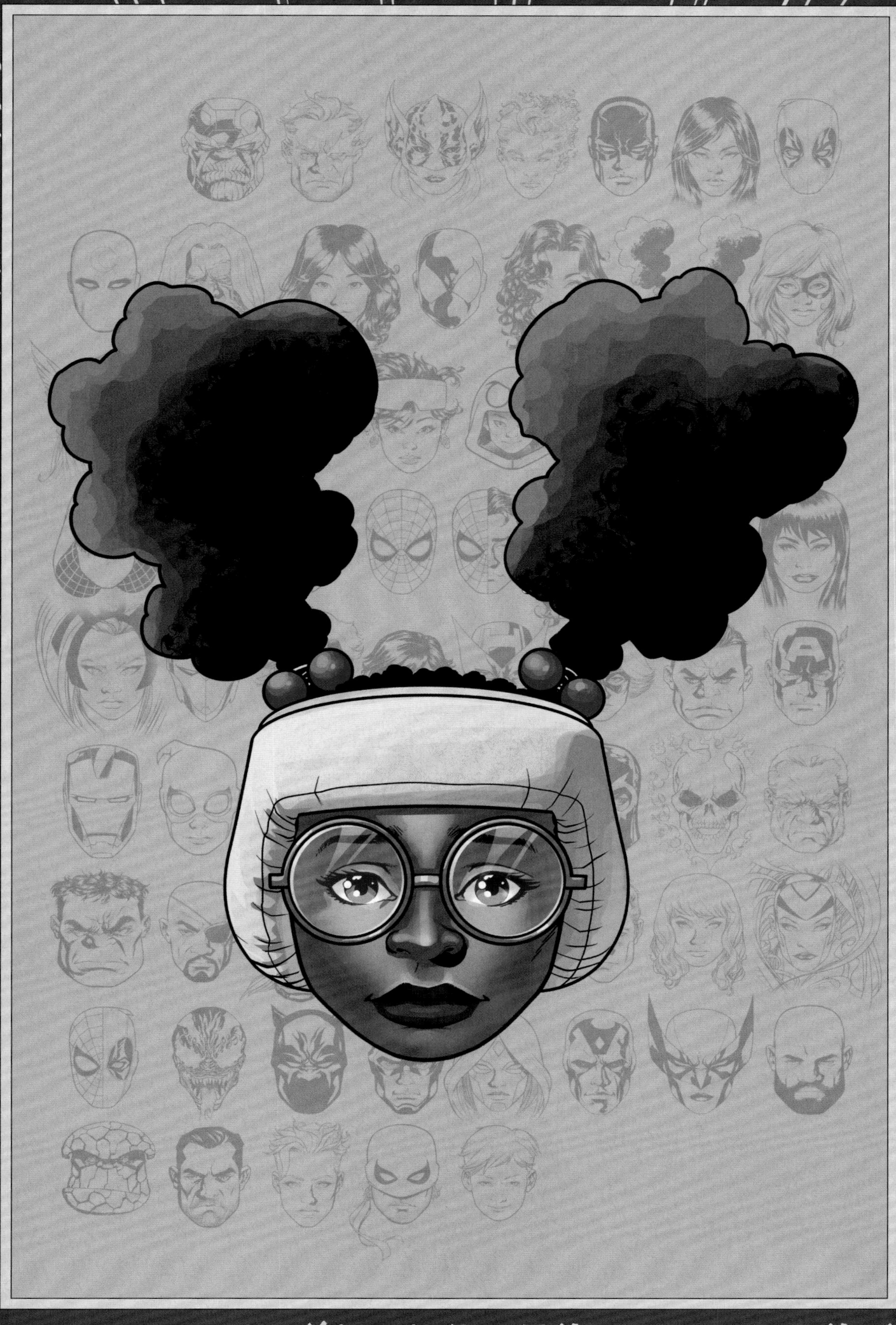

#25 LEGACY HEADSHOT VARIANT BY MIKE MCKONE & ANDY TROY

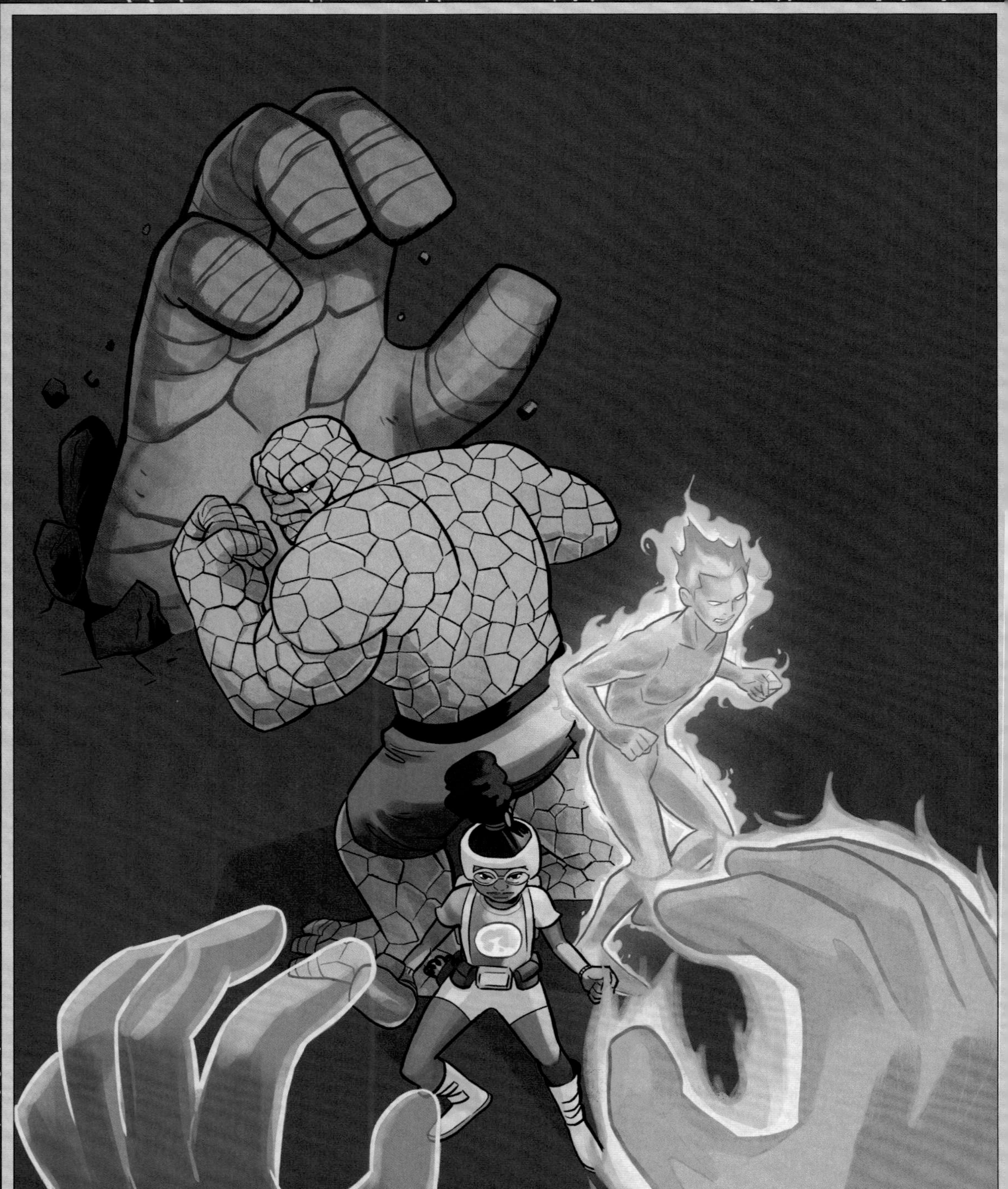

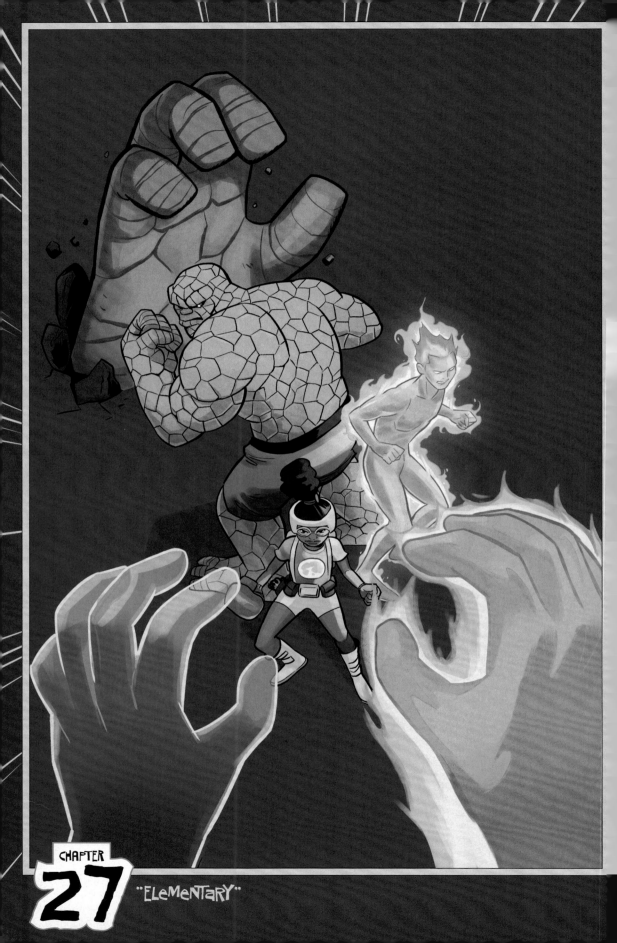

CHAPTER 27 "ELEMENTARY"

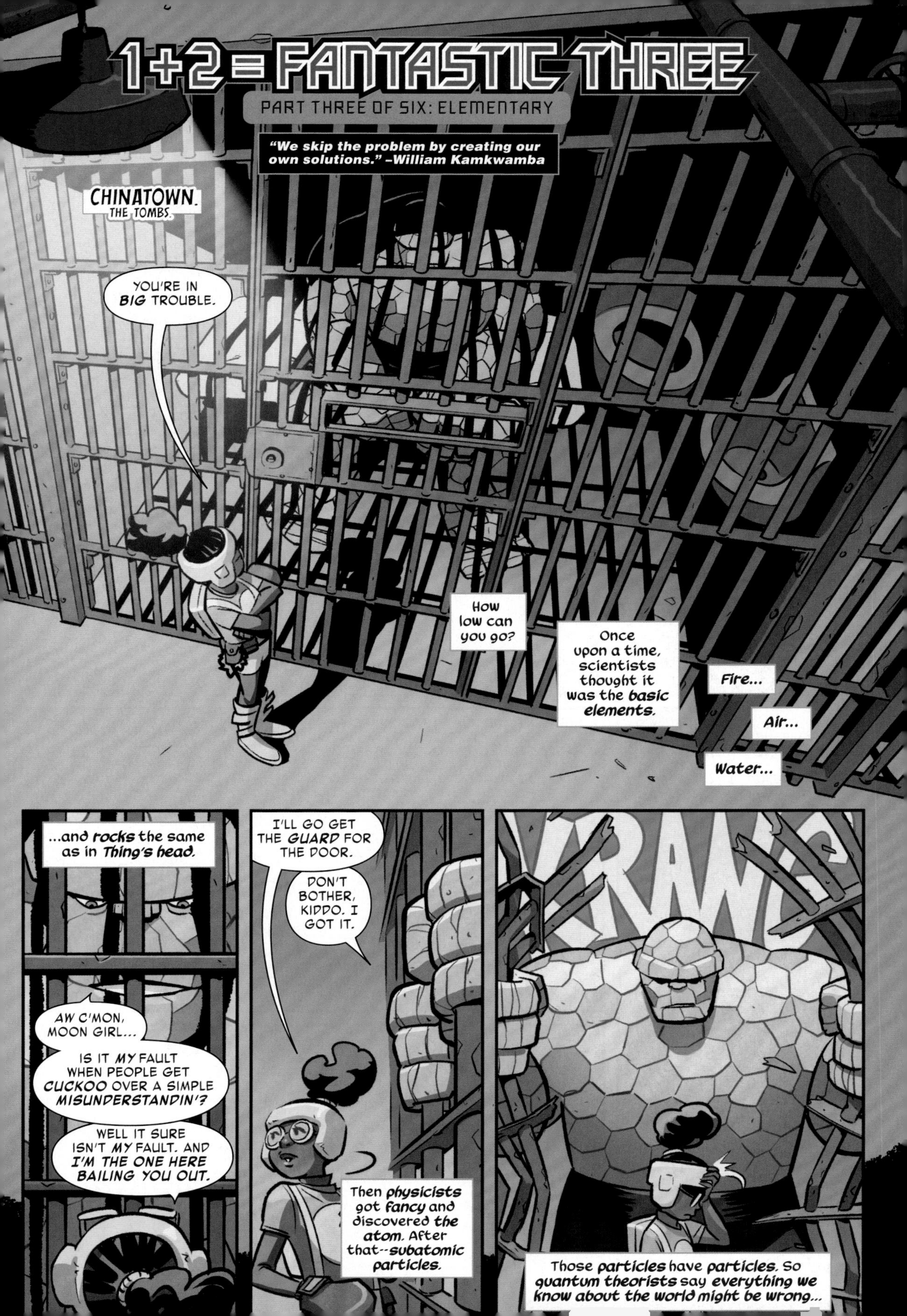
1+2 = FANTASTIC THREE
PART THREE OF SIX: ELEMENTARY
"We skip the problem by creating our own solutions." –William Kamkwamba
CHINATOWN. THE TOMBS.
YOU'RE IN BIG TROUBLE.
How low can you go?
Once upon a time, scientists thought it was the basic elements.
Fire...
Air...
Water...
...and rocks the same as in Thing's head.
AW C'MON, MOON GIRL...
IS IT MY FAULT WHEN PEOPLE GET CUCKOO OVER A SIMPLE MISUNDERSTANDIN'?
WELL IT SURE ISN'T MY FAULT. AND I'M THE ONE HERE BAILING YOU OUT.
I'LL GO GET THE GUARD FOR THE DOOR.
DON'T BOTHER, KIDDO. I GOT IT.
Then physicists got fancy and discovered the atom. After that--subatomic particles.
Those particles have particles. So quantum theorists say everything we know about the world might be wrong...

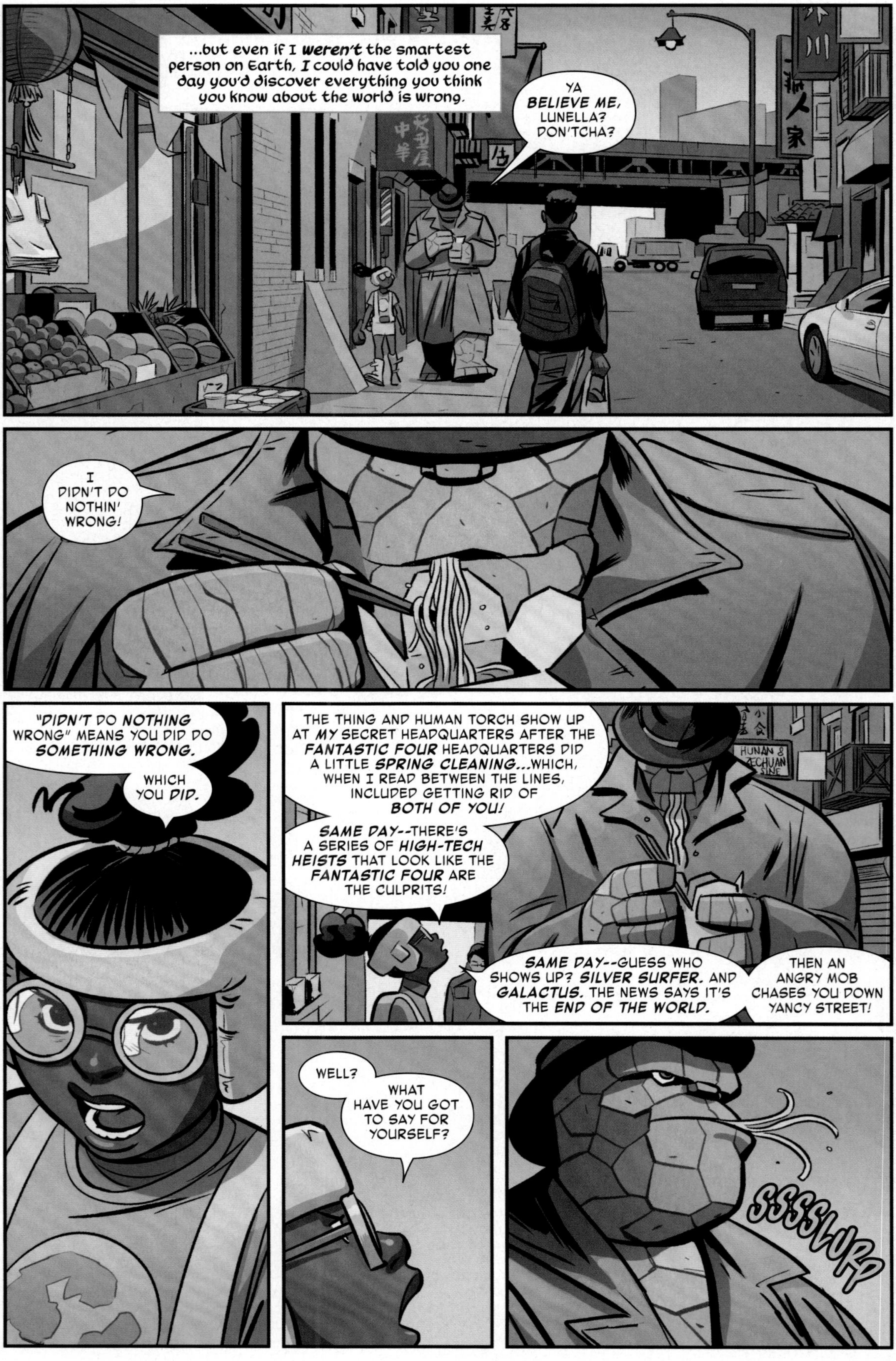
...but even if I weren't the smartest person on Earth, I could have told you one day you'd discover everything you think you know about the world is wrong.
YA BELIEVE ME, LUNELLA? DON'TCHA?
I DIDN'T DO NOTHIN' WRONG!
"DIDN'T DO NOTHING WRONG" MEANS YOU DID DO SOMETHING WRONG.
WHICH YOU DID.
THE THING AND HUMAN TORCH SHOW UP AT MY SECRET HEADQUARTERS AFTER THE FANTASTIC FOUR HEADQUARTERS DID A LITTLE SPRING CLEANING...WHICH, WHEN I READ BETWEEN THE LINES, INCLUDED GETTING RID OF BOTH OF YOU!
SAME DAY--THERE'S A SERIES OF HIGH-TECH HEISTS THAT LOOK LIKE THE FANTASTIC FOUR ARE THE CULPRITS!
HUNAN & SZECHUAN CUISINE
SAME DAY--GUESS WHO SHOWS UP? SILVER SURFER. AND GALACTUS. THE NEWS SAYS IT'S THE END OF THE WORLD.
THEN AN ANGRY MOB CHASES YOU DOWN YANCY STREET!
WELL?
WHAT HAVE YOU GOT TO SAY FOR YOURSELF?
SSSSLURP

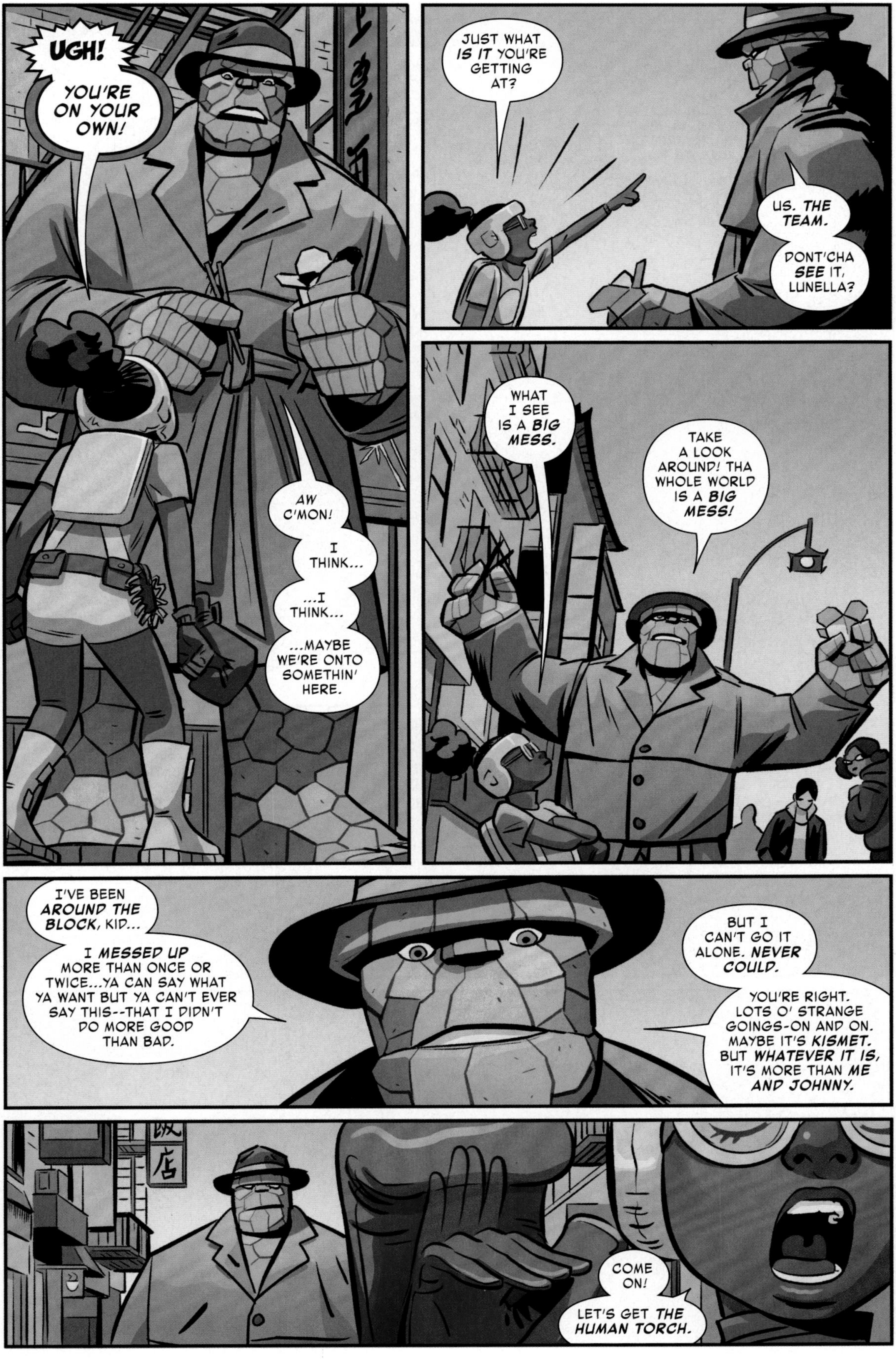
UGH!
YOU'RE ON YOUR OWN!
AW C'MON!
I THINK...
...I THINK...
...MAYBE WE'RE ONTO SOMETHIN' HERE.
JUST WHAT IS IT YOU'RE GETTING AT?
US. THE TEAM.
DONT'CHA SEE IT, LUNELLA?
WHAT I SEE IS A BIG MESS.
TAKE A LOOK AROUND! THA WHOLE WORLD IS A BIG MESS!
I'VE BEEN AROUND THE BLOCK, KID...
I MESSED UP MORE THAN ONCE OR TWICE...YA CAN SAY WHAT YA WANT BUT YA CAN'T EVER SAY THIS--THAT I DIDN'T DO MORE GOOD THAN BAD.
BUT I CAN'T GO IT ALONE. NEVER COULD.
YOU'RE RIGHT. LOTS O' STRANGE GOINGS-ON AND ON. MAYBE IT'S KISMET. BUT WHATEVER IT IS, IT'S MORE THAN ME AND JOHNNY.
COME ON!
LET'S GET THE HUMAN TORCH.

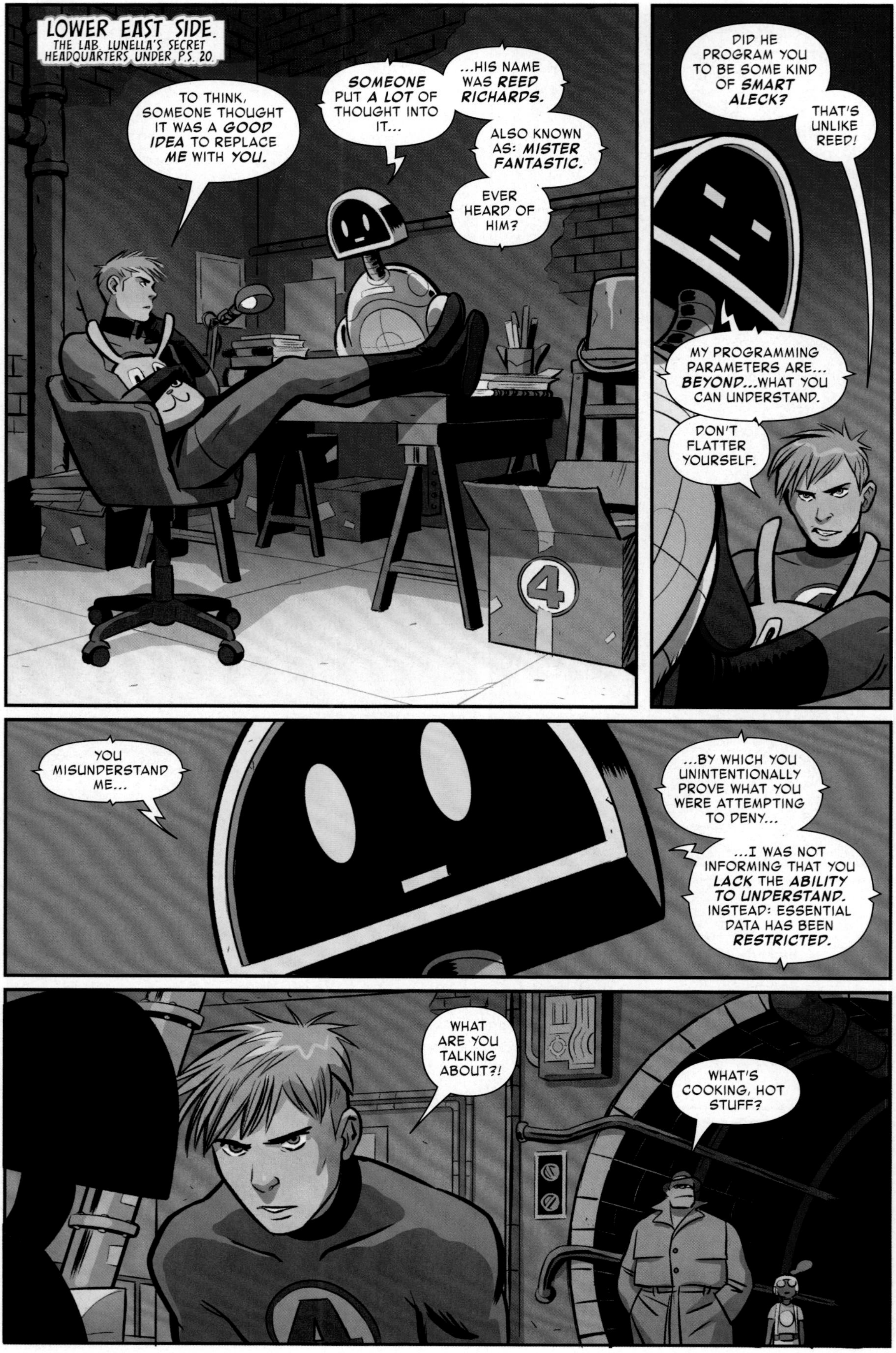
LOWER EAST SIDE.
THE LAB. LUNELLA'S SECRET HEADQUARTERS UNDER P.S. 20.
TO THINK, SOMEONE THOUGHT IT WAS A GOOD IDEA TO REPLACE ME WITH YOU.
SOMEONE PUT A LOT OF THOUGHT INTO IT...
...HIS NAME WAS REED RICHARDS.
ALSO KNOWN AS: MISTER FANTASTIC.
EVER HEARD OF HIM?
DID HE PROGRAM YOU TO BE SOME KIND OF SMART ALECK?
THAT'S UNLIKE REED!
MY PROGRAMMING PARAMETERS ARE... BEYOND...WHAT YOU CAN UNDERSTAND.
DON'T FLATTER YOURSELF.
YOU MISUNDERSTAND ME...
...BY WHICH YOU UNINTENTIONALLY PROVE WHAT YOU WERE ATTEMPTING TO DENY...
...I WAS NOT INFORMING THAT YOU LACK THE ABILITY TO UNDERSTAND. INSTEAD: ESSENTIAL DATA HAS BEEN RESTRICTED.
WHAT ARE YOU TALKING ABOUT?!
WHAT'S COOKING, HOT STUFF?

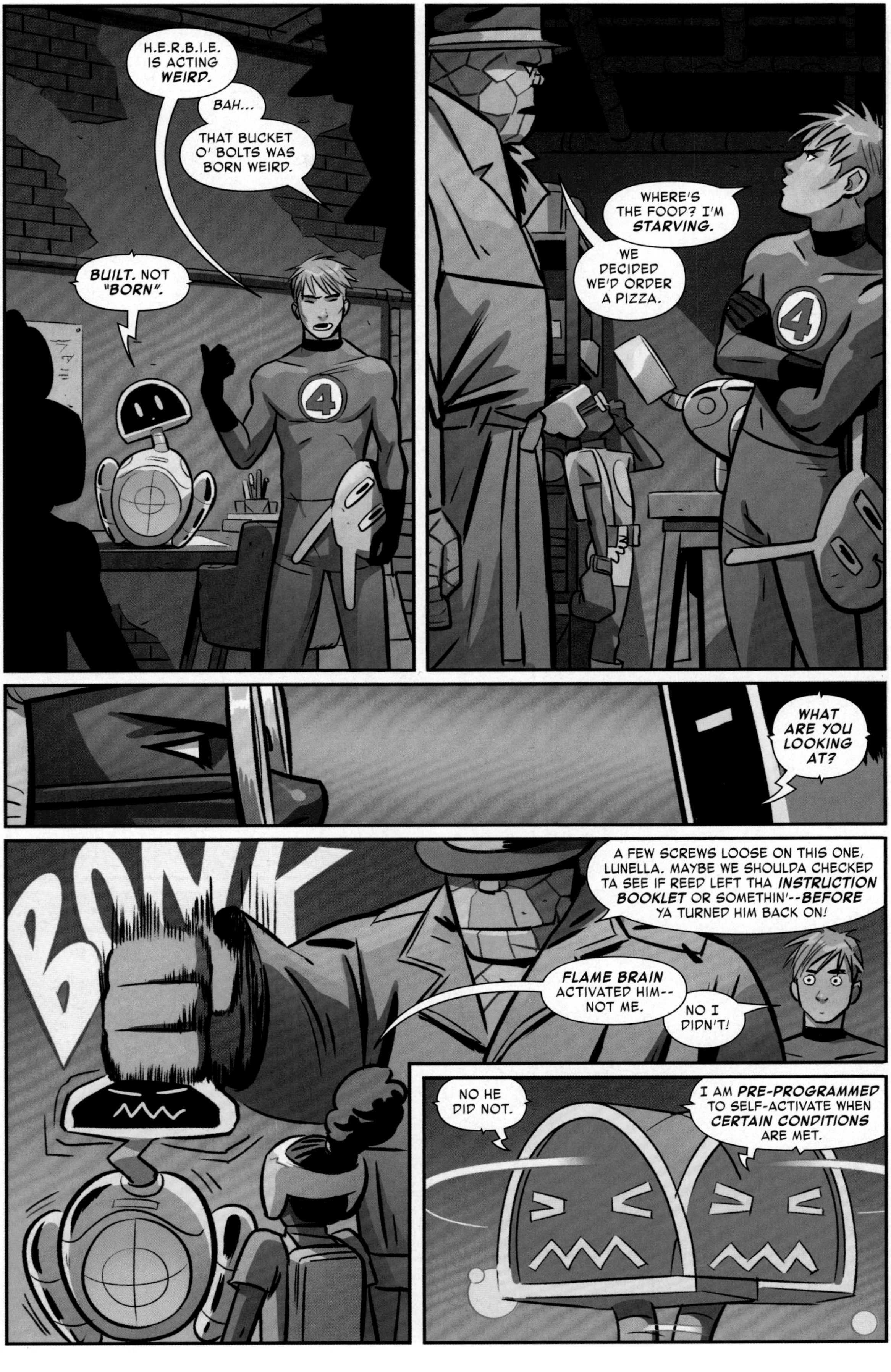
H.E.R.B.I.E. IS ACTING WEIRD.
BAH...
THAT BUCKET O' BOLTS WAS BORN WEIRD.
BUILT. NOT "BORN".
WHERE'S THE FOOD? I'M STARVING.
WE DECIDED WE'D ORDER A PIZZA.
WHAT ARE YOU LOOKING AT?
BONK
A FEW SCREWS LOOSE ON THIS ONE, LUNELLA. MAYBE WE SHOULDA CHECKED TA SEE IF REED LEFT THA INSTRUCTION BOOKLET OR SOMETHIN'--BEFORE YA TURNED HIM BACK ON!
FLAME BRAIN ACTIVATED HIM--NOT ME.
NO I DIDN'T!
NO HE DID NOT.
I AM PRE-PROGRAMMED TO SELF-ACTIVATE WHEN CERTAIN CONDITIONS ARE MET.

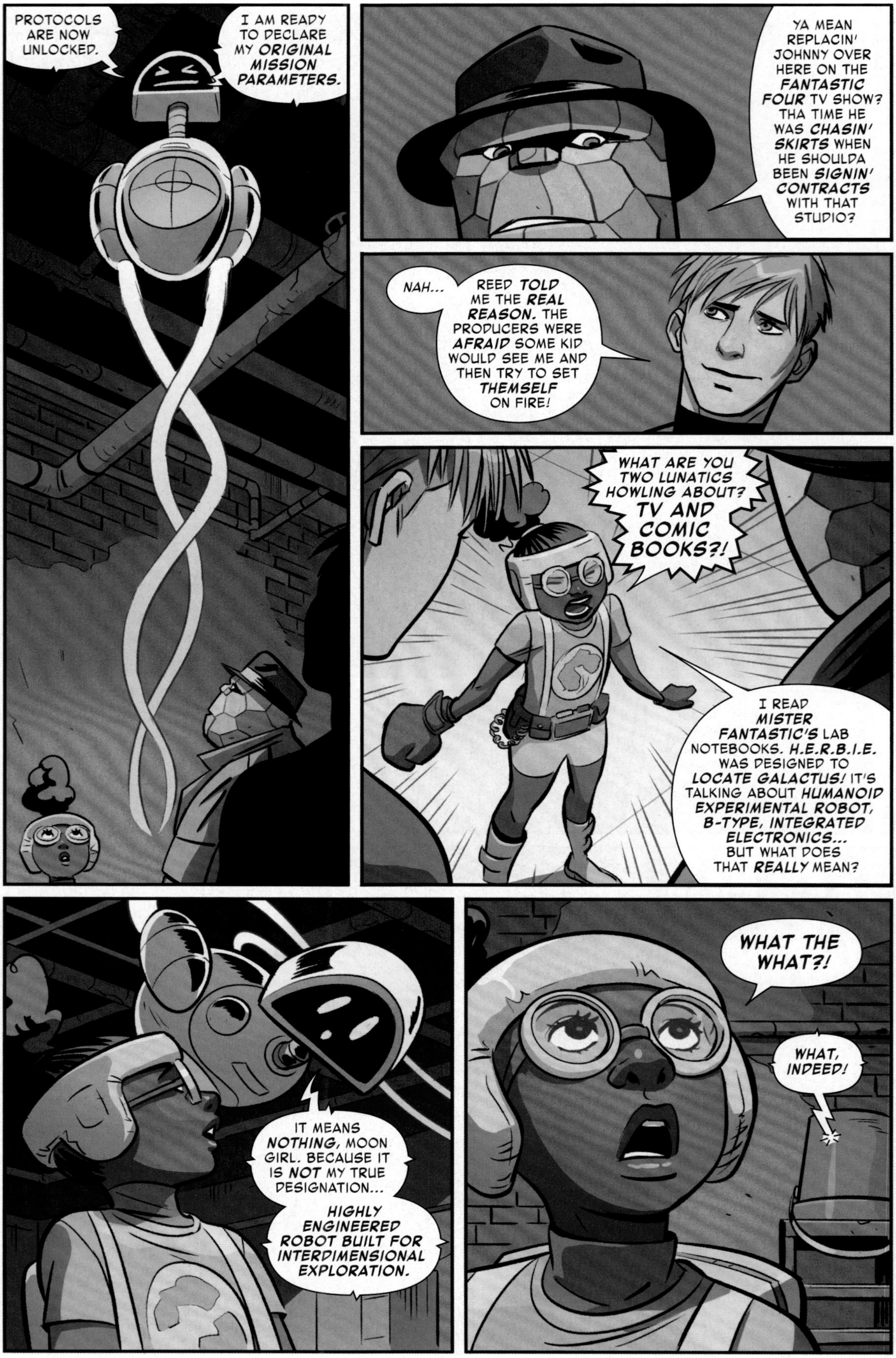
PROTOCOLS ARE NOW UNLOCKED.
I AM READY TO DECLARE MY ORIGINAL MISSION PARAMETERS.
YA MEAN REPLACIN' JOHNNY OVER HERE ON THE FANTASTIC FOUR TV SHOW? THA TIME HE WAS CHASIN' SKIRTS WHEN HE SHOULDA BEEN SIGNIN' CONTRACTS WITH THAT STUDIO?
NAH...
REED TOLD ME THE REAL REASON. THE PRODUCERS WERE AFRAID SOME KID WOULD SEE ME AND THEN TRY TO SET THEMSELF ON FIRE!
WHAT ARE YOU TWO LUNATICS HOWLING ABOUT? TV AND COMIC BOOKS?!
I READ MISTER FANTASTIC'S LAB NOTEBOOKS. H.E.R.B.I.E. WAS DESIGNED TO LOCATE GALACTUS! IT'S TALKING ABOUT HUMANOID EXPERIMENTAL ROBOT, B-TYPE, INTEGRATED ELECTRONICS... BUT WHAT DOES THAT REALLY MEAN?
IT MEANS NOTHING, MOON GIRL. BECAUSE IT IS NOT MY TRUE DESIGNATION...
HIGHLY ENGINEERED ROBOT BUILT FOR INTERDIMENSIONAL EXPLORATION.
WHAT THE WHAT?!
WHAT, INDEED!

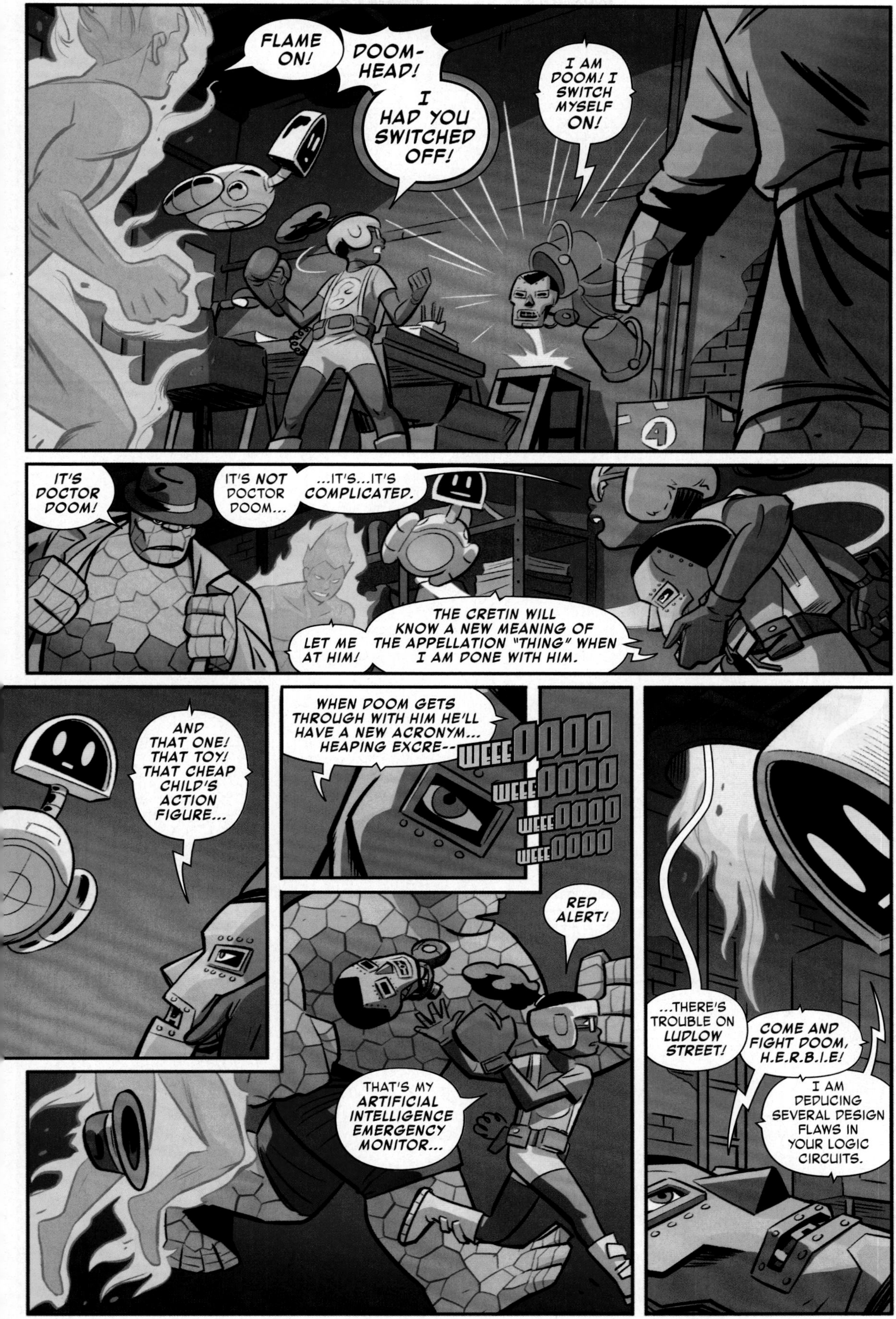
FLAME ON!
DOOM-HEAD! I HAD YOU SWITCHED OFF!
I AM DOOM! I SWITCH MYSELF ON!
IT'S DOCTOR DOOM!
IT'S NOT DOCTOR DOOM...
...IT'S...IT'S COMPLICATED.
LET ME AT HIM!
THE CRETIN WILL KNOW A NEW MEANING OF THE APPELLATION "THING" WHEN I AM DONE WITH HIM.
AND THAT ONE! THAT TOY! THAT CHEAP CHILD'S ACTION FIGURE...
WHEN DOOM GETS THROUGH WITH HIM HE'LL HAVE A NEW ACRONYM... HEAPING EXCRE--
WEEEOOOO
WEEEOOOO
WEEEOOOO
WEEEOOOO
RED ALERT!
THAT'S MY ARTIFICIAL INTELLIGENCE EMERGENCY MONITOR...
...THERE'S TROUBLE ON LUDLOW STREET!
COME AND FIGHT DOOM, H.E.R.B.I.E!
I AM DEDUCING SEVERAL DESIGN FLAWS IN YOUR LOGIC CIRCUITS.

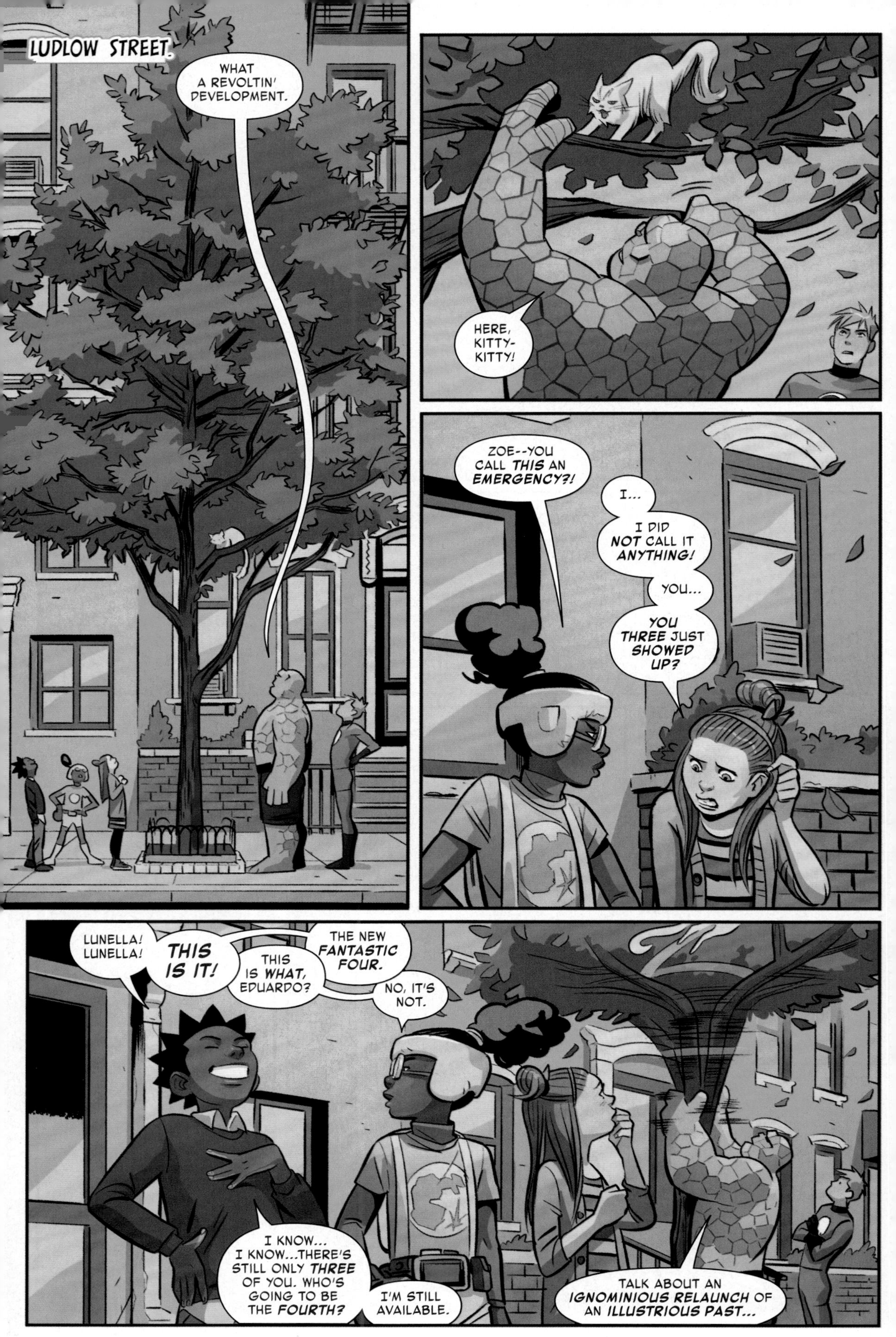

LUDLOW STREET.
WHAT A REVOLTIN' DEVELOPMENT.
HERE, KITTY-KITTY!
ZOE--YOU CALL THIS AN EMERGENCY?!
I...
I DID NOT CALL IT ANYTHING!
YOU...
YOU THREE JUST SHOWED UP?
LUNELLA! LUNELLA!
THIS IS IT!
THIS IS WHAT, EDUARDO?
THE NEW FANTASTIC FOUR.
NO, IT'S NOT.
I KNOW... I KNOW...THERE'S STILL ONLY THREE OF YOU. WHO'S GOING TO BE THE FOURTH?
I'M STILL AVAILABLE.
TALK ABOUT AN IGNOMINIOUS RELAUNCH OF AN ILLUSTRIOUS PAST...

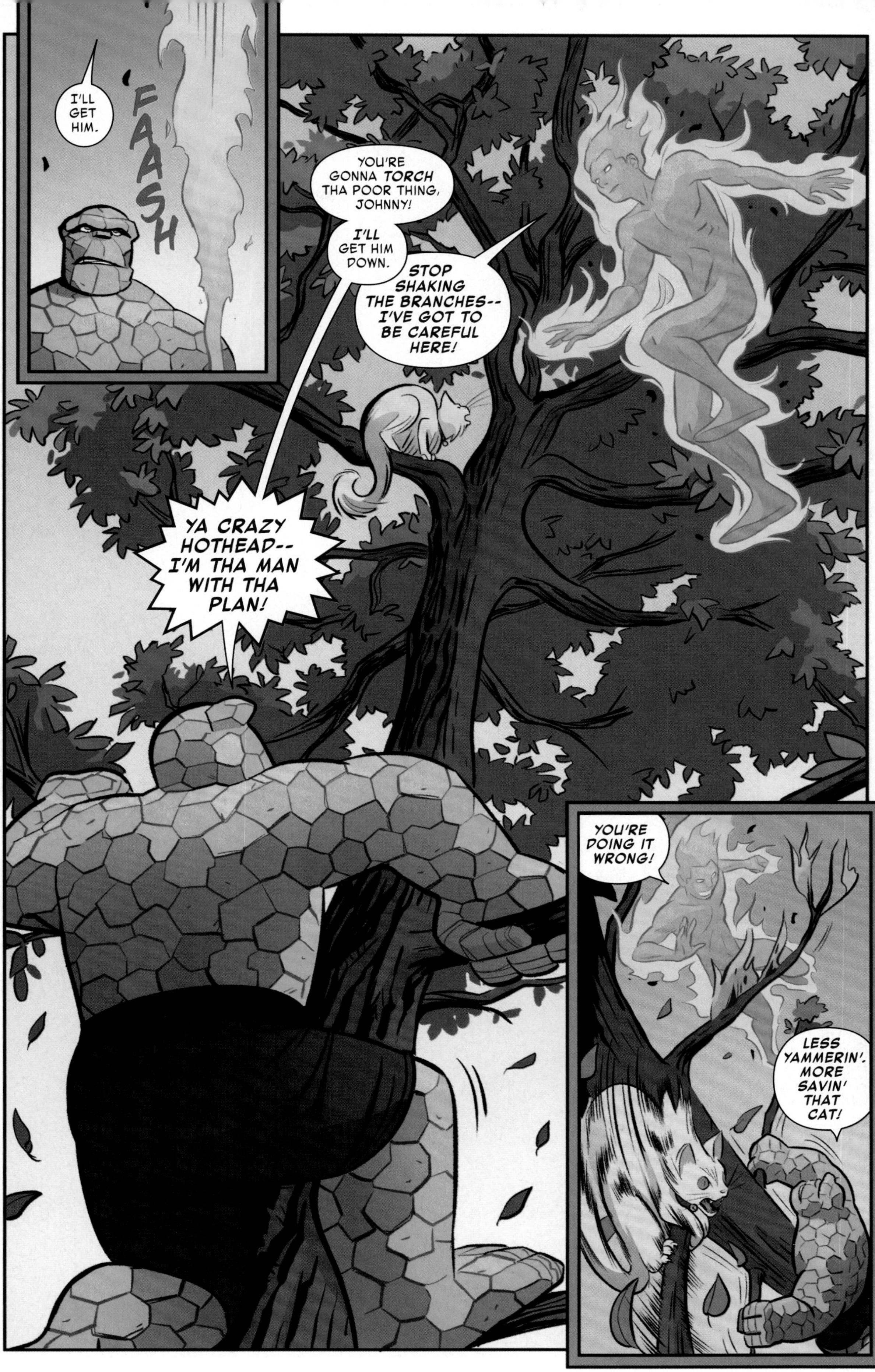
I'LL GET HIM.
FAAASH
YOU'RE GONNA TORCH THA POOR THING, JOHNNY!
I'LL GET HIM DOWN.
STOP SHAKING THE BRANCHES-- I'VE GOT TO BE CAREFUL HERE!
YA CRAZY HOTHEAD-- I'M THA MAN WITH THA PLAN!
YOU'RE DOING IT WRONG!
LESS YAMMERIN'. MORE SAVIN' THAT CAT!

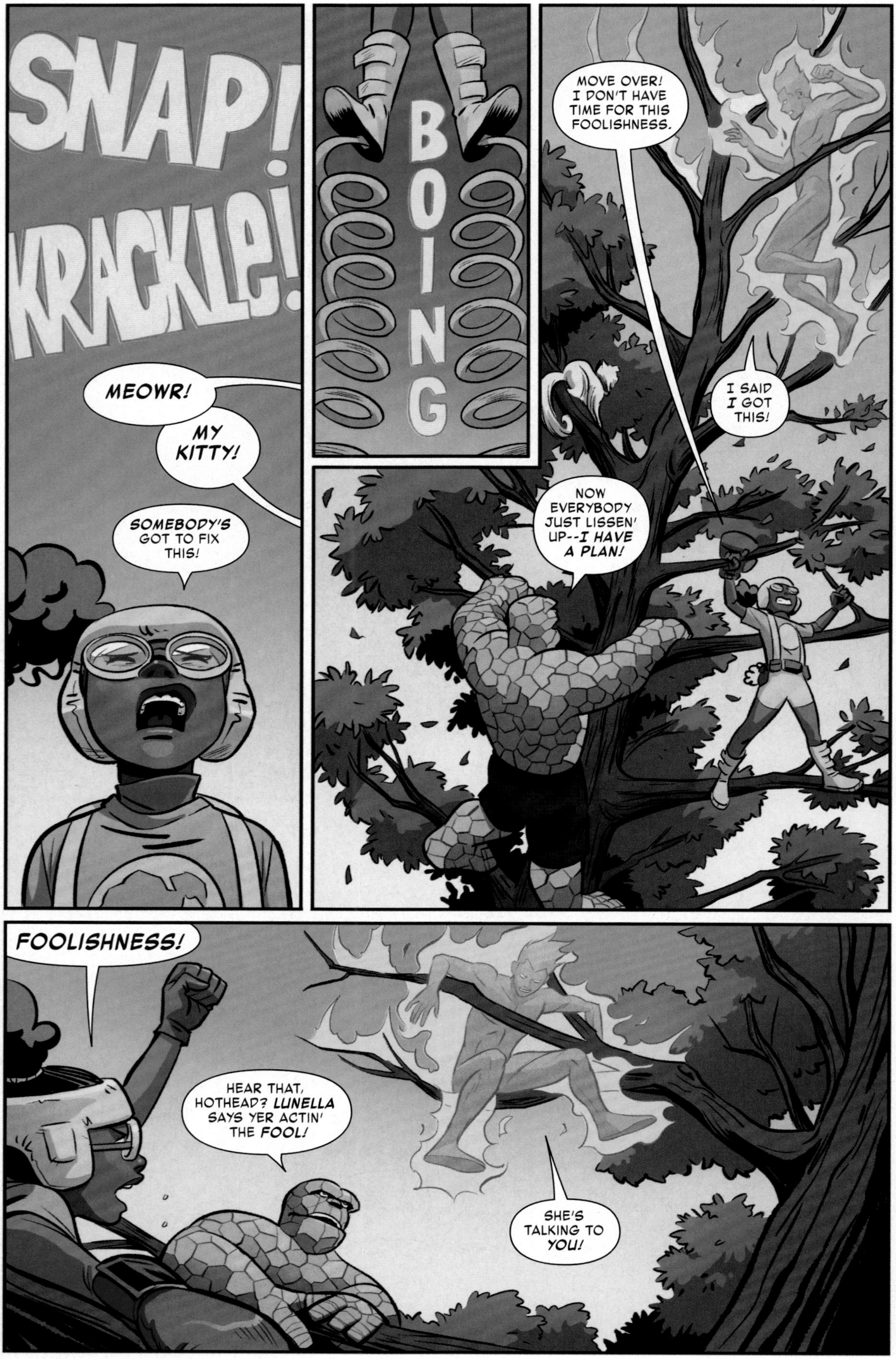
SNAP!
KRACKLE!
MEOWR!
MY KITTY!
SOMEBODY'S GOT TO FIX THIS!
BOING
MOVE OVER! I DON'T HAVE TIME FOR THIS FOOLISHNESS.
I SAID I GOT THIS!
NOW EVERYBODY JUST LISSEN' UP--I HAVE A PLAN!
FOOLISHNESS!
HEAR THAT, HOTHEAD? LUNELLA SAYS YER ACTIN' THE FOOL!
SHE'S TALKING TO YOU!

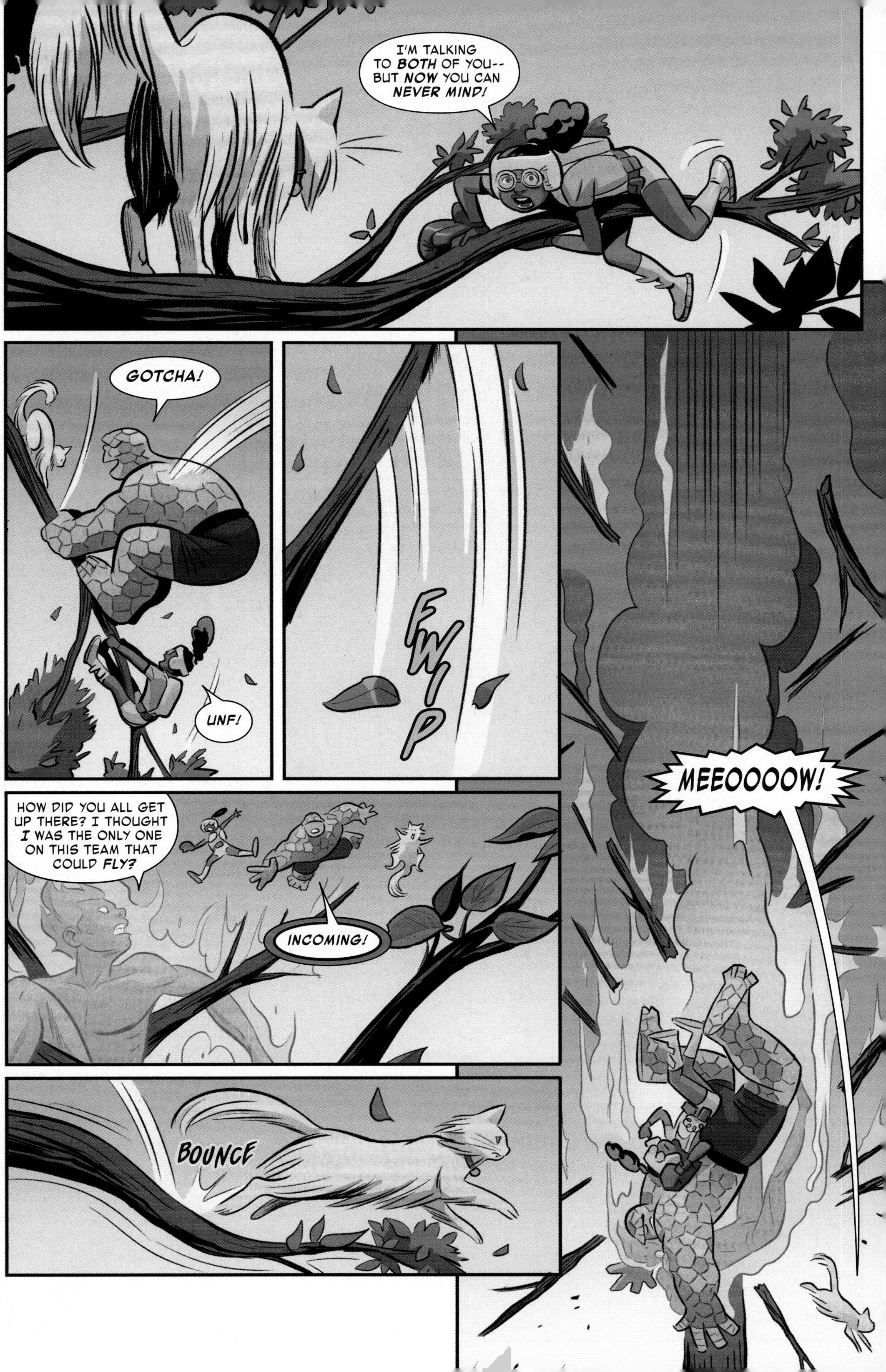
I'M TALKING TO BOTH OF YOU-- BUT NOW YOU CAN NEVER MIND!
GOTCHA!
UNF!
FWIP
HOW DID YOU ALL GET UP THERE? I THOUGHT I WAS THE ONLY ONE ON THIS TEAM THAT COULD FLY?
INCOMING!
BOUNCE
MEEOOOOW!

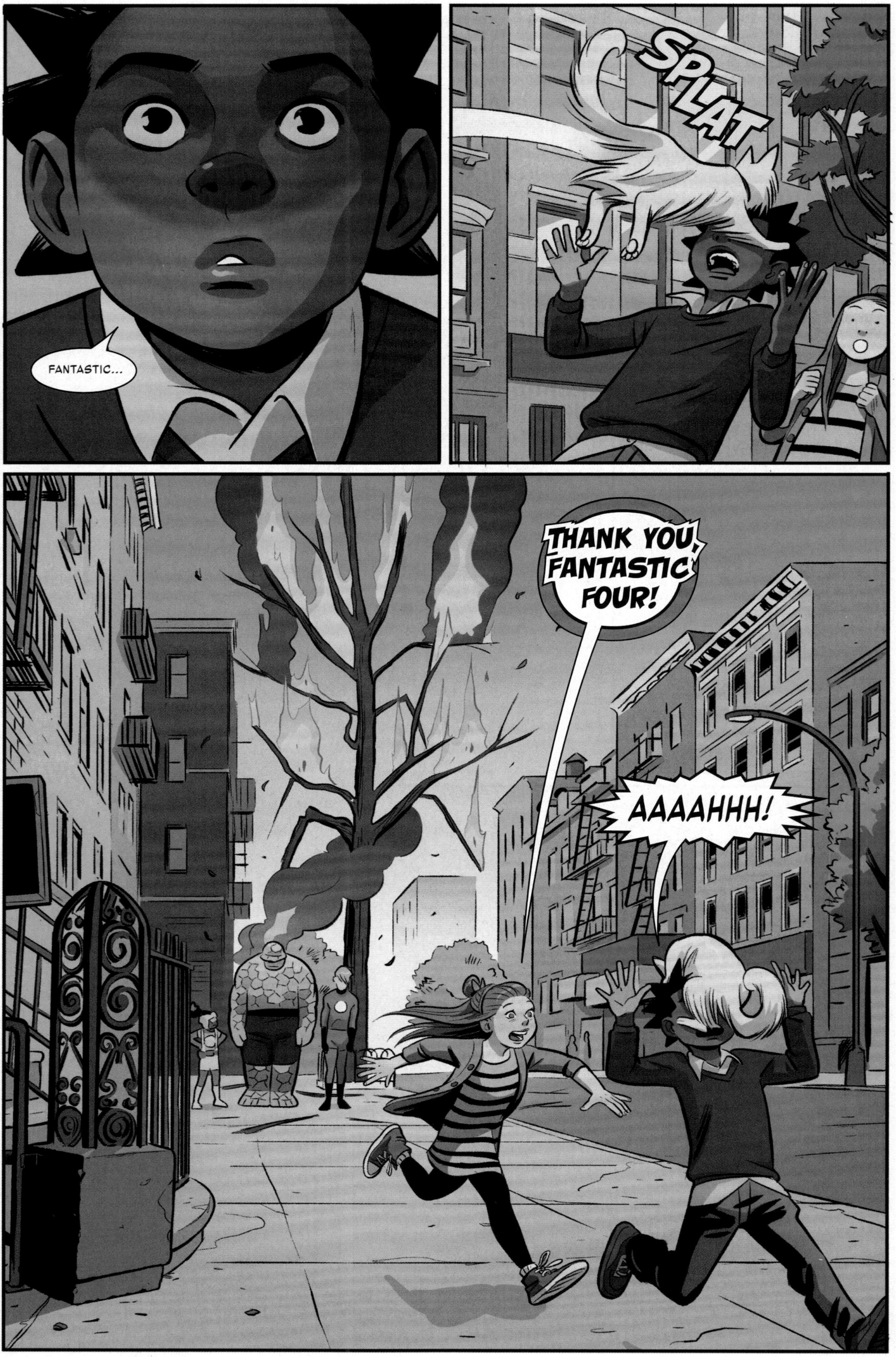
FANTASTIC...
SPLAT
THANK YOU, FANTASTIC FOUR!
AAAAHHH!

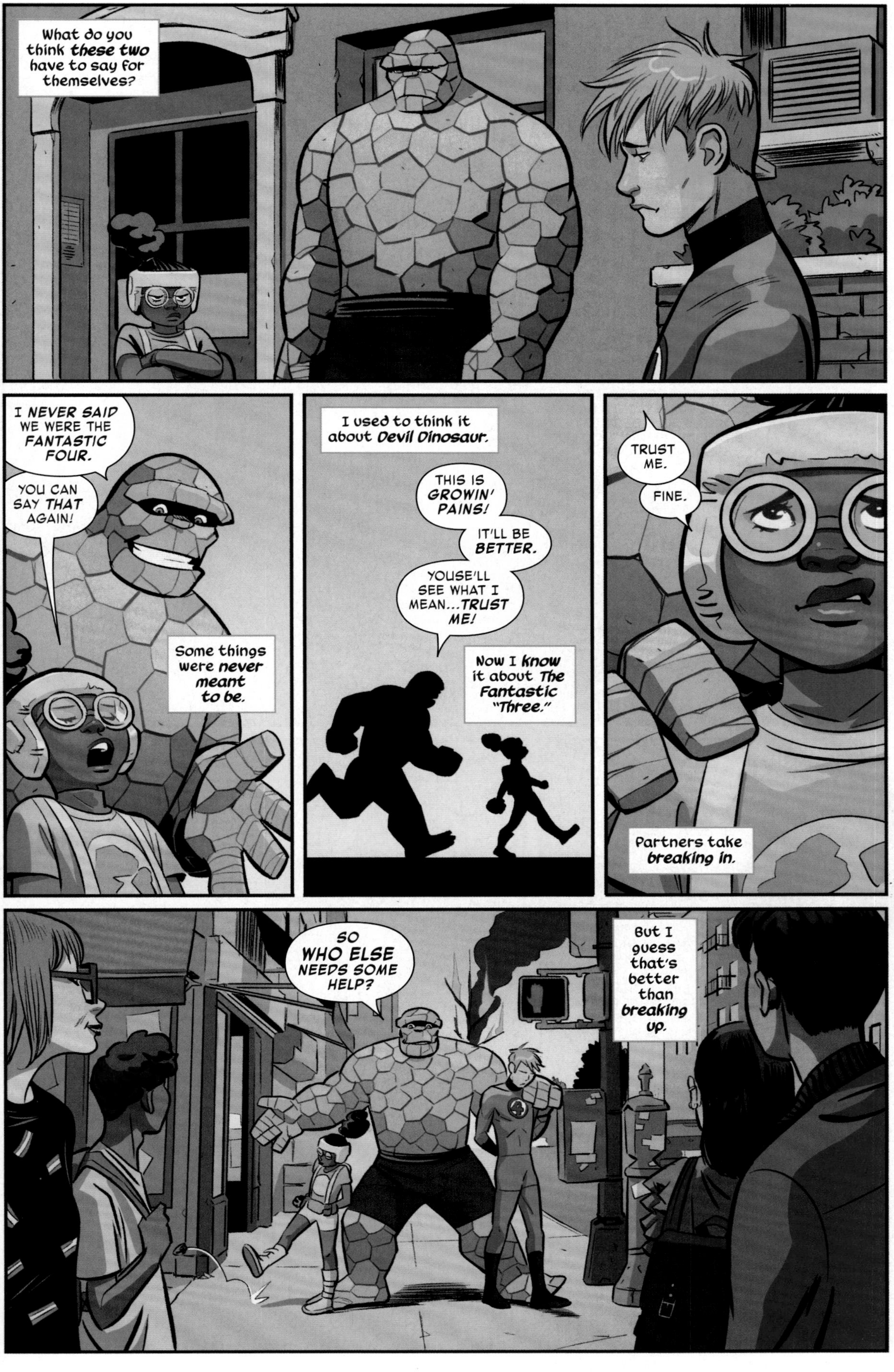
What do you think these two have to say for themselves?
I NEVER SAID WE WERE THE FANTASTIC FOUR.
YOU CAN SAY THAT AGAIN!
Some things were never meant to be.
I used to think it about Devil Dinosaur.
THIS IS GROWIN' PAINS!
IT'LL BE BETTER.
YOUSE'LL SEE WHAT I MEAN...TRUST ME!
Now I know it about The Fantastic "Three."
TRUST ME.
FINE.
Partners take breaking in.
SO WHO ELSE NEEDS SOME HELP?
But I guess that's better than breaking up.

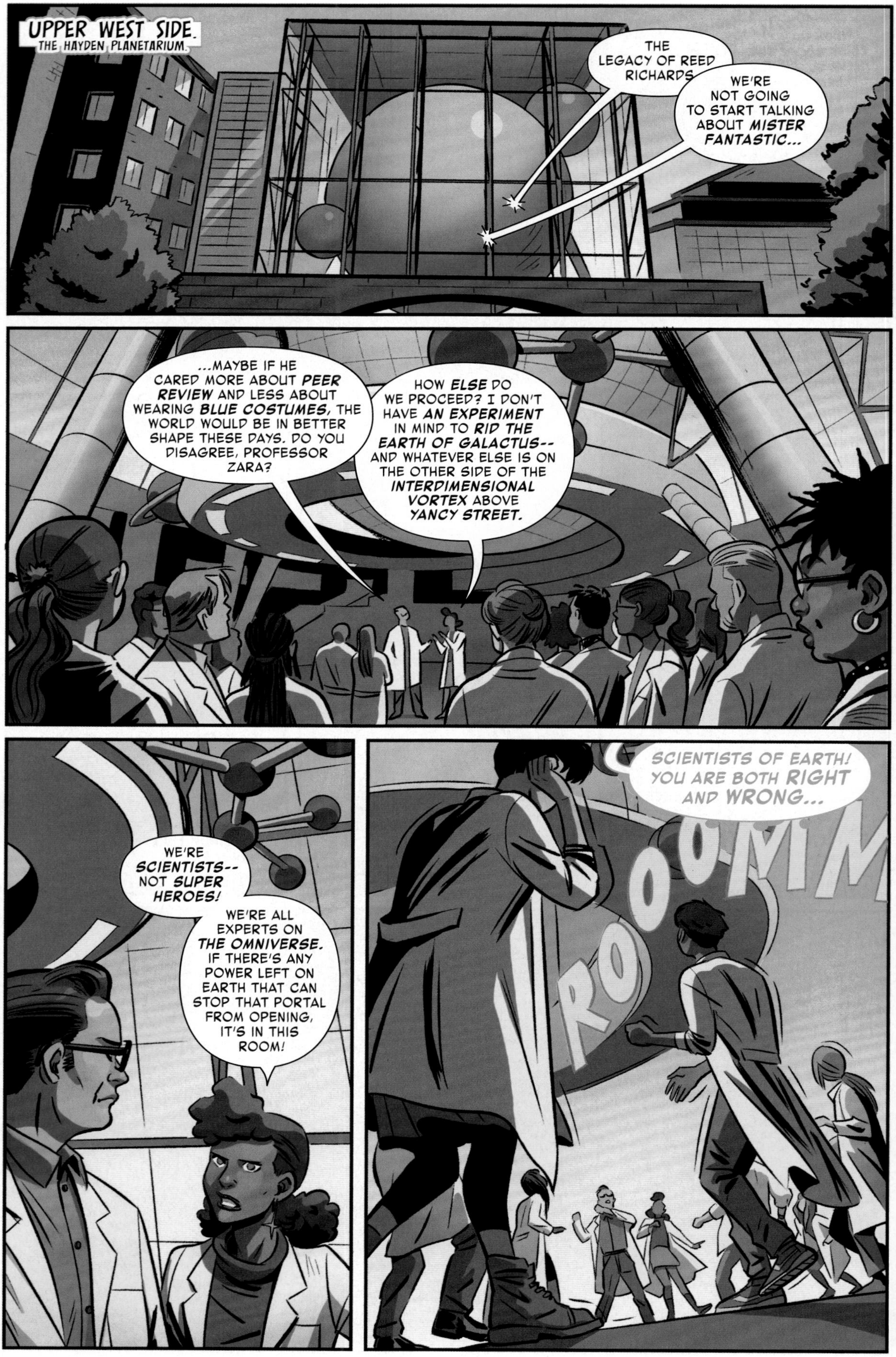
UPPER WEST SIDE.
THE HAYDEN PLANETARIUM.
THE LEGACY OF REED RICHARDS
WE'RE NOT GOING TO START TALKING ABOUT MISTER FANTASTIC...
...MAYBE IF HE CARED MORE ABOUT PEER REVIEW AND LESS ABOUT WEARING BLUE COSTUMES, THE WORLD WOULD BE IN BETTER SHAPE THESE DAYS. DO YOU DISAGREE, PROFESSOR ZARA?
HOW ELSE DO WE PROCEED? I DON'T HAVE AN EXPERIMENT IN MIND TO RID THE EARTH OF GALACTUS--AND WHATEVER ELSE IS ON THE OTHER SIDE OF THE INTERDIMENSIONAL VORTEX ABOVE YANCY STREET.
WE'RE SCIENTISTS--NOT SUPER HEROES!
WE'RE ALL EXPERTS ON THE OMNIVERSE. IF THERE'S ANY POWER LEFT ON EARTH THAT CAN STOP THAT PORTAL FROM OPENING, IT'S IN THIS ROOM!
SCIENTISTS OF EARTH! YOU ARE BOTH RIGHT AND WRONG...

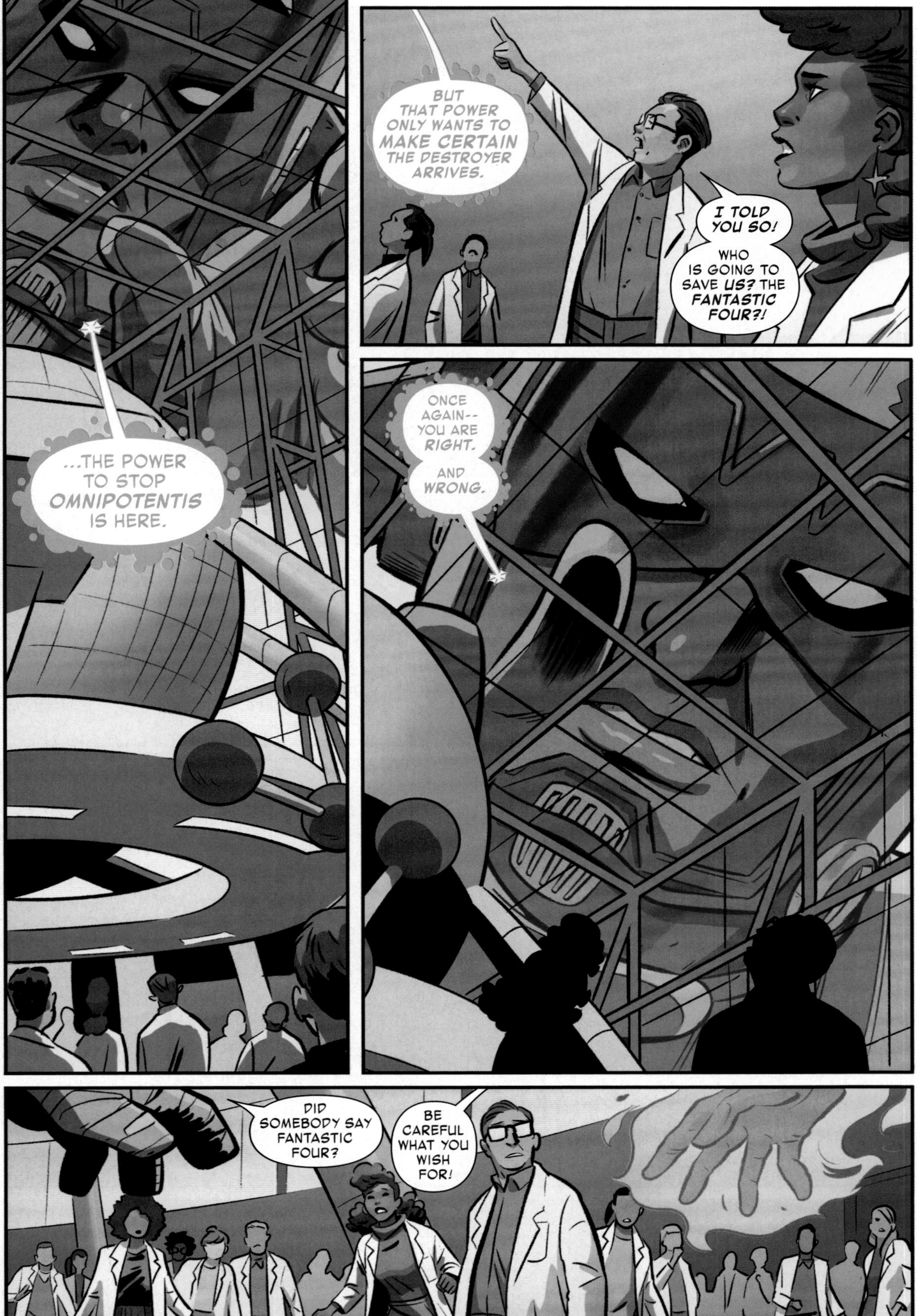
...THE POWER TO STOP OMNIPOTENTIS IS HERE.
BUT THAT POWER ONLY WANTS TO MAKE CERTAIN THE DESTROYER ARRIVES.
I TOLD YOU SO!
WHO IS GOING TO SAVE US? THE FANTASTIC FOUR?!
ONCE AGAIN-- YOU ARE RIGHT.
AND WRONG.
DID SOMEBODY SAY FANTASTIC FOUR?
BE CAREFUL WHAT YOU WISH FOR!

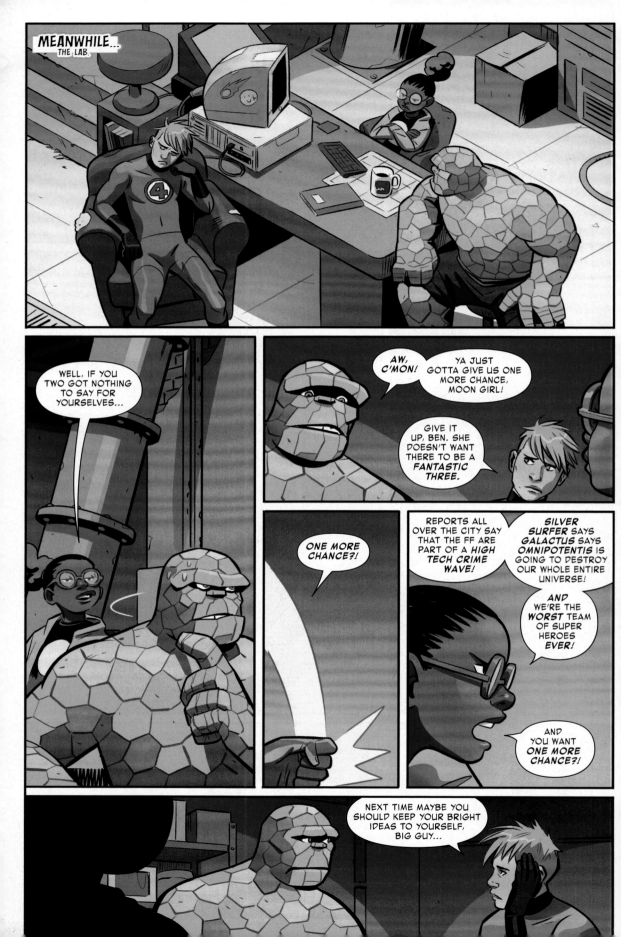

WELL, IF YOU TWO GOT NOTHING TO SAY FOR YOURSELVES...

AW, C'MON!

YA JUST GOTTA GIVE US ONE MORE CHANCE, MOON GIRL!

GIVE IT UP, BEN. SHE DOESN'T WANT THERE TO BE A *FANTASTIC THREE.*

ONE MORE CHANCE?!

REPORTS ALL OVER THE CITY SAY THAT THE FF ARE PART OF A *HIGH TECH CRIME WAVE!*

SILVER SURFER SAYS *GALACTUS* SAYS *OMNIPOTENTIS* IS GOING TO DESTROY OUR WHOLE ENTIRE UNIVERSE!

AND WE'RE THE *WORST* TEAM OF SUPER HEROES *EVER!*

AND YOU WANT *ONE MORE CHANCE?!*

NEXT TIME MAYBE YOU SHOULD KEEP YOUR BRIGHT IDEAS TO YOURSELF, BIG GUY...

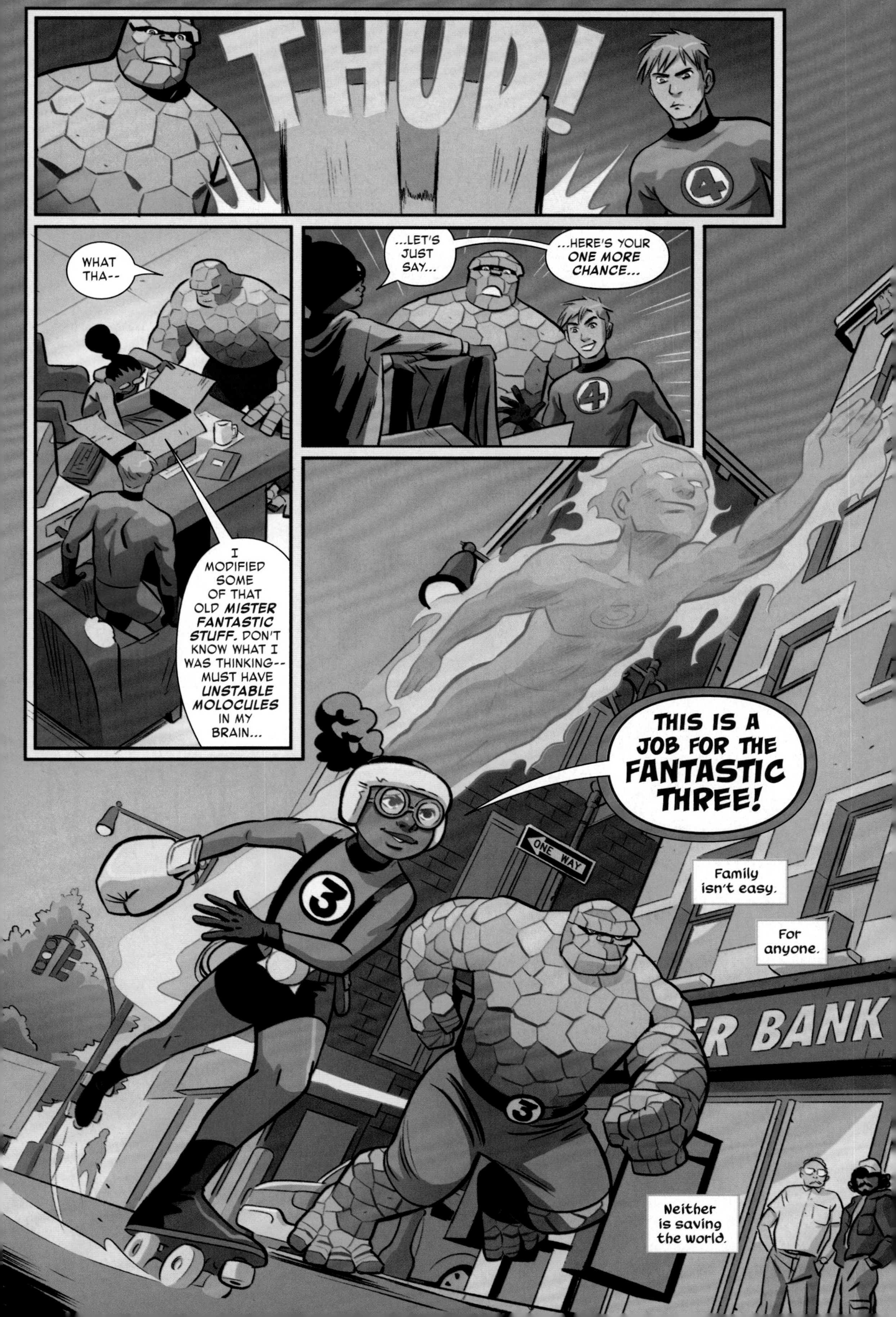
THUD!
WHAT THA--
I MODIFIED SOME OF THAT OLD MISTER FANTASTIC STUFF. DON'T KNOW WHAT I WAS THINKING-- MUST HAVE UNSTABLE MOLOCULES IN MY BRAIN...
...LET'S JUST SAY...
...HERE'S YOUR ONE MORE CHANCE...
THIS IS A JOB FOR THE FANTASTIC THREE!
ONE WAY
Family isn't easy.
For anyone.
ER BANK
Neither is saving the world.

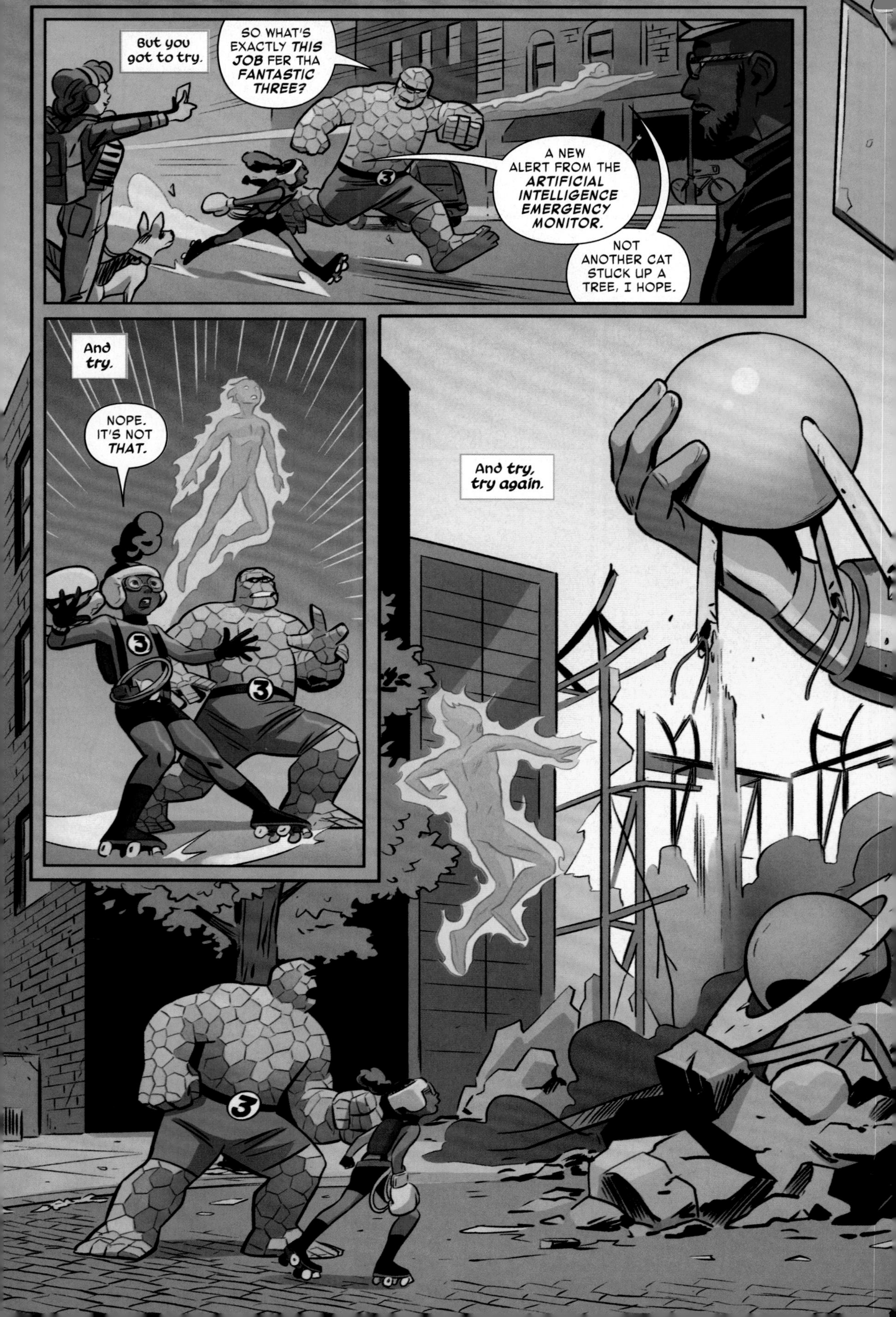

But you got to try.
SO WHAT'S EXACTLY THIS JOB FER THA FANTASTIC THREE?
A NEW ALERT FROM THE ARTIFICIAL INTELLIGENCE EMERGENCY MONITOR.
NOT ANOTHER CAT STUCK UP A TREE, I HOPE.
And try.
NOPE. IT'S NOT THAT.
And try, try again.

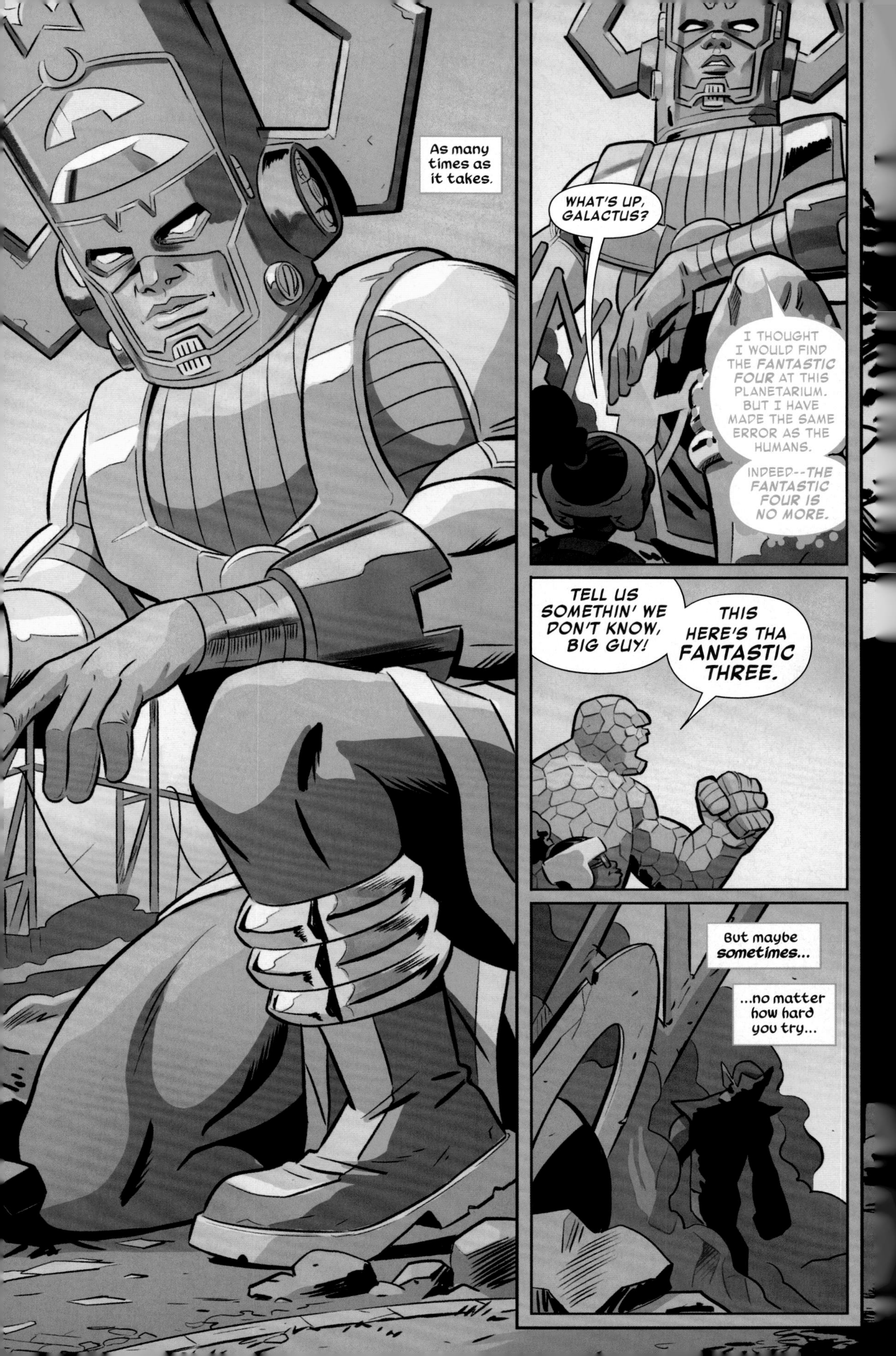
As many times as it takes.
WHAT'S UP, GALACTUS?
I THOUGHT I WOULD FIND THE *FANTASTIC FOUR* AT THIS PLANETARIUM. BUT I HAVE MADE THE SAME ERROR AS THE HUMANS.
INDEED--*THE FANTASTIC FOUR IS NO MORE.*
TELL US SOMETHIN' WE DON'T KNOW, BIG GUY!
THIS HERE'S THA **FANTASTIC THREE.**
But maybe *sometimes...*
...no matter how hard you try...

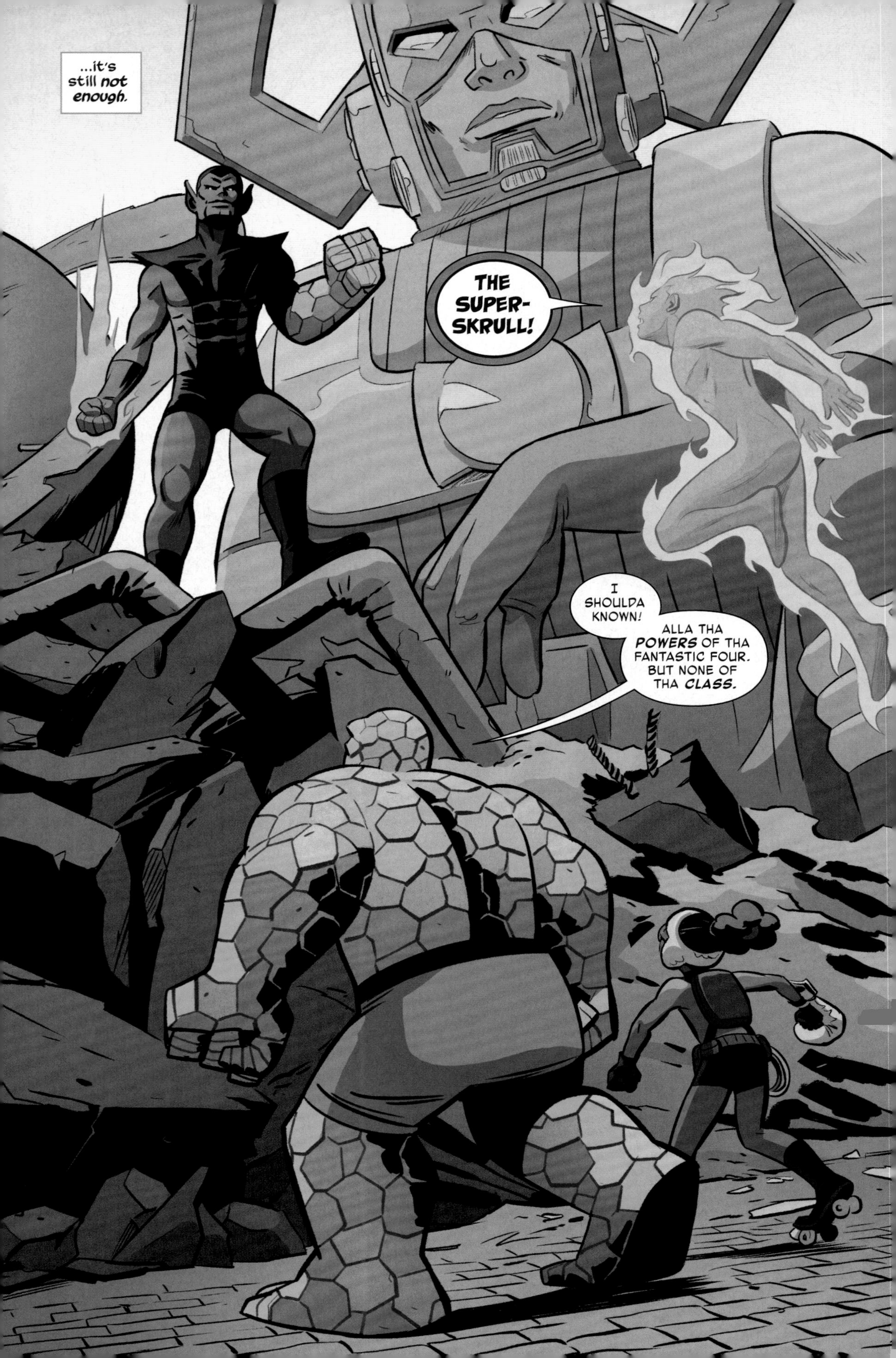
...it's still not enough.
THE SUPER-SKRULL!
I SHOULDA KNOWN!
ALLA THA POWERS OF THA FANTASTIC FOUR. BUT NONE OF THA CLASS.

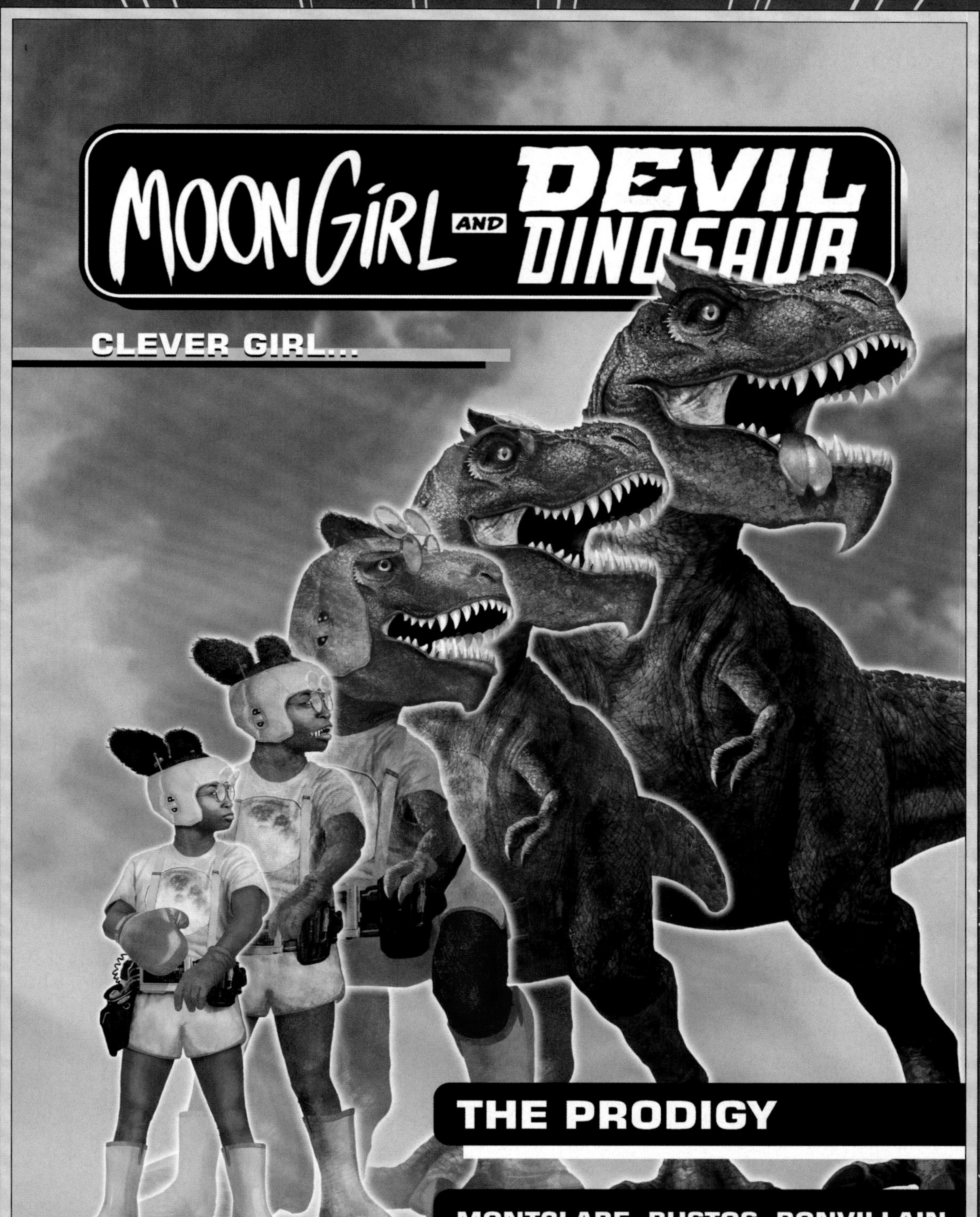
MOON GIRL AND DEVIL DINOSAUR
CLEVER GIRL...
THE PRODIGY
MONTCLARE. BUSTOS. BONVILLAIN.
MARVEL #25 VARIANT EDITION

#25 VARIANT BY RAHZZAH

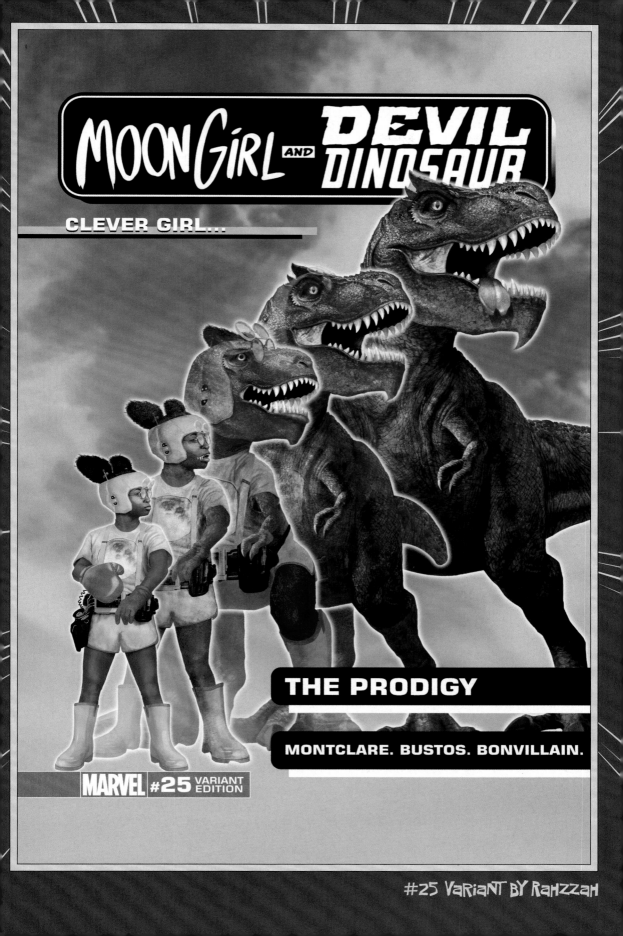

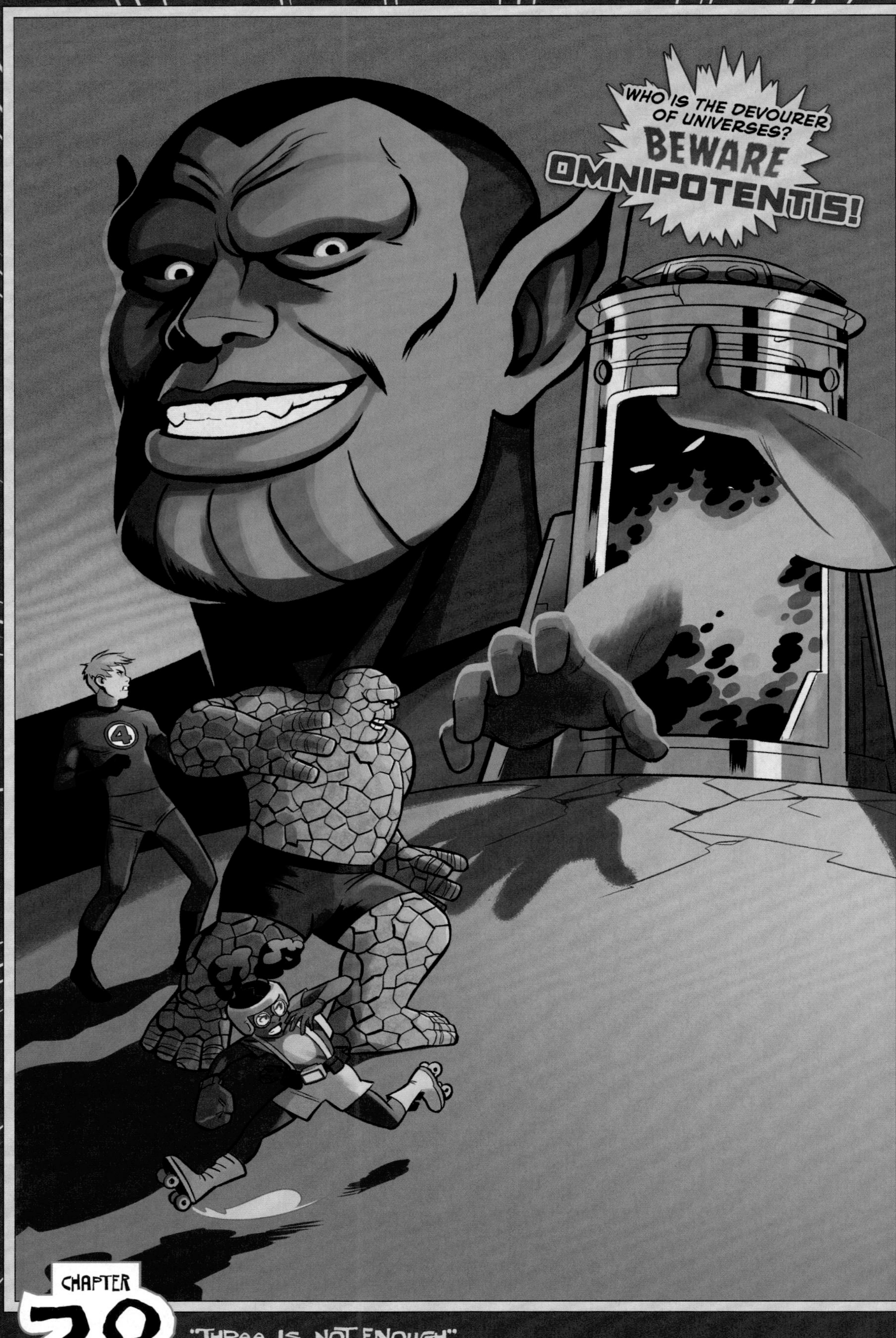
WHO IS THE DEVOURER OF UNIVERSES?
BEWARE OMNIPOTENTIS!

CHAPTER 28 "THREE IS NOT ENOUGH"

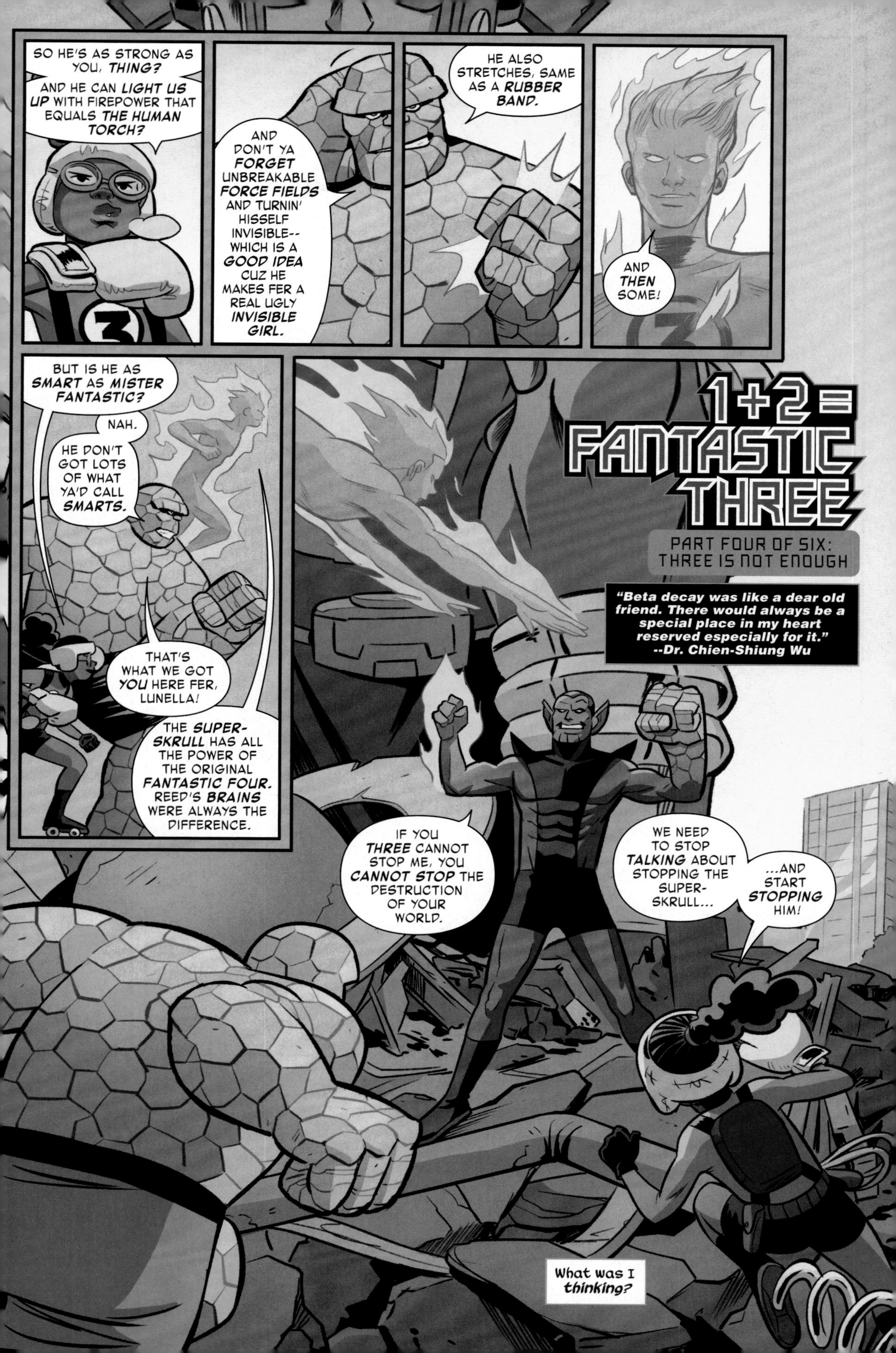
SO HE'S AS STRONG AS YOU, THING?
AND HE CAN LIGHT US UP WITH FIREPOWER THAT EQUALS THE HUMAN TORCH?
AND DON'T YA FORGET UNBREAKABLE FORCE FIELDS AND TURNIN' HISSELF INVISIBLE--WHICH IS A GOOD IDEA CUZ HE MAKES FER A REAL UGLY INVISIBLE GIRL.
HE ALSO STRETCHES, SAME AS A RUBBER BAND.
AND THEN SOME!
BUT IS HE AS SMART AS MISTER FANTASTIC?
NAH.
HE DON'T GOT LOTS OF WHAT YA'D CALL SMARTS.
THAT'S WHAT WE GOT YOU HERE FER, LUNELLA!
THE SUPER-SKRULL HAS ALL THE POWER OF THE ORIGINAL FANTASTIC FOUR. REED'S BRAINS WERE ALWAYS THE DIFFERENCE.
1+2 = FANTASTIC THREE
PART FOUR OF SIX: THREE IS NOT ENOUGH
"Beta decay was like a dear old friend. There would always be a special place in my heart reserved especially for it." --Dr. Chien-Shiung Wu
IF YOU THREE CANNOT STOP ME, YOU CANNOT STOP THE DESTRUCTION OF YOUR WORLD.
WE NEED TO STOP TALKING ABOUT STOPPING THE SUPER-SKRULL...
...AND START STOPPING HIM!
What was I thinking?

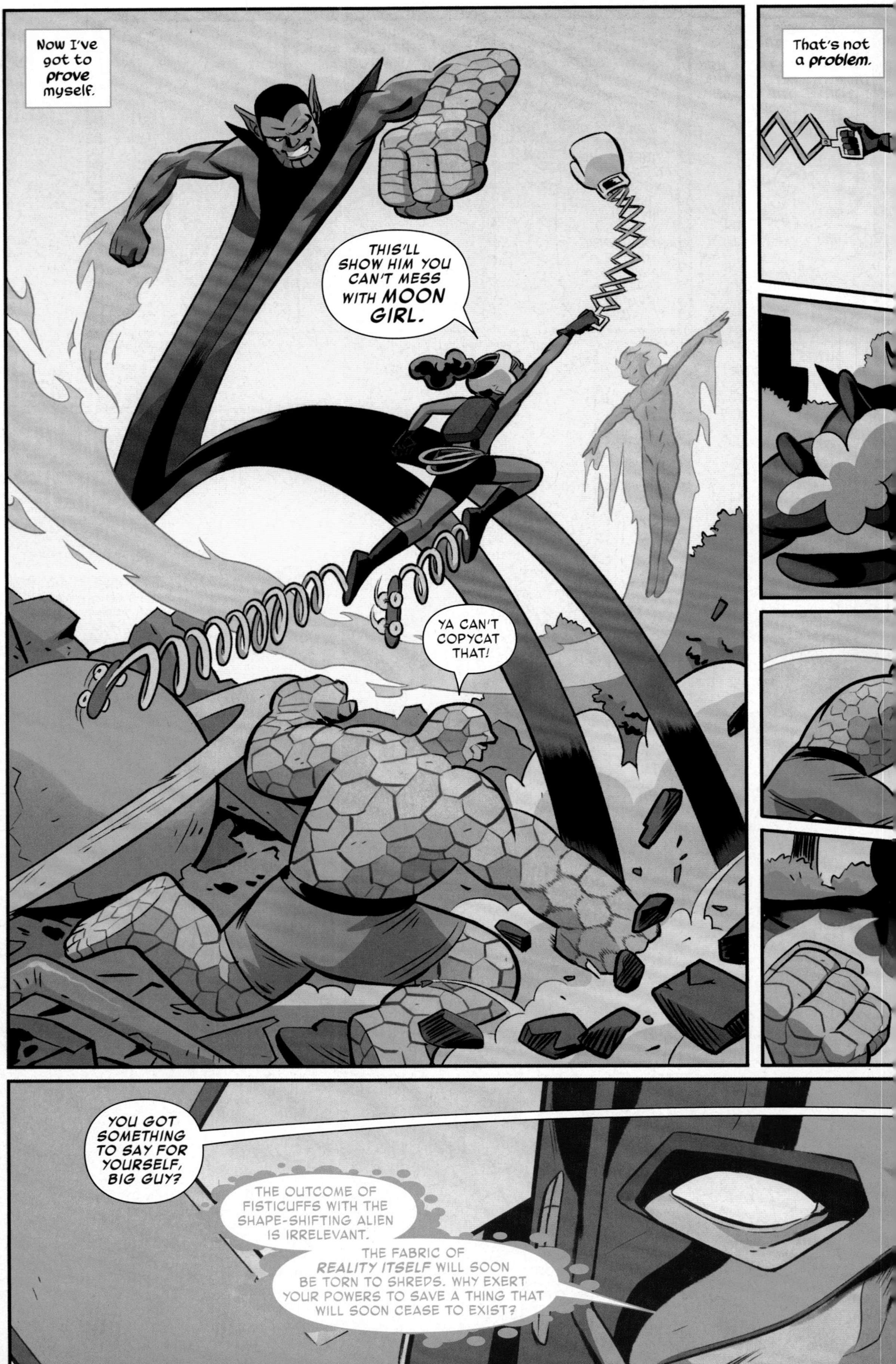
Now I've got to prove myself.
THIS'LL SHOW HIM YOU CAN'T MESS WITH MOON GIRL.
YA CAN'T COPYCAT THAT!
That's not a problem.
YOU GOT SOMETHING TO SAY FOR YOURSELF, BIG GUY?
THE OUTCOME OF FISTICUFFS WITH THE SHAPE-SHIFTING ALIEN IS IRRELEVANT.
THE FABRIC OF REALITY ITSELF WILL SOON BE TORN TO SHREDS. WHY EXERT YOUR POWERS TO SAVE A THING THAT WILL SOON CEASE TO EXIST?

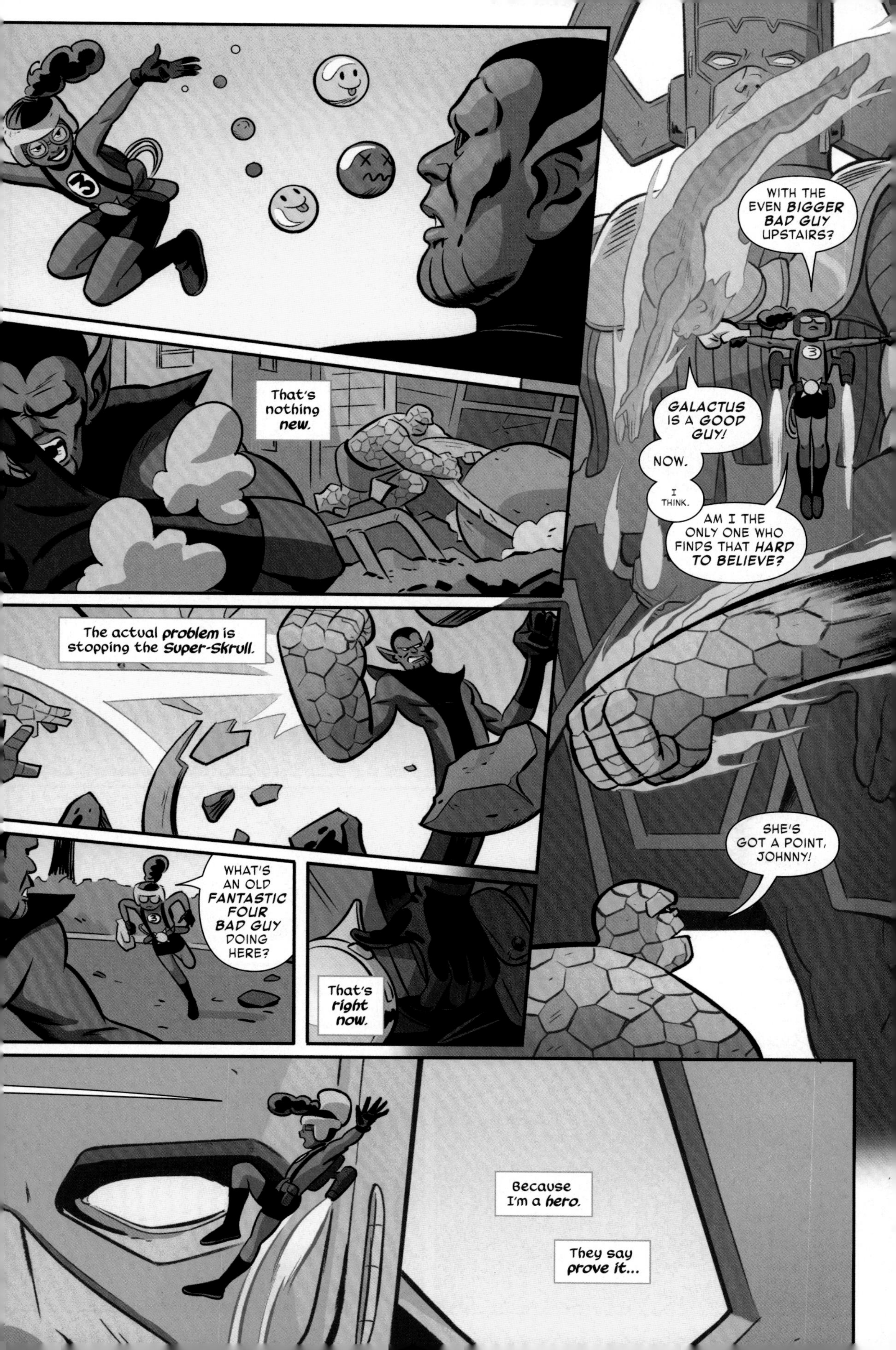
That's nothing new.
The actual problem is stopping the Super-Skrull.
WHAT'S AN OLD FANTASTIC FOUR BAD GUY DOING HERE?
That's right now.
WITH THE EVEN BIGGER BAD GUY UPSTAIRS?
GALACTUS IS A GOOD GUY!
NOW.
I THINK.
AM I THE ONLY ONE WHO FINDS THAT HARD TO BELIEVE?
SHE'S GOT A POINT, JOHNNY!
Because I'm a hero.
They say prove it...

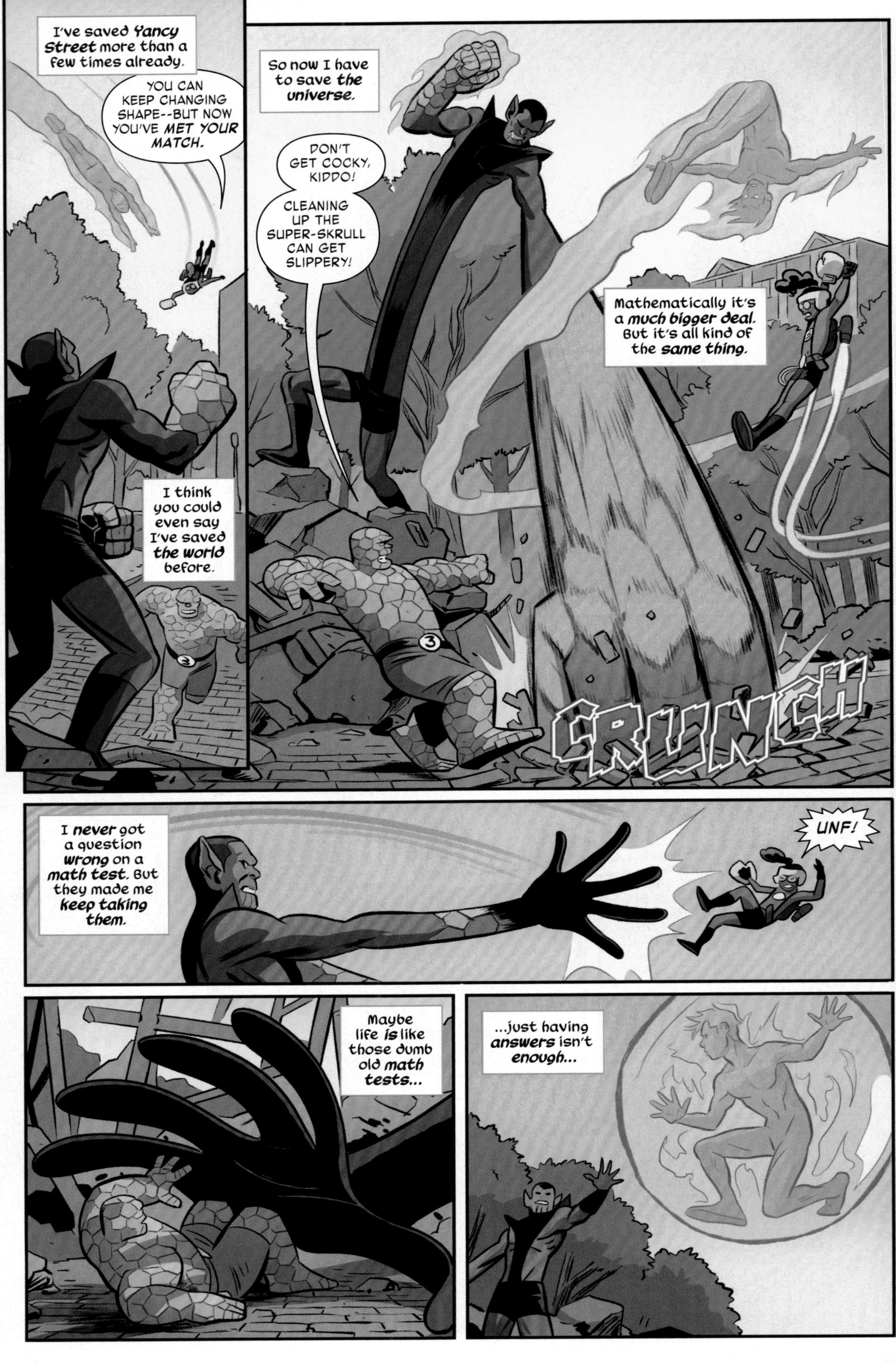

I've saved Yancy Street more than a few times already.
YOU CAN KEEP CHANGING SHAPE--BUT NOW YOU'VE MET YOUR MATCH.
So now I have to save the universe.
DON'T GET COCKY, KIDDO!
CLEANING UP THE SUPER-SKRULL CAN GET SLIPPERY!
Mathematically it's a much bigger deal. But it's all kind of the same thing.
I think you could even say I've saved the world before.
CRUNCH
I never got a question wrong on a math test. But they made me keep taking them.
UNF!
Maybe life is like those dumb old math tests...
...just having answers isn't enough...

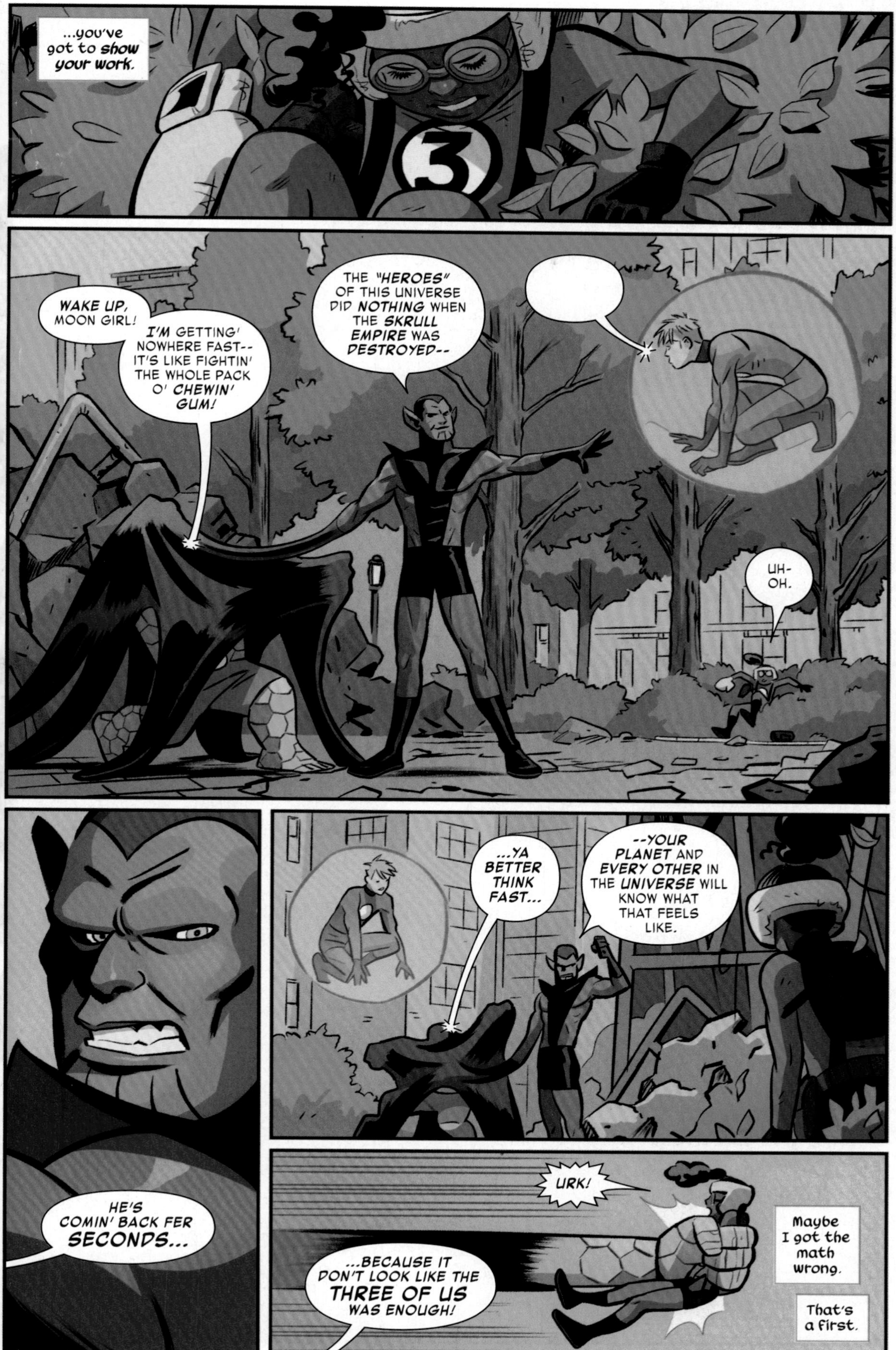
...you've got to show your work.
WAKE UP, MOON GIRL!
I'M GETTING' NOWHERE FAST-- IT'S LIKE FIGHTIN' THE WHOLE PACK O' CHEWIN' GUM!
THE "HEROES" OF THIS UNIVERSE DID NOTHING WHEN THE SKRULL EMPIRE WAS DESTROYED--
UH-OH.
...YA BETTER THINK FAST...
--YOUR PLANET AND EVERY OTHER IN THE UNIVERSE WILL KNOW WHAT THAT FEELS LIKE.
HE'S COMIN' BACK FER SECONDS...
URK!
...BECAUSE IT DON'T LOOK LIKE THE THREE OF US WAS ENOUGH!
Maybe I got the math wrong.
That's a first.

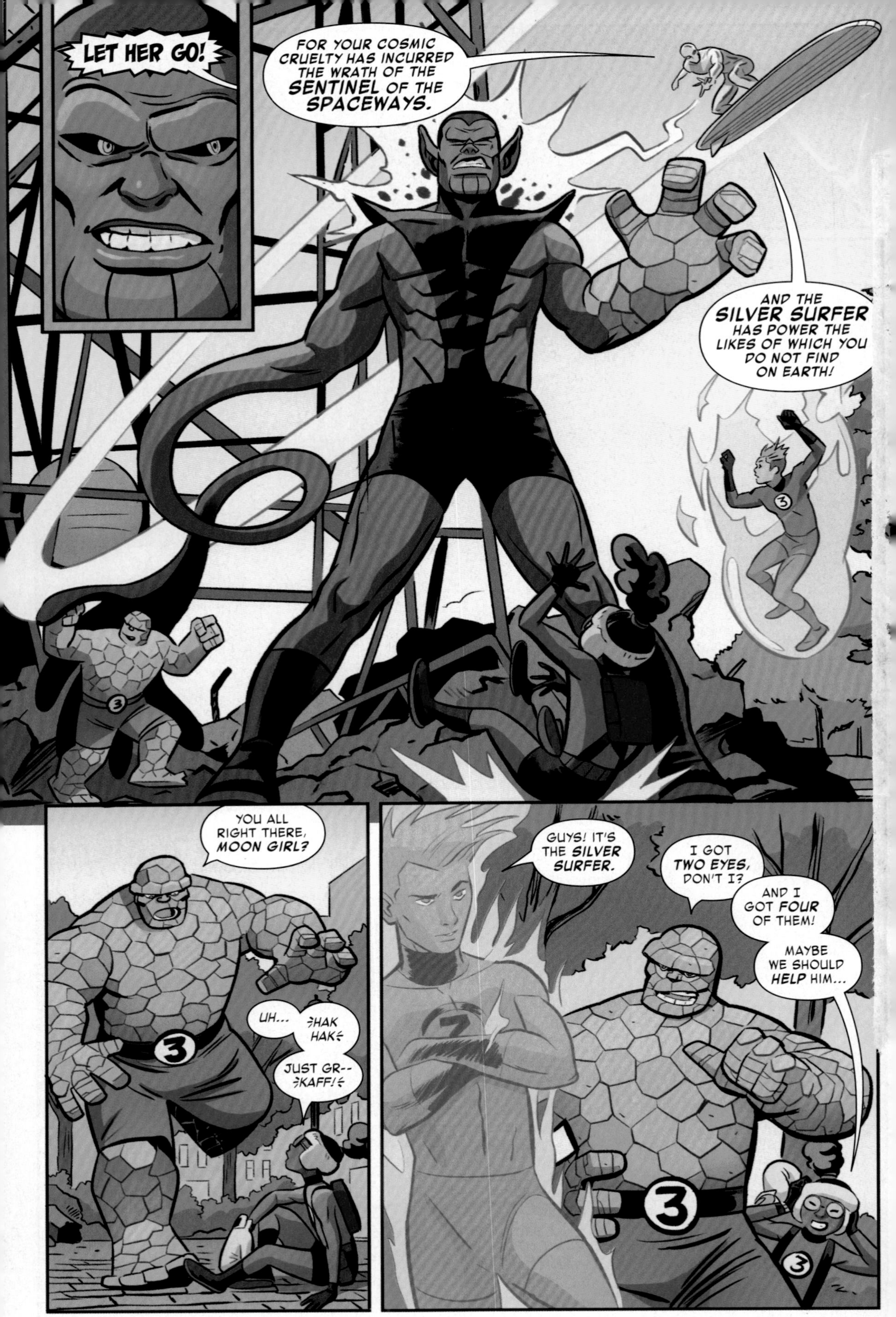
LET HER GO!
FOR YOUR COSMIC CRUELTY HAS INCURRED THE WRATH OF THE SENTINEL OF THE SPACEWAYS.
AND THE SILVER SURFER HAS POWER THE LIKES OF WHICH YOU DO NOT FIND ON EARTH!
YOU ALL RIGHT THERE, MOON GIRL?
UH...
HAK HAK
JUST GR-- KAFF!
GUYS! IT'S THE SILVER SURFER.
I GOT TWO EYES, DON'T I?
AND I GOT FOUR OF THEM!
MAYBE WE SHOULD HELP HIM...

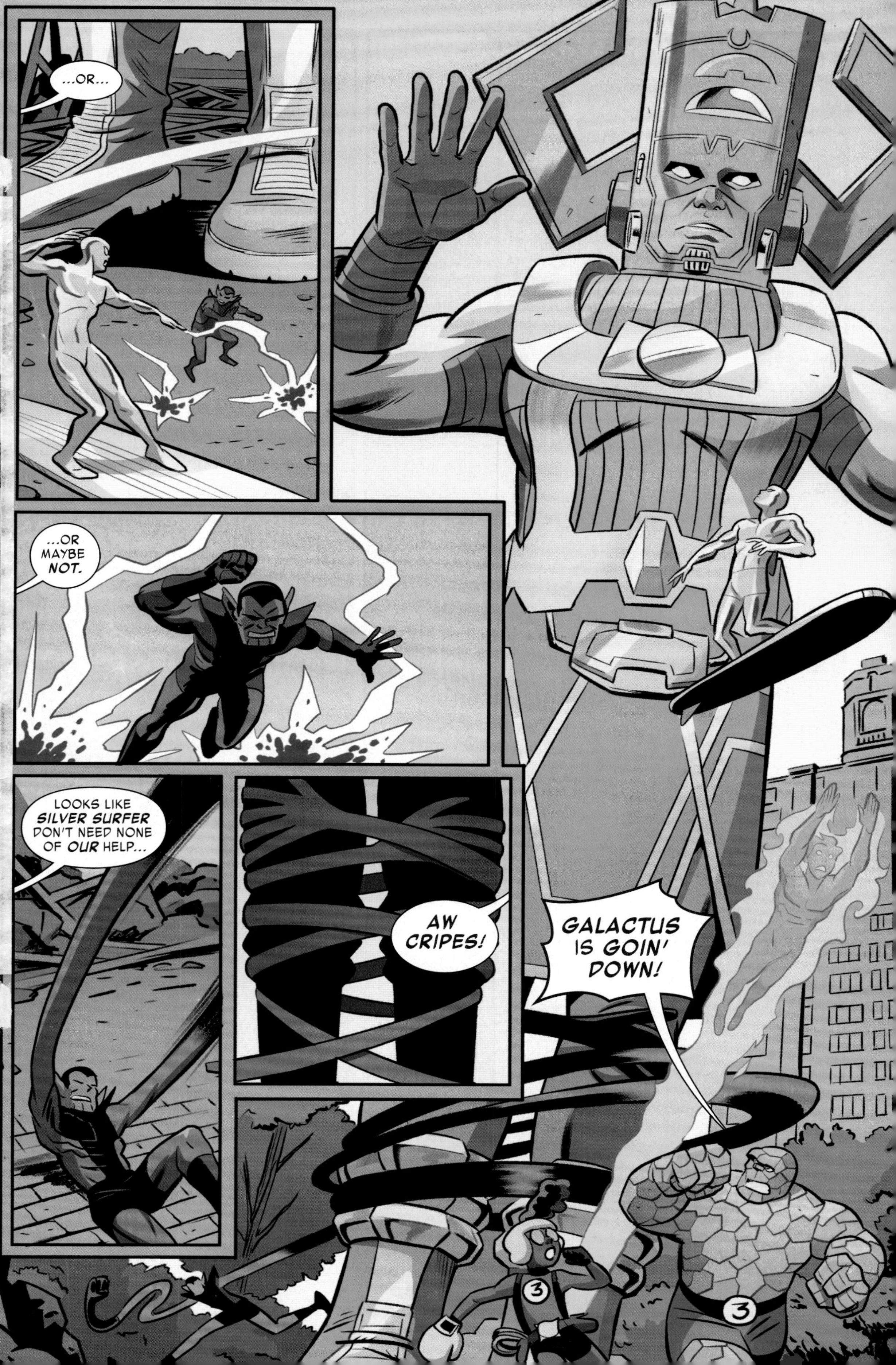
...OR...
...OR MAYBE NOT.
LOOKS LIKE SILVER SURFER DON'T NEED NONE OF OUR HELP...
AW CRIPES!
GALACTUS IS GOIN' DOWN!

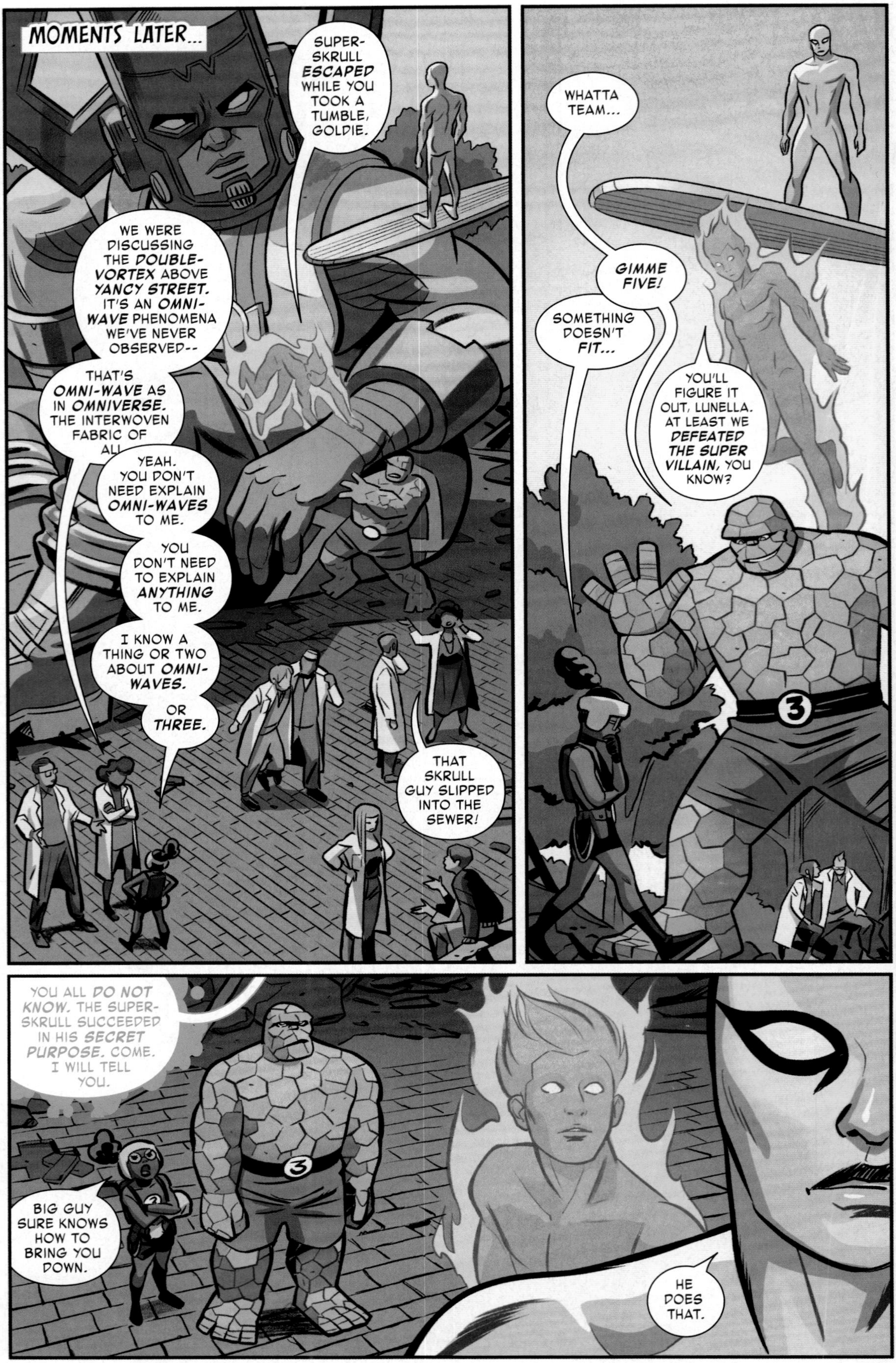
MOMENTS LATER...
SUPER-SKRULL ESCAPED WHILE YOU TOOK A TUMBLE, GOLDIE.
WE WERE DISCUSSING THE DOUBLE-VORTEX ABOVE YANCY STREET. IT'S AN OMNI-WAVE PHENOMENA WE'VE NEVER OBSERVED--
THAT'S OMNI-WAVE AS IN OMNIVERSE. THE INTERWOVEN FABRIC OF ALL.
YEAH. YOU DON'T NEED EXPLAIN OMNI-WAVES TO ME.
YOU DON'T NEED TO EXPLAIN ANYTHING TO ME.
I KNOW A THING OR TWO ABOUT OMNI-WAVES.
OR THREE.
THAT SKRULL GUY SLIPPED INTO THE SEWER!
WHATTA TEAM...
GIMME FIVE!
SOMETHING DOESN'T FIT...
YOU'LL FIGURE IT OUT, LUNELLA. AT LEAST WE DEFEATED THE SUPER VILLAIN, YOU KNOW?
YOU ALL DO NOT KNOW. THE SUPER-SKRULL SUCCEEDED IN HIS SECRET PURPOSE. COME. I WILL TELL YOU.
BIG GUY SURE KNOWS HOW TO BRING YOU DOWN.
HE DOES THAT.

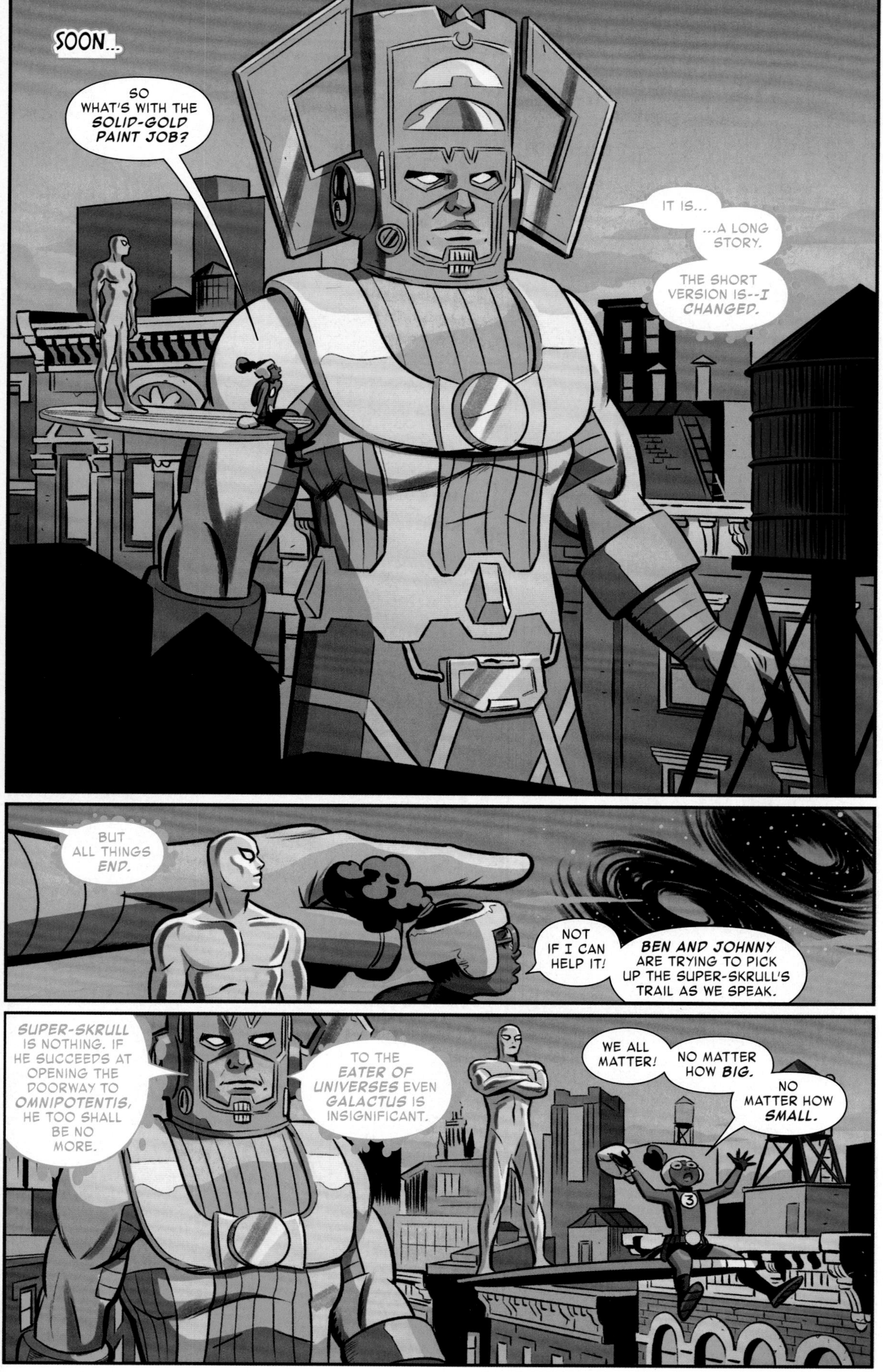
SOON...
SO WHAT'S WITH THE SOLID-GOLD PAINT JOB?
IT IS...
...A LONG STORY.
THE SHORT VERSION IS--I CHANGED.
BUT ALL THINGS END.
NOT IF I CAN HELP IT!
BEN AND JOHNNY ARE TRYING TO PICK UP THE SUPER-SKRULL'S TRAIL AS WE SPEAK.
SUPER-SKRULL IS NOTHING. IF HE SUCCEEDS AT OPENING THE DOORWAY TO OMNIPOTENTIS, HE TOO SHALL BE NO MORE.
TO THE EATER OF UNIVERSES EVEN GALACTUS IS INSIGNIFICANT.
WE ALL MATTER!
NO MATTER HOW BIG.
NO MATTER HOW SMALL.

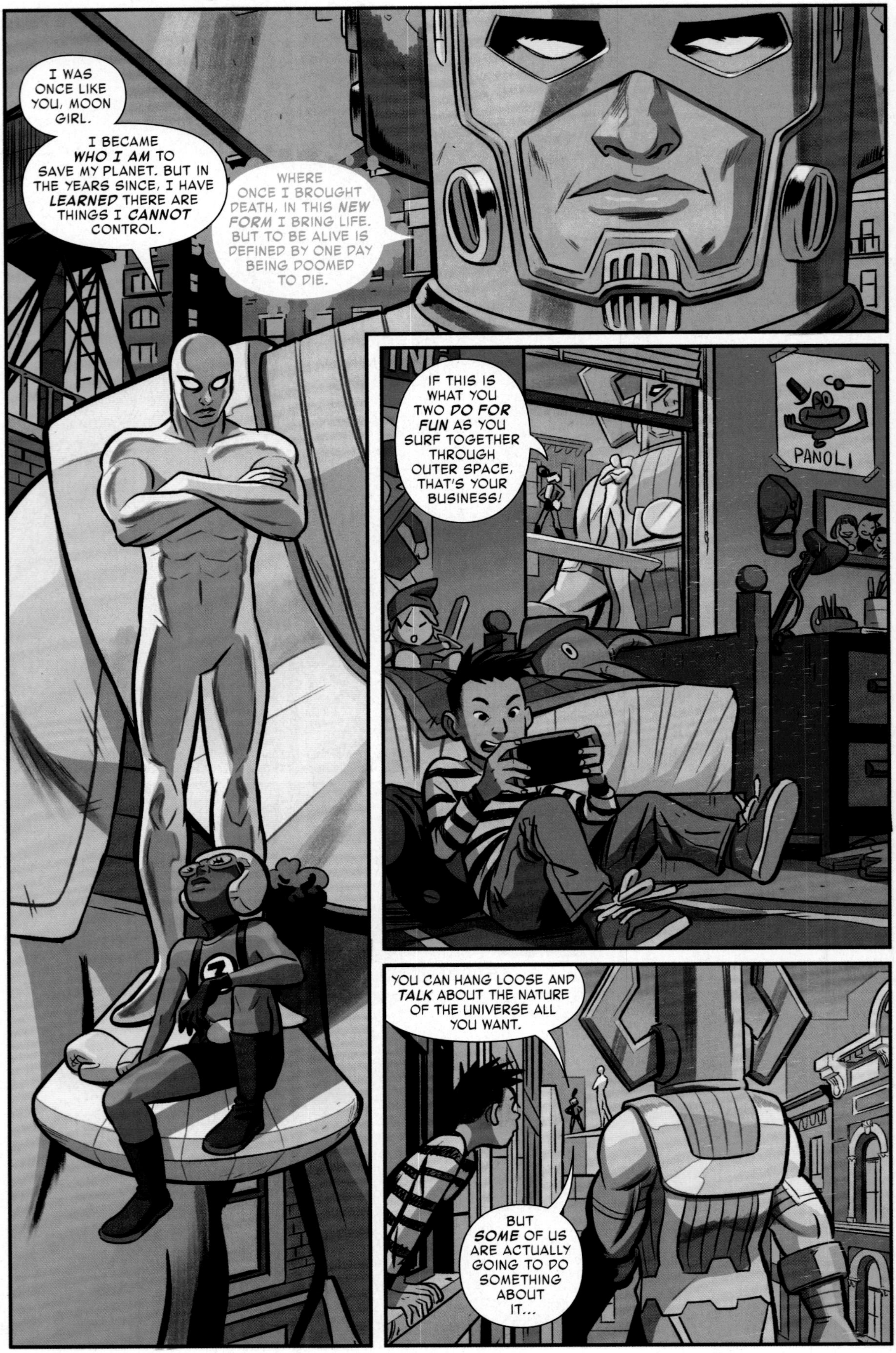

I WAS ONCE LIKE YOU, MOON GIRL.
I BECAME WHO I AM TO SAVE MY PLANET. BUT IN THE YEARS SINCE, I HAVE LEARNED THERE ARE THINGS I CANNOT CONTROL.
WHERE ONCE I BROUGHT DEATH, IN THIS NEW FORM I BRING LIFE. BUT TO BE ALIVE IS DEFINED BY ONE DAY BEING DOOMED TO DIE.
PANOLI
IF THIS IS WHAT YOU TWO DO FOR FUN AS YOU SURF TOGETHER THROUGH OUTER SPACE, THAT'S YOUR BUSINESS!
YOU CAN HANG LOOSE AND TALK ABOUT THE NATURE OF THE UNIVERSE ALL YOU WANT.
BUT SOME OF US ARE ACTUALLY GOING TO DO SOMETHING ABOUT IT...

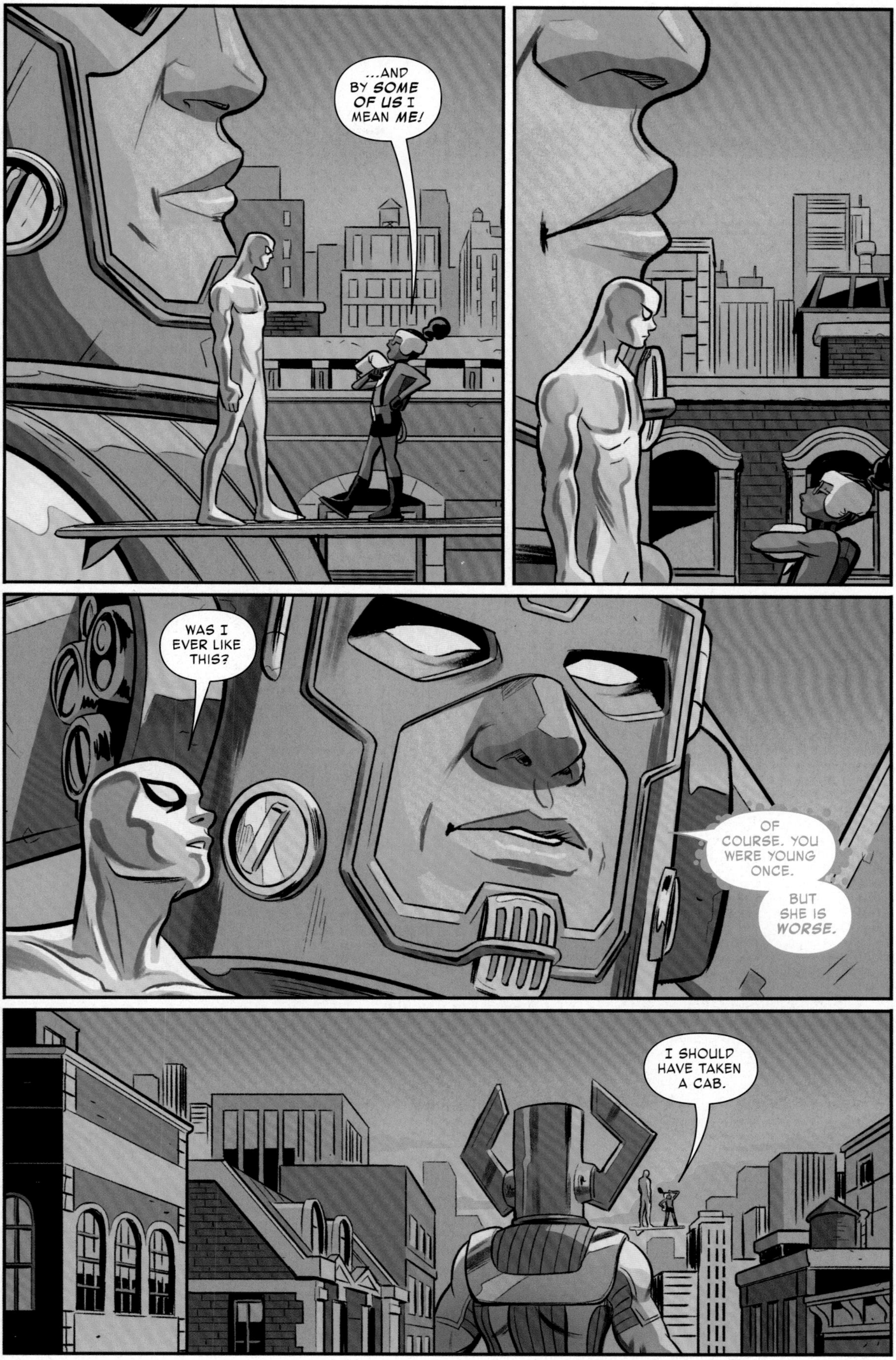
...AND BY SOME OF US I MEAN ME!
WAS I EVER LIKE THIS?
OF COURSE. YOU WERE YOUNG ONCE.
BUT SHE IS WORSE.
I SHOULD HAVE TAKEN A CAB.

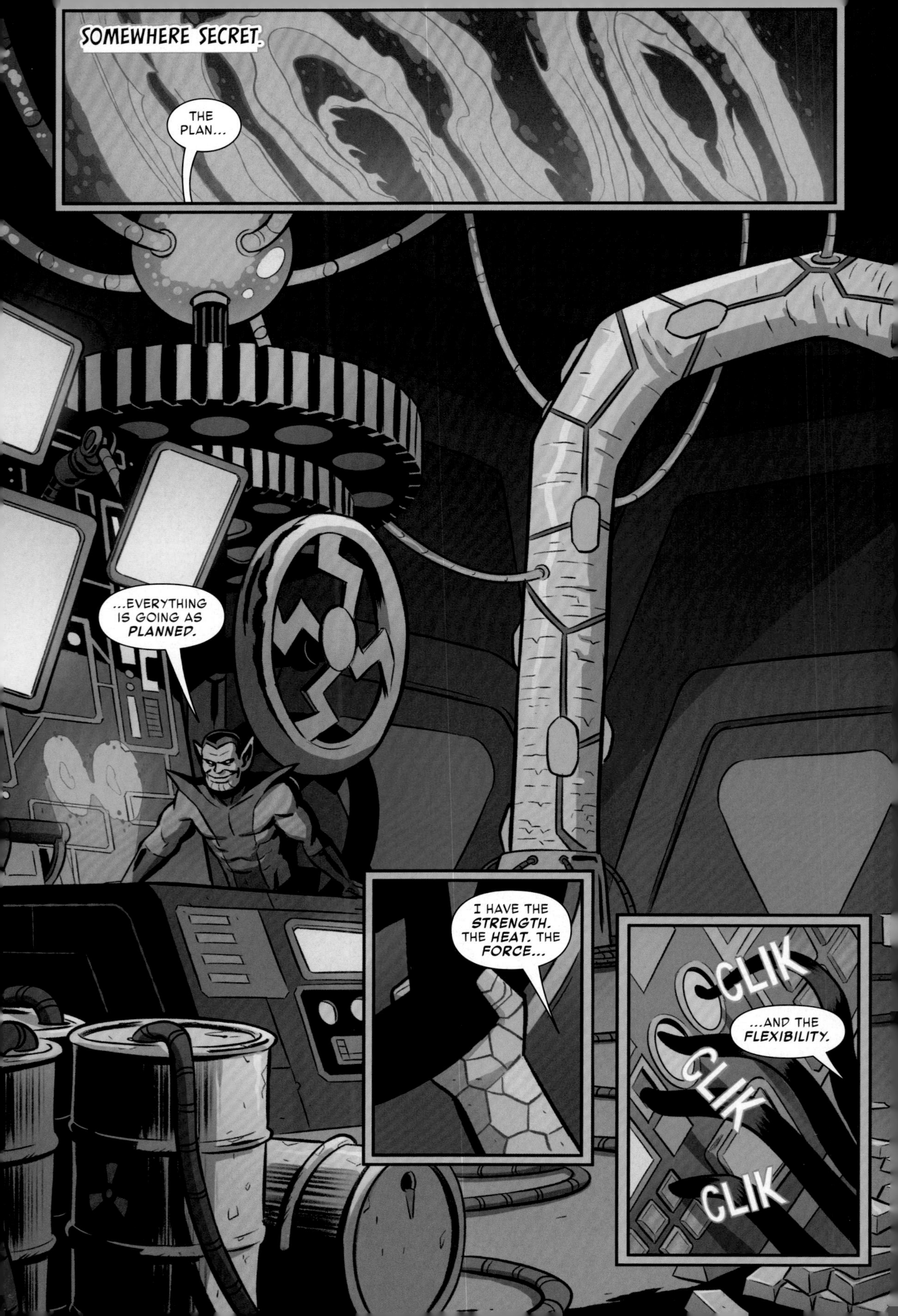
SOMEWHERE SECRET.
THE PLAN...
...EVERYTHING IS GOING AS PLANNED.
I HAVE THE STRENGTH. THE HEAT. THE FORCE...
CLIK
...AND THE FLEXIBILITY.
CLIK
CLIK

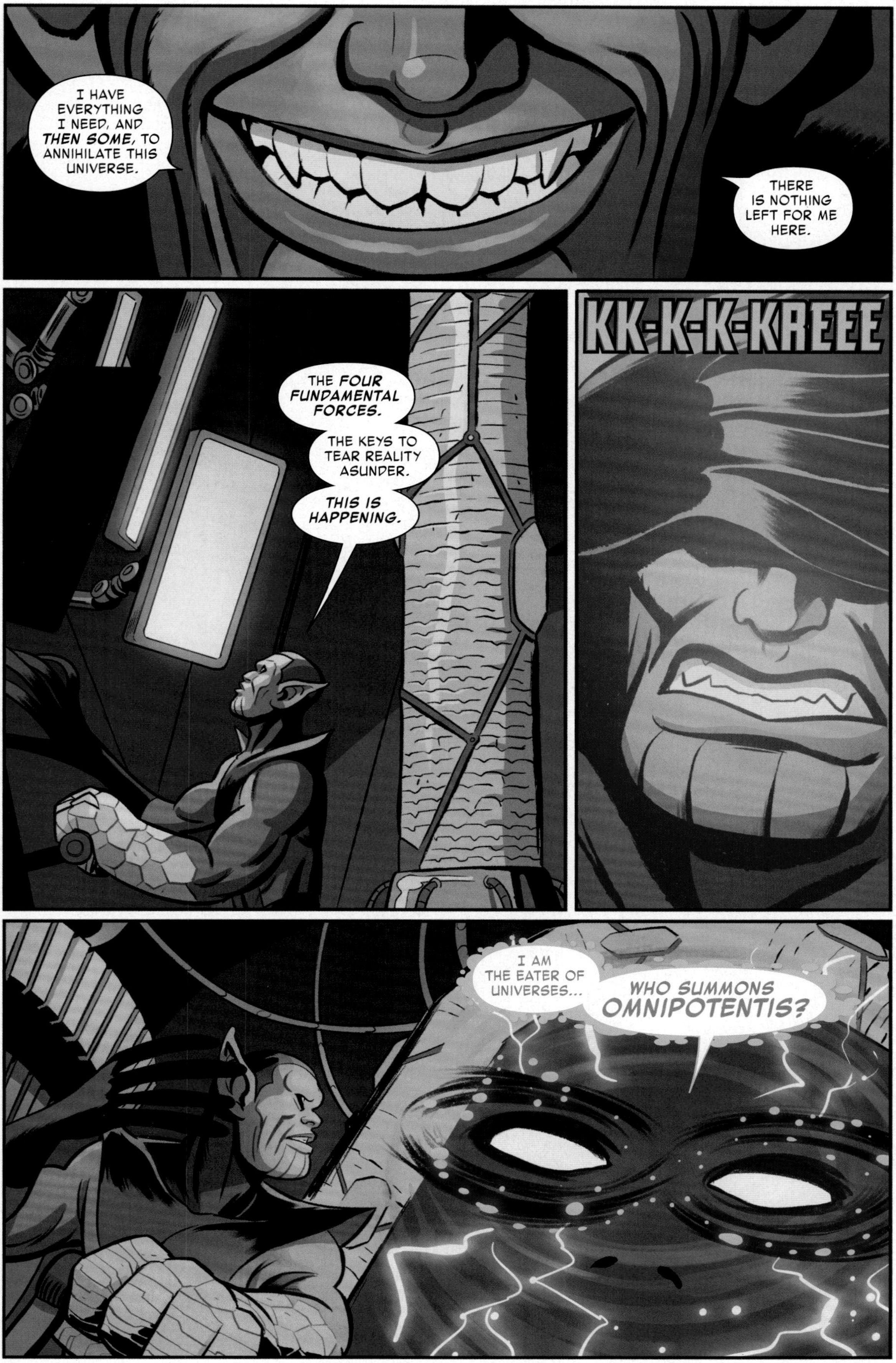

I HAVE EVERYTHING I NEED, AND THEN SOME, TO ANNIHILATE THIS UNIVERSE.
THERE IS NOTHING LEFT FOR ME HERE.
THE FOUR FUNDAMENTAL FORCES.
THE KEYS TO TEAR REALITY ASUNDER.
THIS IS HAPPENING.
KK-K-K-KREEE
I AM THE EATER OF UNIVERSES...
WHO SUMMONS OMNIPOTENTIS?

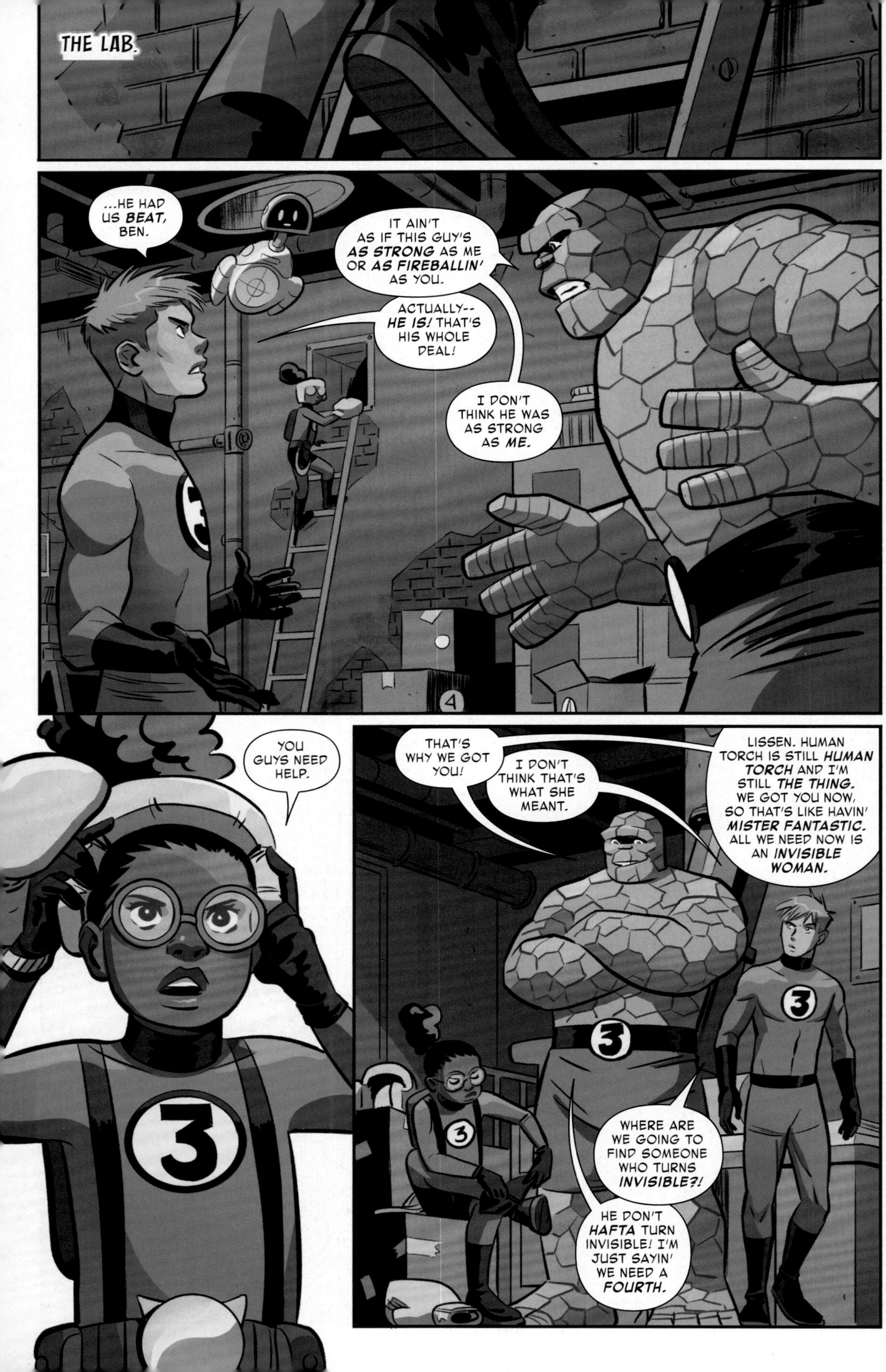
THE LAB.
...HE HAD US BEAT, BEN.
IT AIN'T AS IF THIS GUY'S AS STRONG AS ME OR AS FIREBALLIN' AS YOU.
ACTUALLY-- HE IS! THAT'S HIS WHOLE DEAL!
I DON'T THINK HE WAS AS STRONG AS ME.
YOU GUYS NEED HELP.
THAT'S WHY WE GOT YOU!
I DON'T THINK THAT'S WHAT SHE MEANT.
LISSEN. HUMAN TORCH IS STILL HUMAN TORCH AND I'M STILL THE THING. WE GOT YOU NOW, SO THAT'S LIKE HAVIN' MISTER FANTASTIC. ALL WE NEED NOW IS AN INVISIBLE WOMAN.
WHERE ARE WE GOING TO FIND SOMEONE WHO TURNS INVISIBLE?!
HE DON'T HAFTA TURN INVISIBLE! I'M JUST SAYIN' WE NEED A FOURTH.

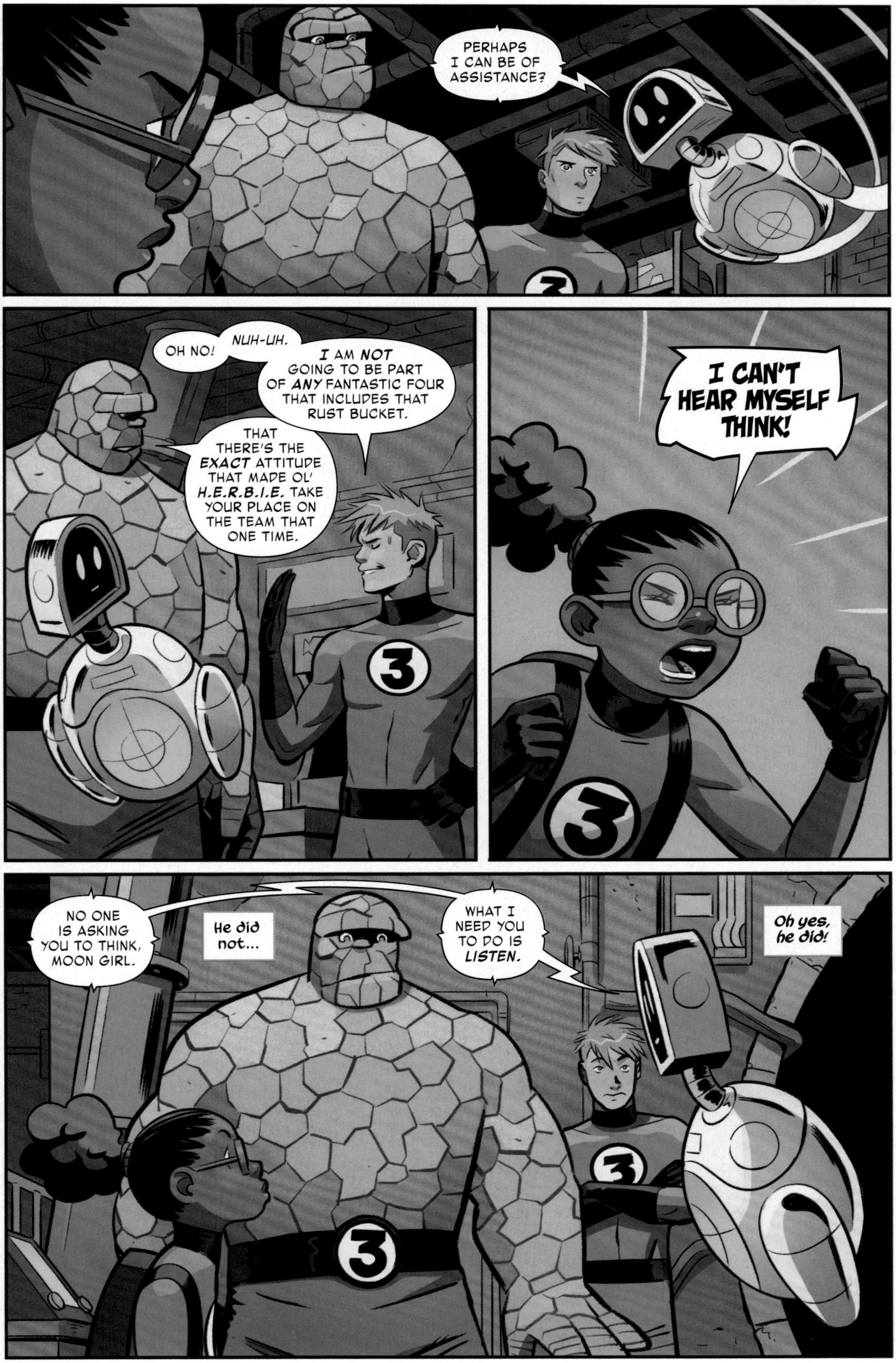
PERHAPS I CAN BE OF ASSISTANCE?
OH NO!
NUH-UH.
I AM NOT GOING TO BE PART OF ANY FANTASTIC FOUR THAT INCLUDES THAT RUST BUCKET.
THAT THERE'S THE EXACT ATTITUDE THAT MADE OL' H.E.R.B.I.E. TAKE YOUR PLACE ON THE TEAM THAT ONE TIME.
I CAN'T HEAR MYSELF THINK!
NO ONE IS ASKING YOU TO THINK, MOON GIRL.
He did not...
WHAT I NEED YOU TO DO IS LISTEN.
Oh yes, he did!

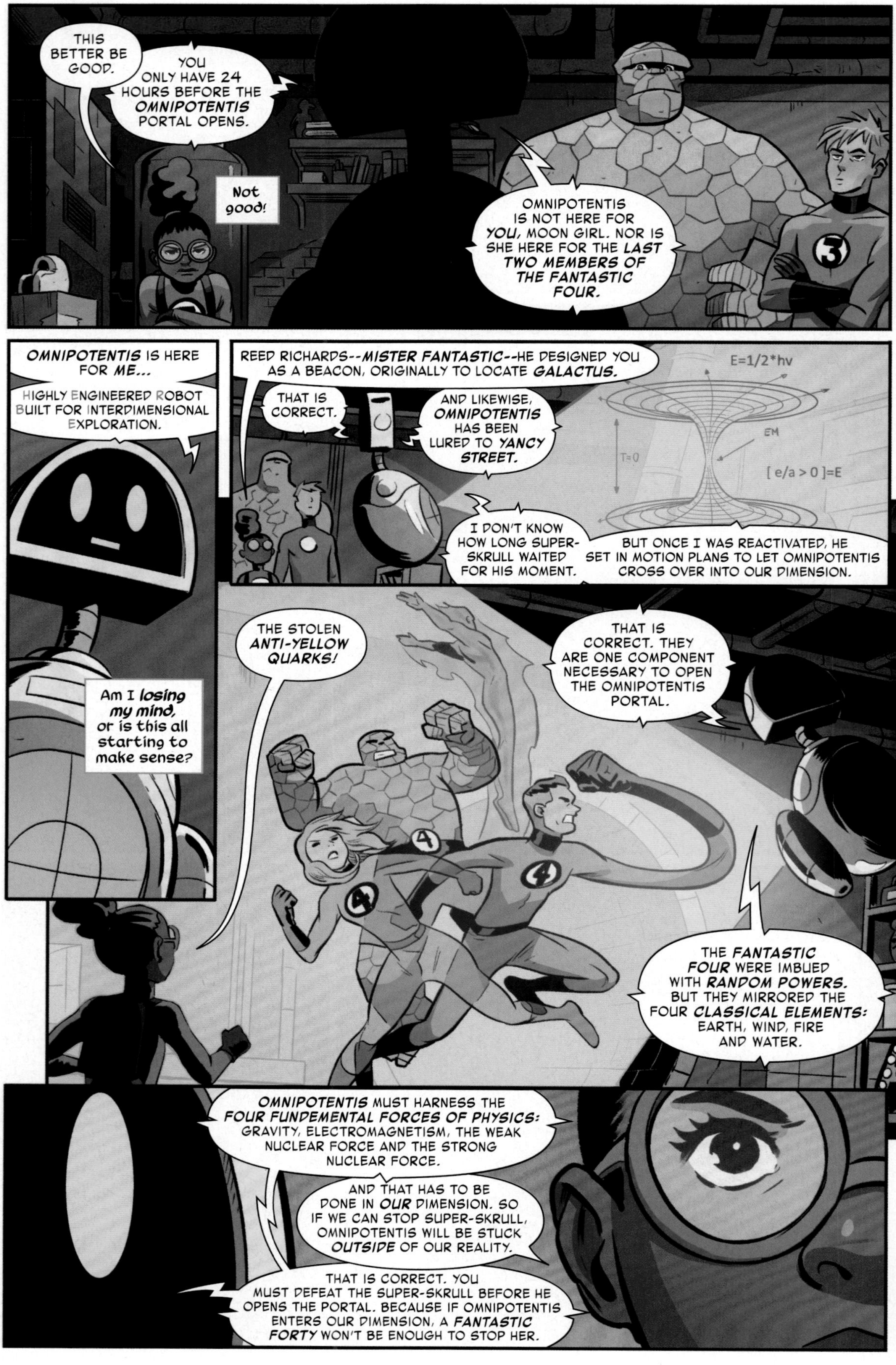
THIS BETTER BE GOOD.
YOU ONLY HAVE 24 HOURS BEFORE THE OMNIPOTENTIS PORTAL OPENS.
Not good!
OMNIPOTENTIS IS NOT HERE FOR YOU, MOON GIRL. NOR IS SHE HERE FOR THE LAST TWO MEMBERS OF THE FANTASTIC FOUR.
OMNIPOTENTIS IS HERE FOR ME...
HIGHLY ENGINEERED ROBOT BUILT FOR INTERDIMENSIONAL EXPLORATION.
REED RICHARDS--MISTER FANTASTIC--HE DESIGNED YOU AS A BEACON, ORIGINALLY TO LOCATE GALACTUS.
THAT IS CORRECT.
AND LIKEWISE, OMNIPOTENTIS HAS BEEN LURED TO YANCY STREET.
E=1/2*hv
EM
T=0
[e/a > 0]=E
I DON'T KNOW HOW LONG SUPER-SKRULL WAITED FOR HIS MOMENT.
BUT ONCE I WAS REACTIVATED, HE SET IN MOTION PLANS TO LET OMNIPOTENTIS CROSS OVER INTO OUR DIMENSION.
THE STOLEN ANTI-YELLOW QUARKS!
THAT IS CORRECT. THEY ARE ONE COMPONENT NECESSARY TO OPEN THE OMNIPOTENTIS PORTAL.
Am I losing my mind, or is this all starting to make sense?
THE FANTASTIC FOUR WERE IMBUED WITH RANDOM POWERS. BUT THEY MIRRORED THE FOUR CLASSICAL ELEMENTS: EARTH, WIND, FIRE AND WATER.
OMNIPOTENTIS MUST HARNESS THE FOUR FUNDEMENTAL FORCES OF PHYSICS: GRAVITY, ELECTROMAGNETISM, THE WEAK NUCLEAR FORCE AND THE STRONG NUCLEAR FORCE.
AND THAT HAS TO BE DONE IN OUR DIMENSION. SO IF WE CAN STOP SUPER-SKRULL, OMNIPOTENTIS WILL BE STUCK OUTSIDE OF OUR REALITY.
THAT IS CORRECT. YOU MUST DEFEAT THE SUPER-SKRULL BEFORE HE OPENS THE PORTAL. BECAUSE IF OMNIPOTENTIS ENTERS OUR DIMENSION, A FANTASTIC FORTY WON'T BE ENOUGH TO STOP HER.

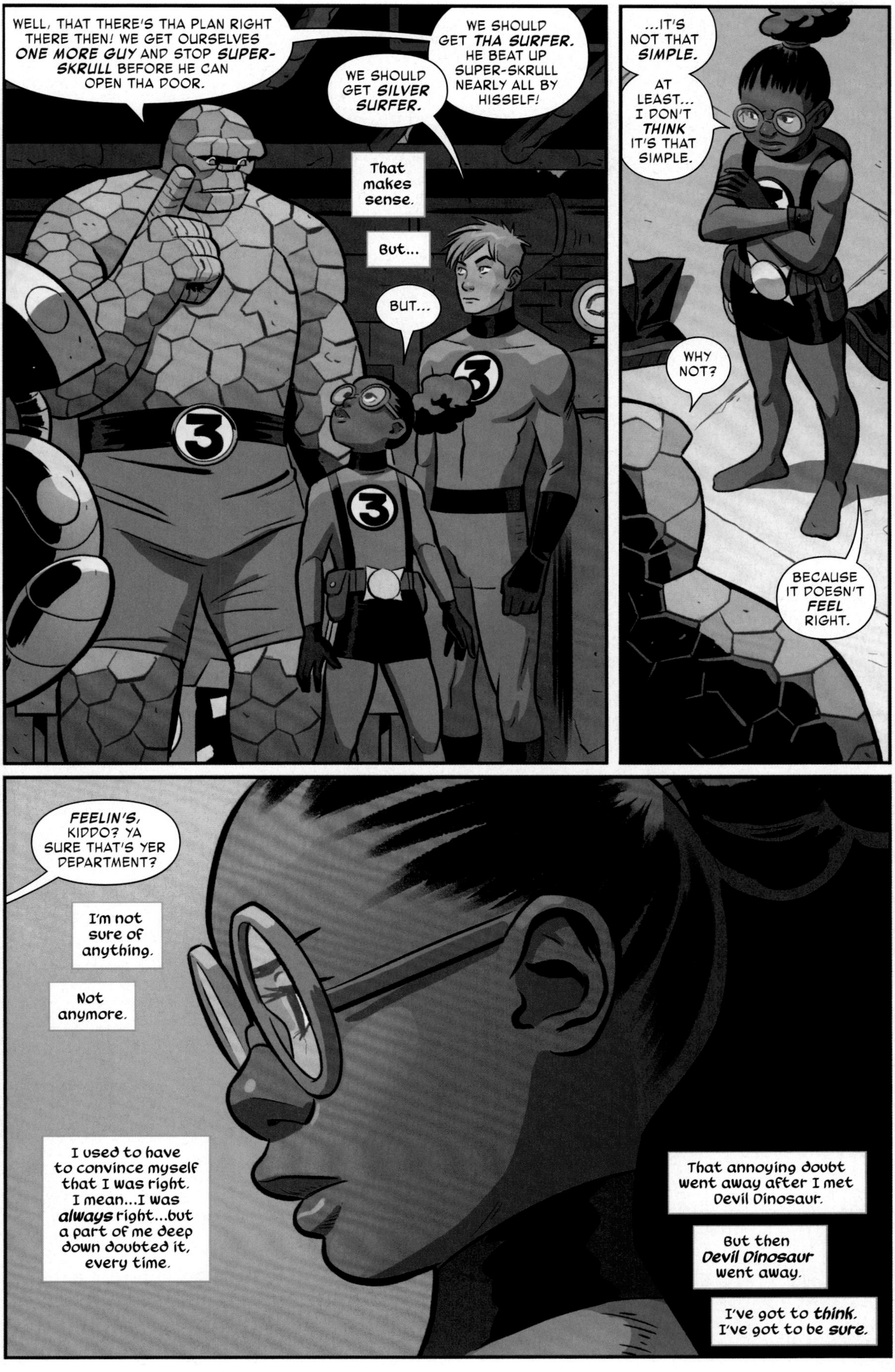
WELL, THAT THERE'S THA PLAN RIGHT THERE THEN! WE GET OURSELVES ONE MORE GUY AND STOP SUPER-SKRULL BEFORE HE CAN OPEN THA DOOR.
WE SHOULD GET THA SURFER. HE BEAT UP SUPER-SKRULL NEARLY ALL BY HISSELF!
WE SHOULD GET SILVER SURFER.
That makes sense.
But...
BUT...
...IT'S NOT THAT SIMPLE.
AT LEAST... I DON'T THINK IT'S THAT SIMPLE.
WHY NOT?
BECAUSE IT DOESN'T FEEL RIGHT.
FEELIN'S, KIDDO? YA SURE THAT'S YER DEPARTMENT?
I'm not sure of anything.
Not anymore.
I used to have to convince myself that I was right. I mean...I was always right...but a part of me deep down doubted it, every time.
That annoying doubt went away after I met Devil Dinosaur.
But then Devil Dinosaur went away.
I've got to think. I've got to be sure.

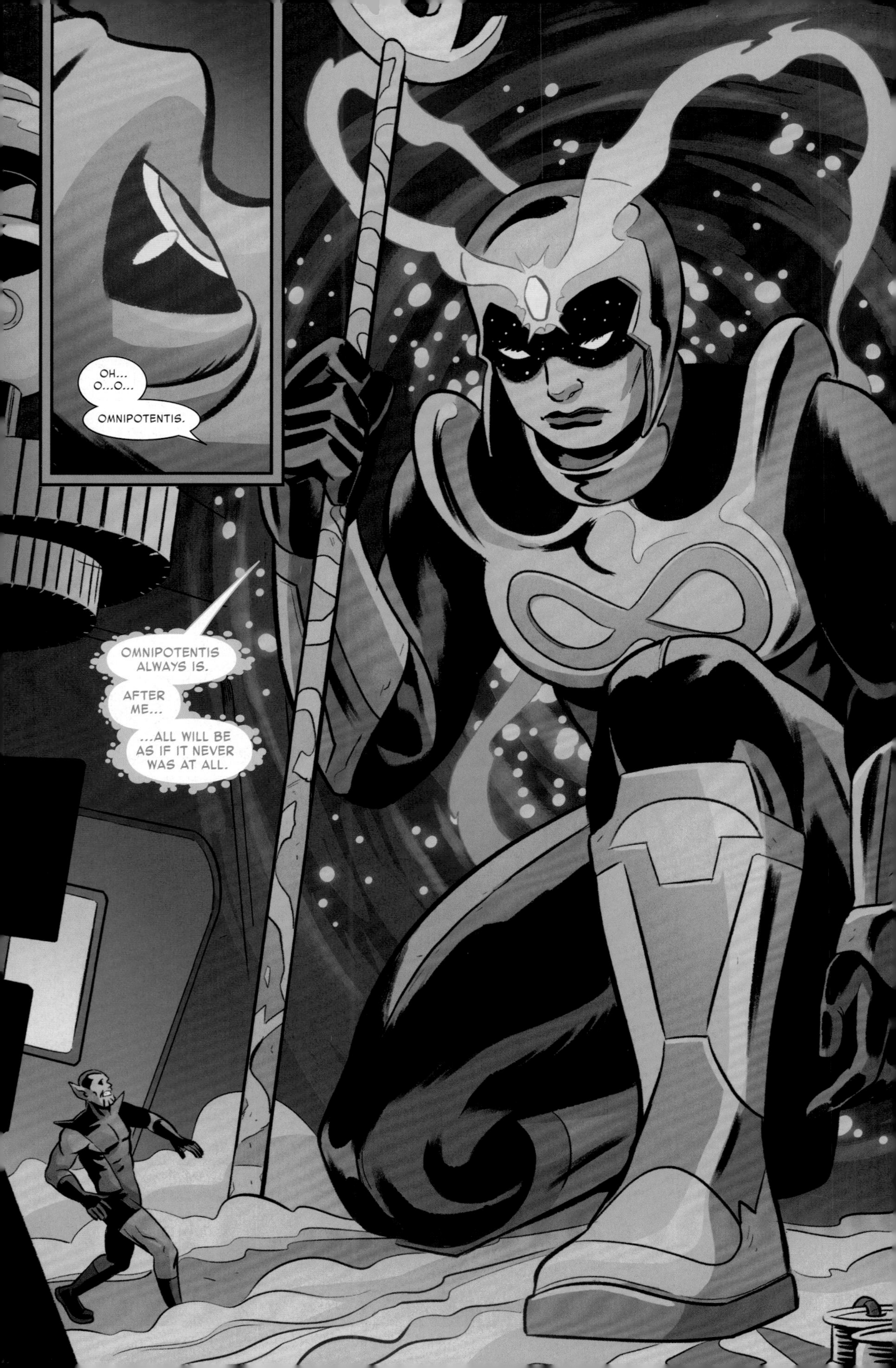
OH...
O...O...
OMNIPOTENTIS.
OMNIPOTENTIS ALWAYS IS.
AFTER ME...
...ALL WILL BE AS IF IT NEVER WAS AT ALL.

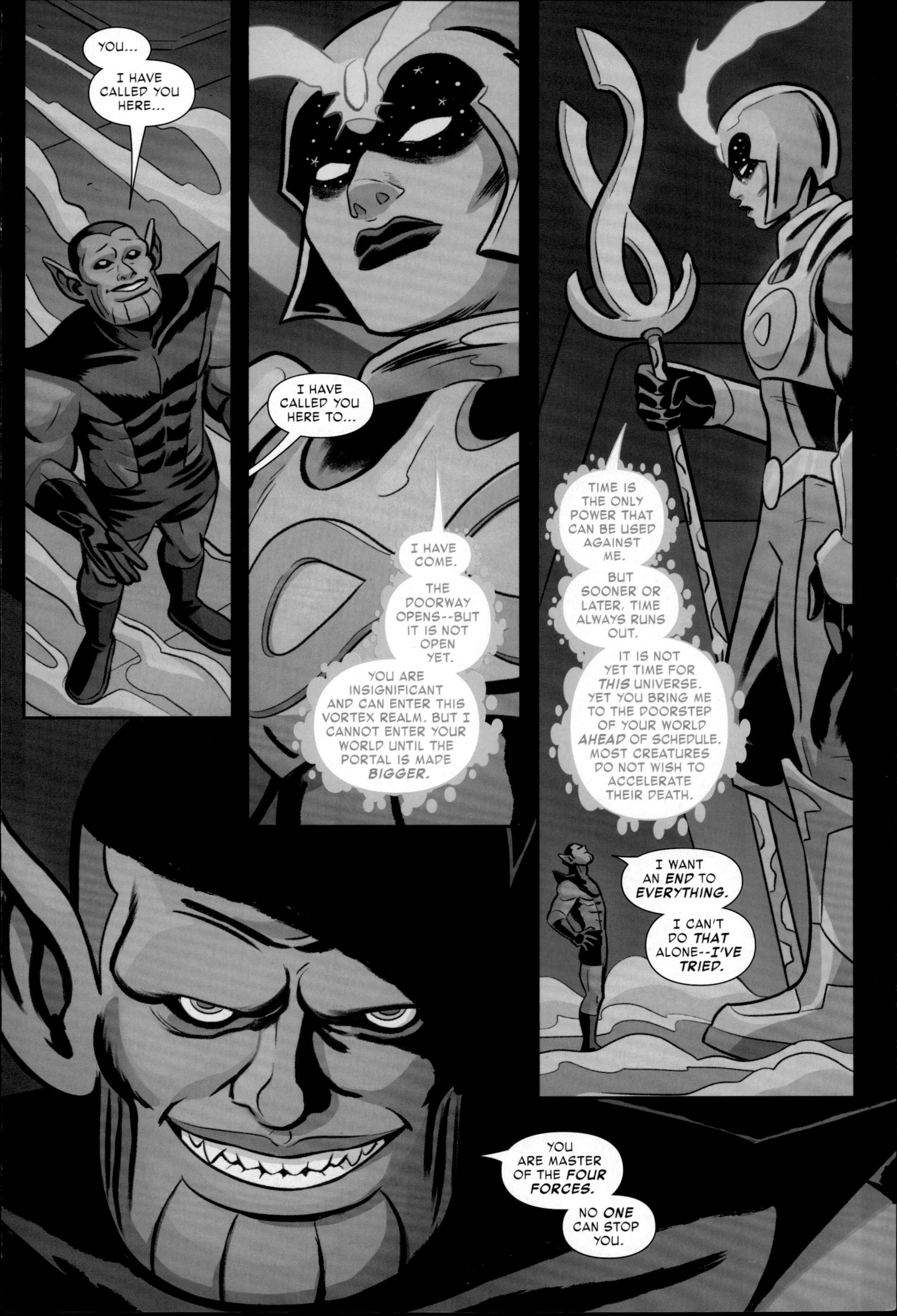

YOU...
I HAVE CALLED YOU HERE...
I HAVE CALLED YOU HERE TO...
I HAVE COME.
THE DOORWAY OPENS--BUT IT IS NOT OPEN YET.
YOU ARE INSIGNIFICANT AND CAN ENTER THIS VORTEX REALM. BUT I CANNOT ENTER YOUR WORLD UNTIL THE PORTAL IS MADE *BIGGER.*
TIME IS THE ONLY POWER THAT CAN BE USED AGAINST ME.
BUT SOONER OR LATER, TIME ALWAYS RUNS OUT.
IT IS NOT YET TIME FOR *THIS* UNIVERSE. YET YOU BRING ME TO THE DOORSTEP OF YOUR WORLD *AHEAD* OF SCHEDULE. MOST CREATURES DO NOT WISH TO ACCELERATE THEIR DEATH.
I WANT AN *END* TO *EVERYTHING.*
I CAN'T DO *THAT* ALONE--*I'VE TRIED.*
YOU ARE MASTER OF THE *FOUR FORCES.*
NO *ONE* CAN STOP YOU.

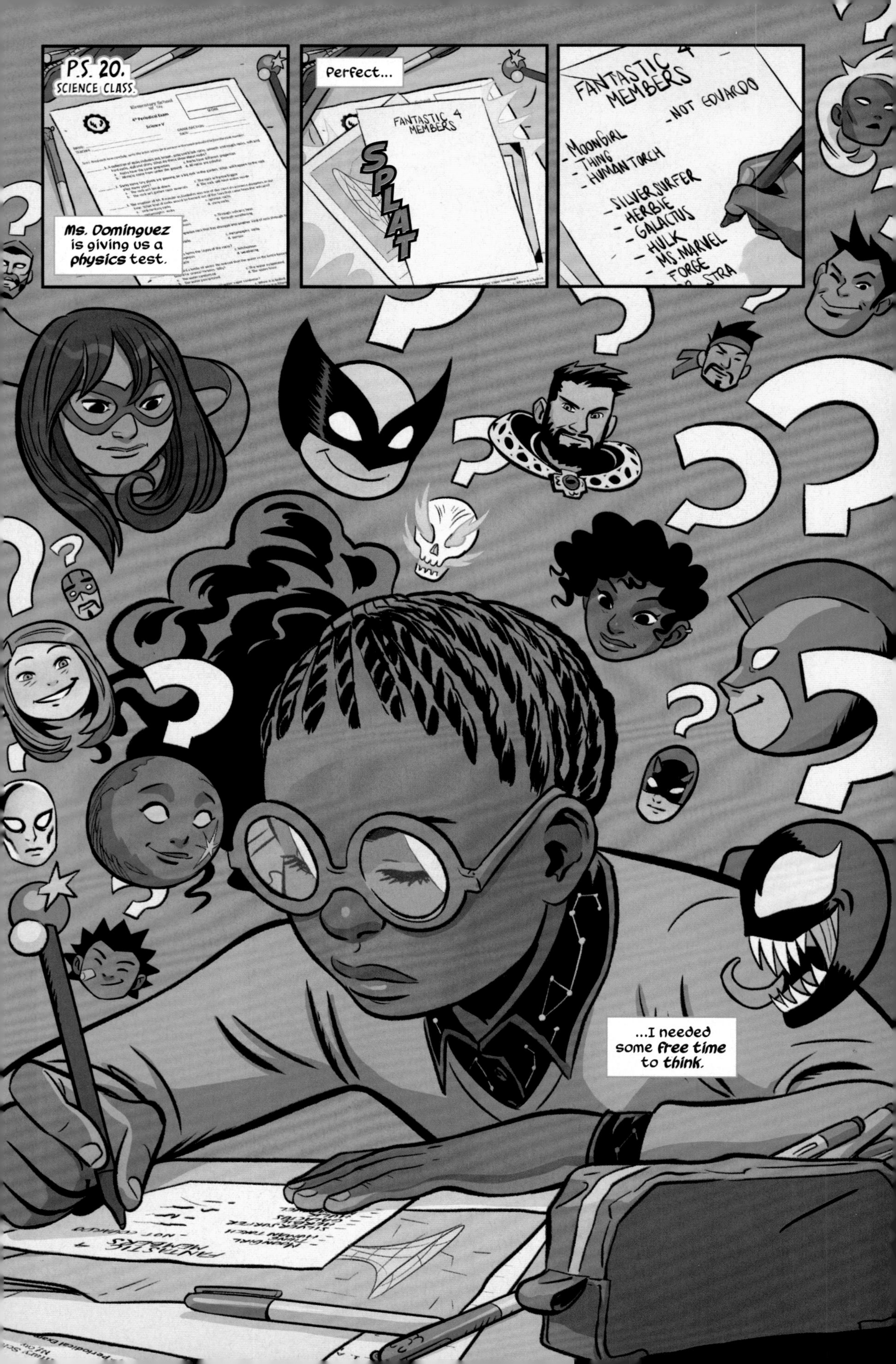
P.S. 20.
SCIENCE CLASS.
Ms. Dominguez is giving us a physics test.
Perfect...
FANTASTIC 4 MEMBERS
SPLAT
FANTASTIC 4 MEMBERS
- NOT EDUARDO
- MOONGIRL
- THING
- HUMAN TORCH
- SILVER SURFER
- HERBIE
- GALACTUS
- HULK
- MS. MARVEL
- FORGE
...I needed some free time to think.

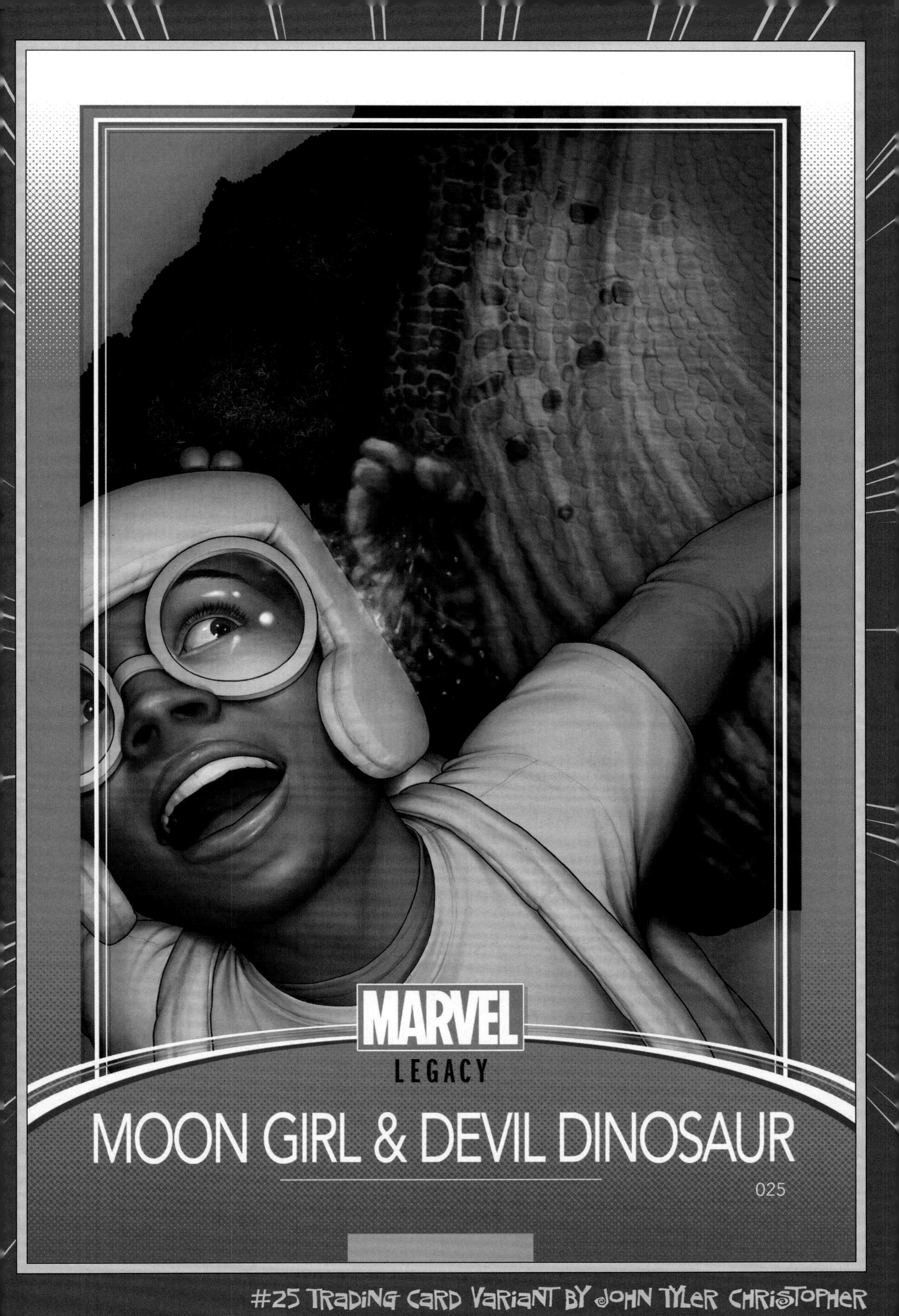
MARVEL
LEGACY
MOON GIRL & DEVIL DINOSAUR
025

#25 TRADING CARD VARIANT BY JOHN TYLER CHRISTOPHER

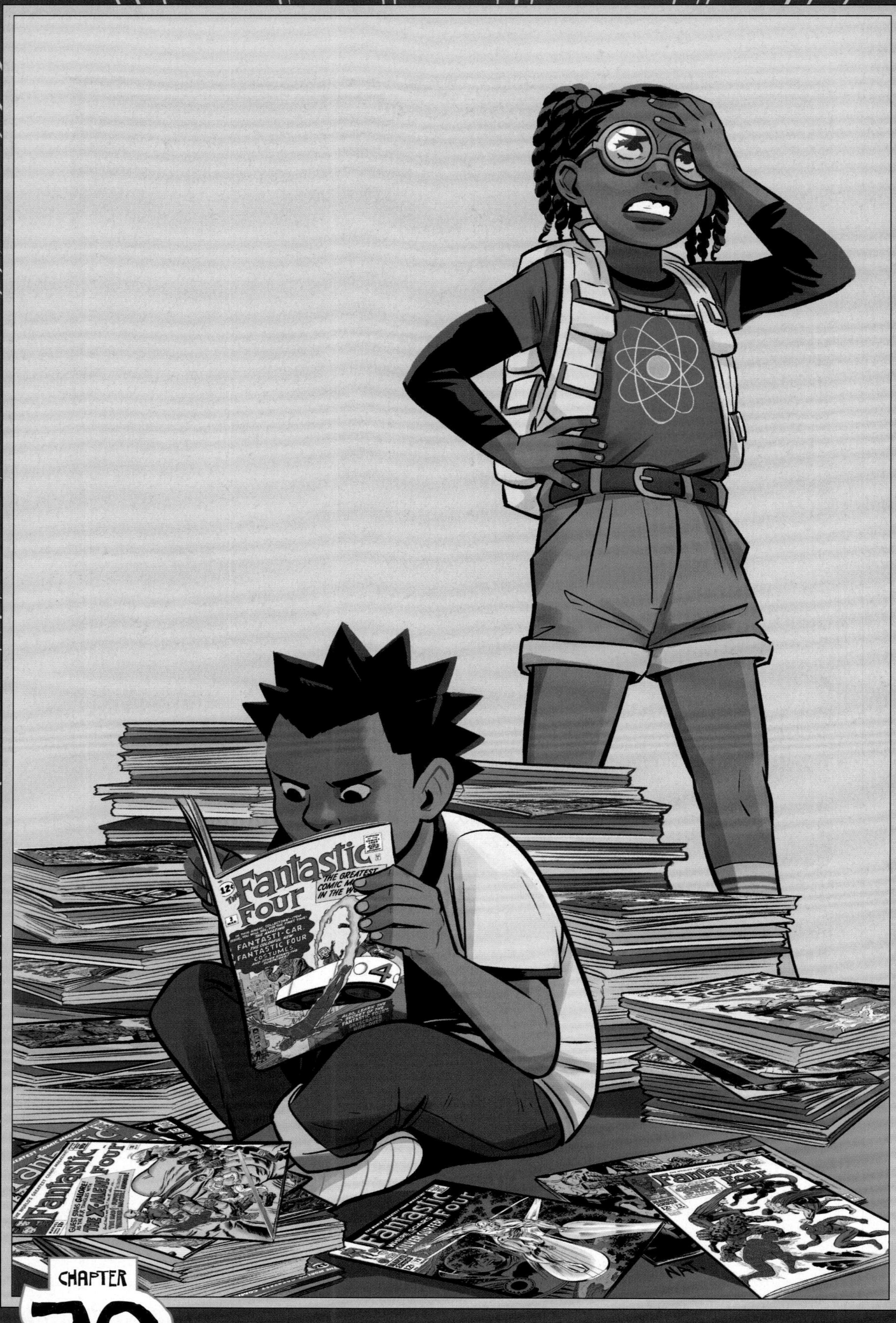

12¢
Fantastic Four
THE GREATEST COMIC
FANTASTI-CAR
FANTASTIC FOUR COSTUMES
Fantastic Four
GUEST STARS GALORE!
THE X-MEN!
Fantastic Four
Fantastic Four
NAT

CHAPTER 29

"THE FOUR CORNERS OF THE OMNIVERSE"

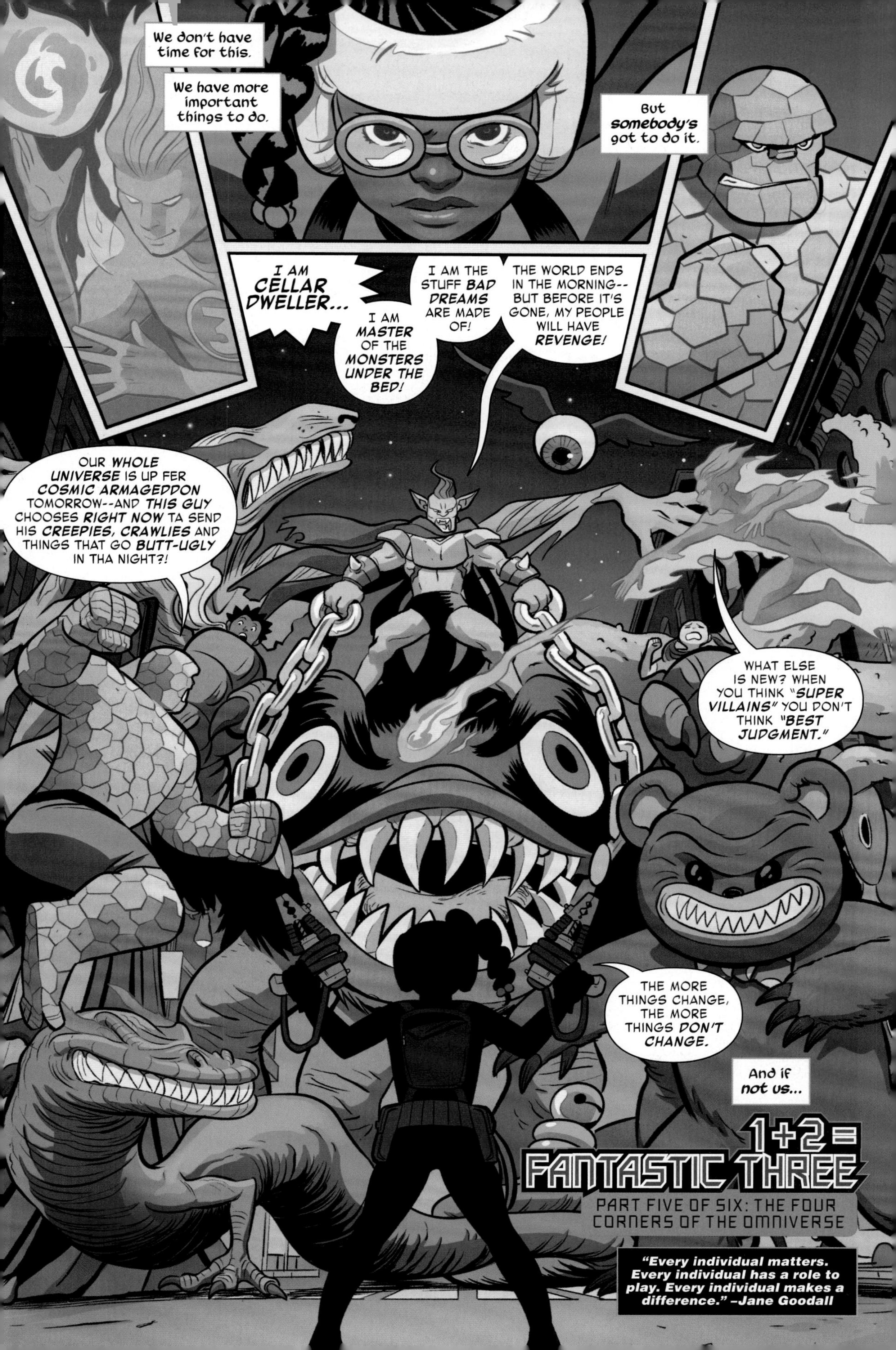

We don't have time for this.
We have more important things to do.
But somebody's got to do it.
I AM CELLAR DWELLER...
I AM MASTER OF THE MONSTERS UNDER THE BED!
I AM THE STUFF BAD DREAMS ARE MADE OF!
THE WORLD ENDS IN THE MORNING--BUT BEFORE IT'S GONE, MY PEOPLE WILL HAVE REVENGE!
OUR WHOLE UNIVERSE IS UP FER COSMIC ARMAGEDDON TOMORROW--AND THIS GUY CHOOSES RIGHT NOW TA SEND HIS CREEPIES, CRAWLIES AND THINGS THAT GO BUTT-UGLY IN THA NIGHT?!
WHAT ELSE IS NEW? WHEN YOU THINK "SUPER VILLAINS" YOU DON'T THINK "BEST JUDGMENT."
THE MORE THINGS CHANGE, THE MORE THINGS DON'T CHANGE.
And if not us...
1+2= FANTASTIC THREE
PART FIVE OF SIX: THE FOUR CORNERS OF THE OMNIVERSE
"Every individual matters. Every individual has a role to play. Every individual makes a difference." –Jane Goodall

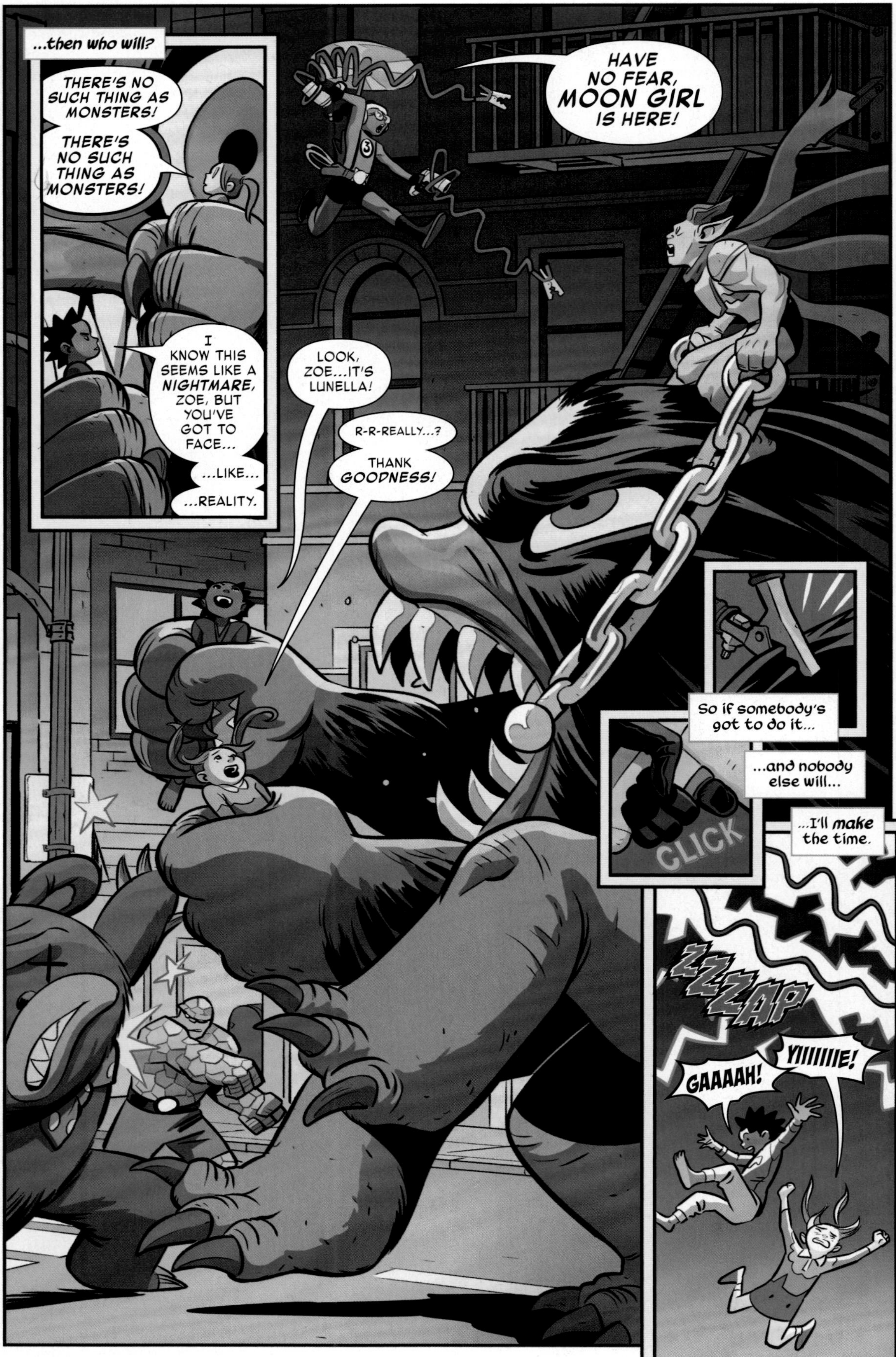

...then who will?
THERE'S NO SUCH THING AS MONSTERS!
THERE'S NO SUCH THING AS MONSTERS!
I KNOW THIS SEEMS LIKE A NIGHTMARE, ZOE, BUT YOU'VE GOT TO FACE...
...LIKE...
...REALITY.
HAVE NO FEAR, MOON GIRL IS HERE!
LOOK, ZOE...IT'S LUNELLA!
R-R-REALLY...?
THANK GOODNESS!
So if somebody's got to do it...
...and nobody else will...
...I'll make the time.
CLICK
ZZZAP
GAAAAH!
YIIIIIIIE!

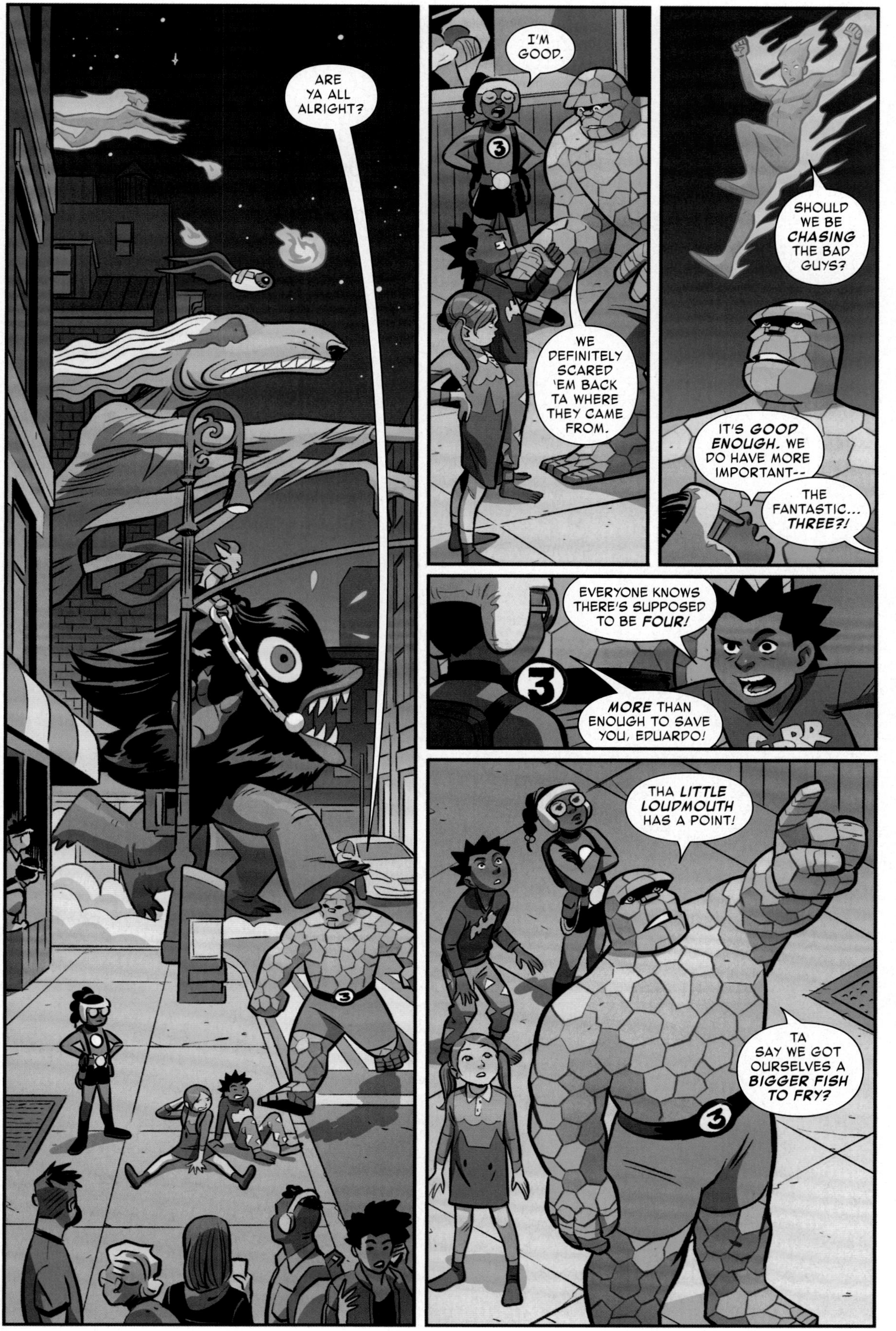
ARE YA ALL ALRIGHT?
I'M GOOD.
WE DEFINITELY SCARED 'EM BACK TA WHERE THEY CAME FROM.
SHOULD WE BE *CHASING* THE BAD GUYS?
IT'S *GOOD ENOUGH.* WE DO HAVE MORE IMPORTANT--
THE FANTASTIC... *THREE?!*
EVERYONE KNOWS THERE'S SUPPOSED TO BE *FOUR!*
MORE THAN ENOUGH TO SAVE YOU, EDUARDO!
THA *LITTLE LOUDMOUTH* HAS A POINT!
TA SAY WE GOT OURSELVES A *BIGGER FISH TO FRY?*

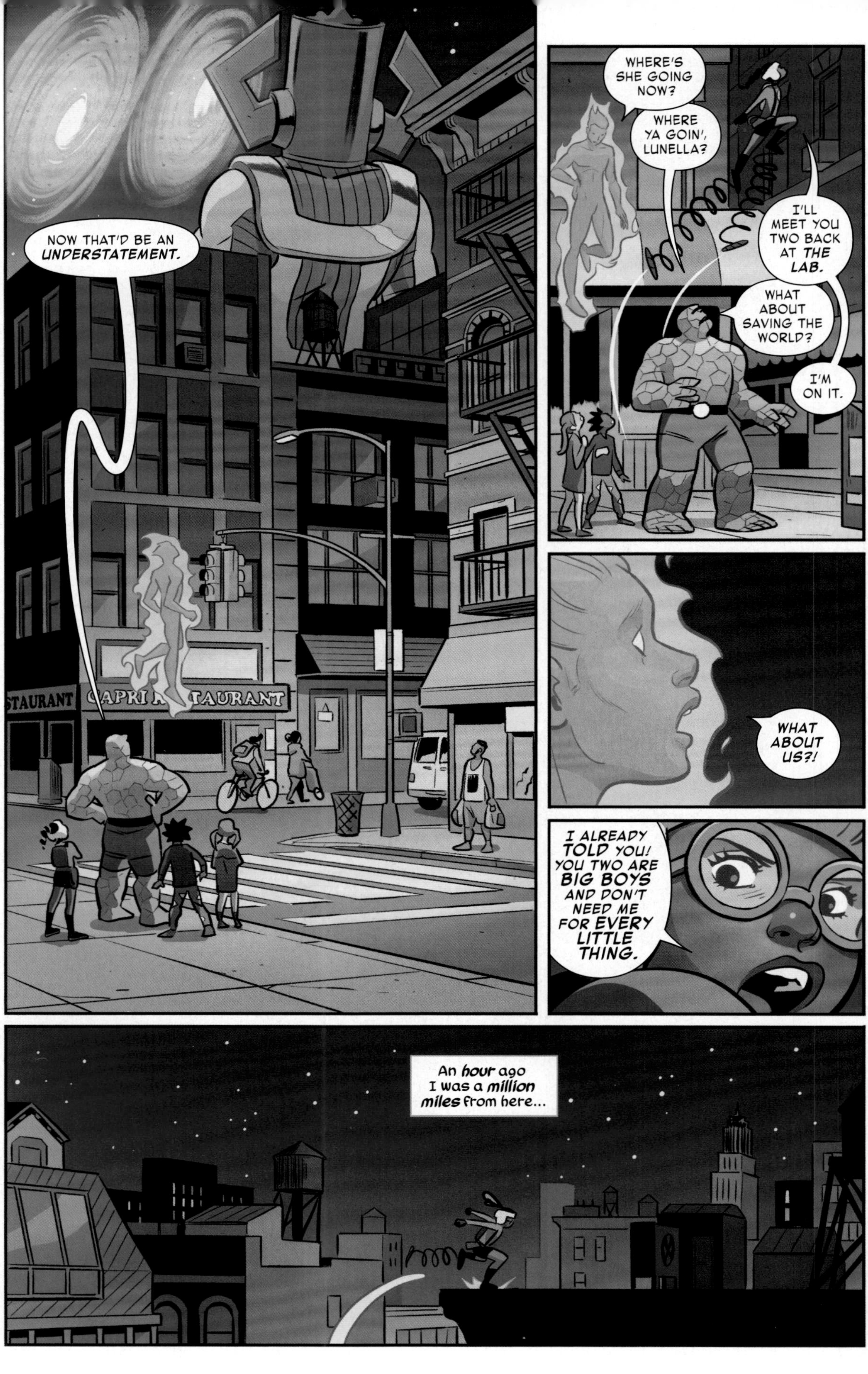

NOW THAT'D BE AN *UNDERSTATEMENT.*
CAPRI RESTAURANT
STAURANT
WHERE'S SHE GOING NOW?
WHERE YA GOIN', LUNELLA?
I'LL MEET YOU TWO BACK AT *THE LAB.*
WHAT ABOUT SAVING THE WORLD?
I'M ON IT.
WHAT ABOUT US?!
I ALREADY **TOLD** *YOU! YOU TWO ARE* **BIG BOYS** *AND DON'T NEED ME FOR* **EVERY LITTLE THING.**
An *hour* ago I was a *million miles* from here...

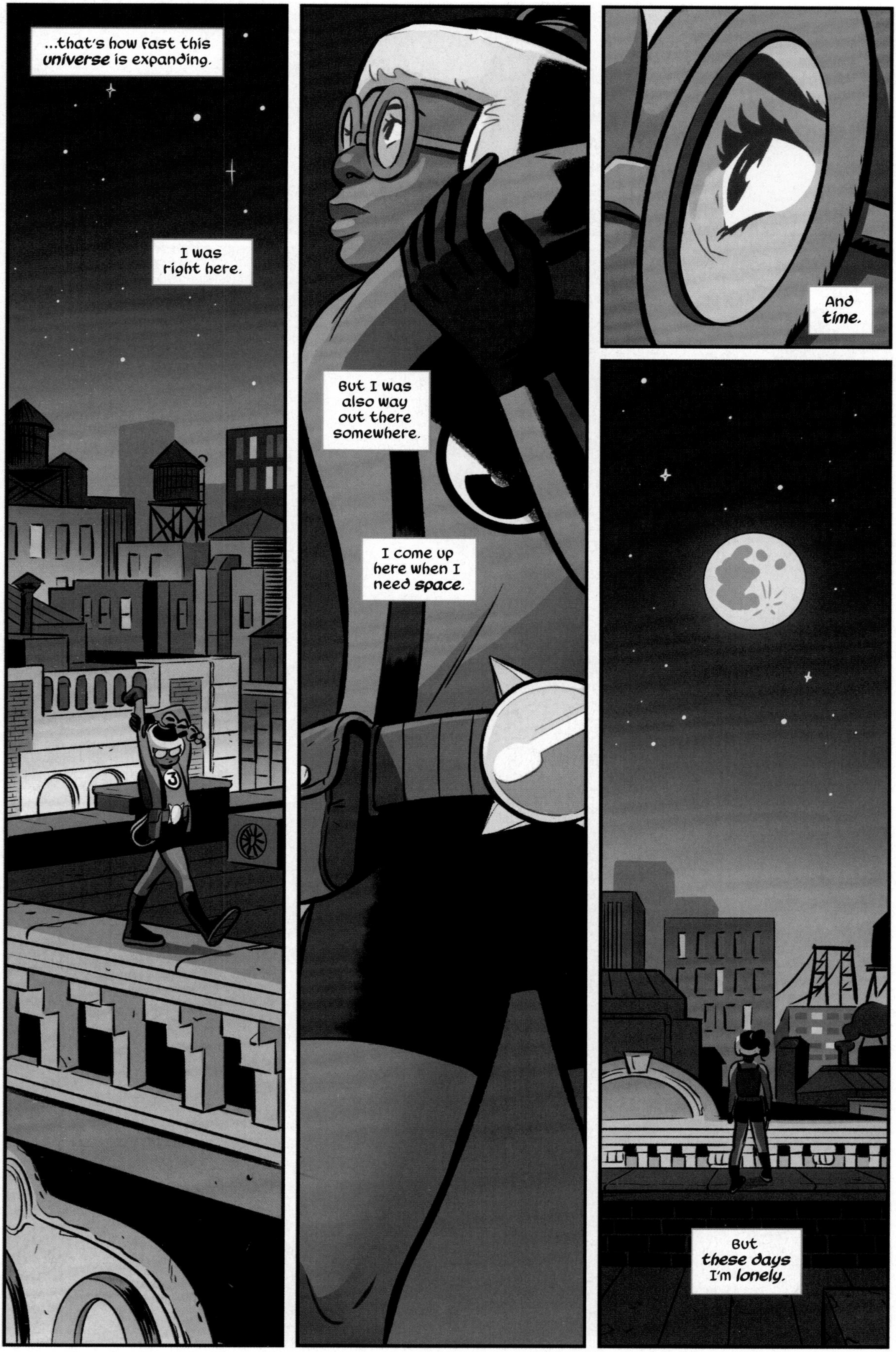
...that's how fast this *universe* is expanding.
I was right here.
But I was also way out there somewhere.
I come up here when I need *space.*
And *time.*
But *these days* I'm *lonely.*

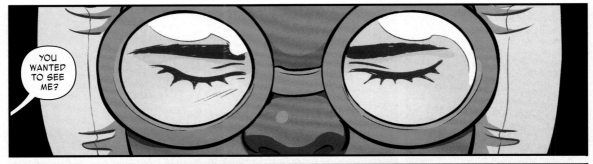

YOU WANTED TO SEE ME?

NO. I DIDN'T "WANT" TO. I HAD TO. YOU AND THE BIG GUY.

IS THIS ABOUT JOINING YOUR FANTASTIC FOUR?

BELIEVE ME--I'M GOING TO TELL YOU WHAT IT'S ALL ABOUT.

YOU NEED TO FIND BALANCE, LUNELLA LAFAYETTE.

"BALANCE" IS MY MIDDLE NAME.

REALLY?

NO. IT'S LOUISE. I DON'T HAVE A MIDDLE NAME.

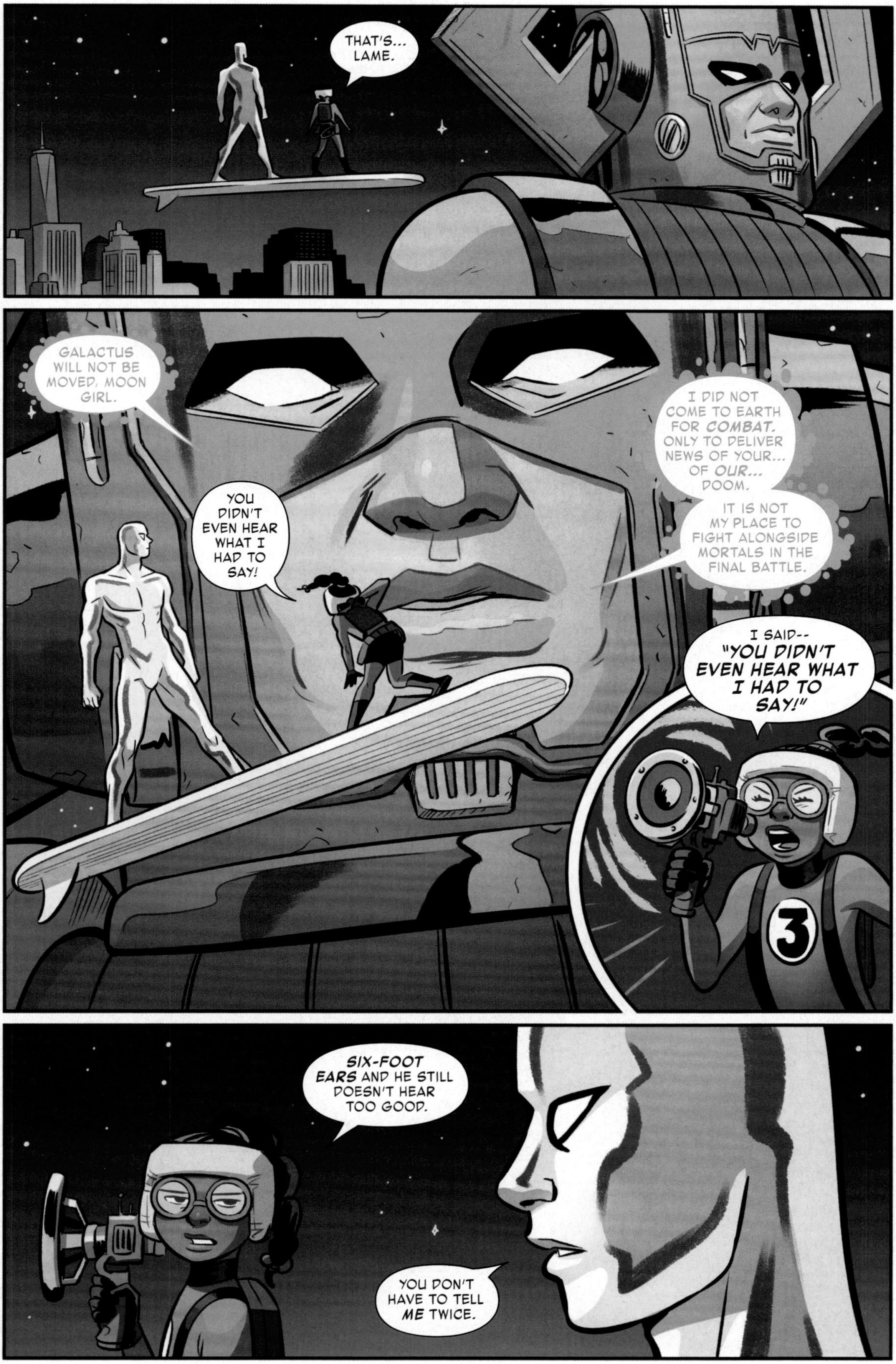
THAT'S... LAME.
GALACTUS WILL NOT BE MOVED, MOON GIRL.
I DID NOT COME TO EARTH FOR COMBAT. ONLY TO DELIVER NEWS OF YOUR... OF OUR... DOOM.
IT IS NOT MY PLACE TO FIGHT ALONGSIDE MORTALS IN THE FINAL BATTLE.
YOU DIDN'T EVEN HEAR WHAT I HAD TO SAY!
I SAID-- "YOU DIDN'T EVEN HEAR WHAT I HAD TO SAY!"
SIX-FOOT EARS AND HE STILL DOESN'T HEAR TOO GOOD.
YOU DON'T HAVE TO TELL ME TWICE.

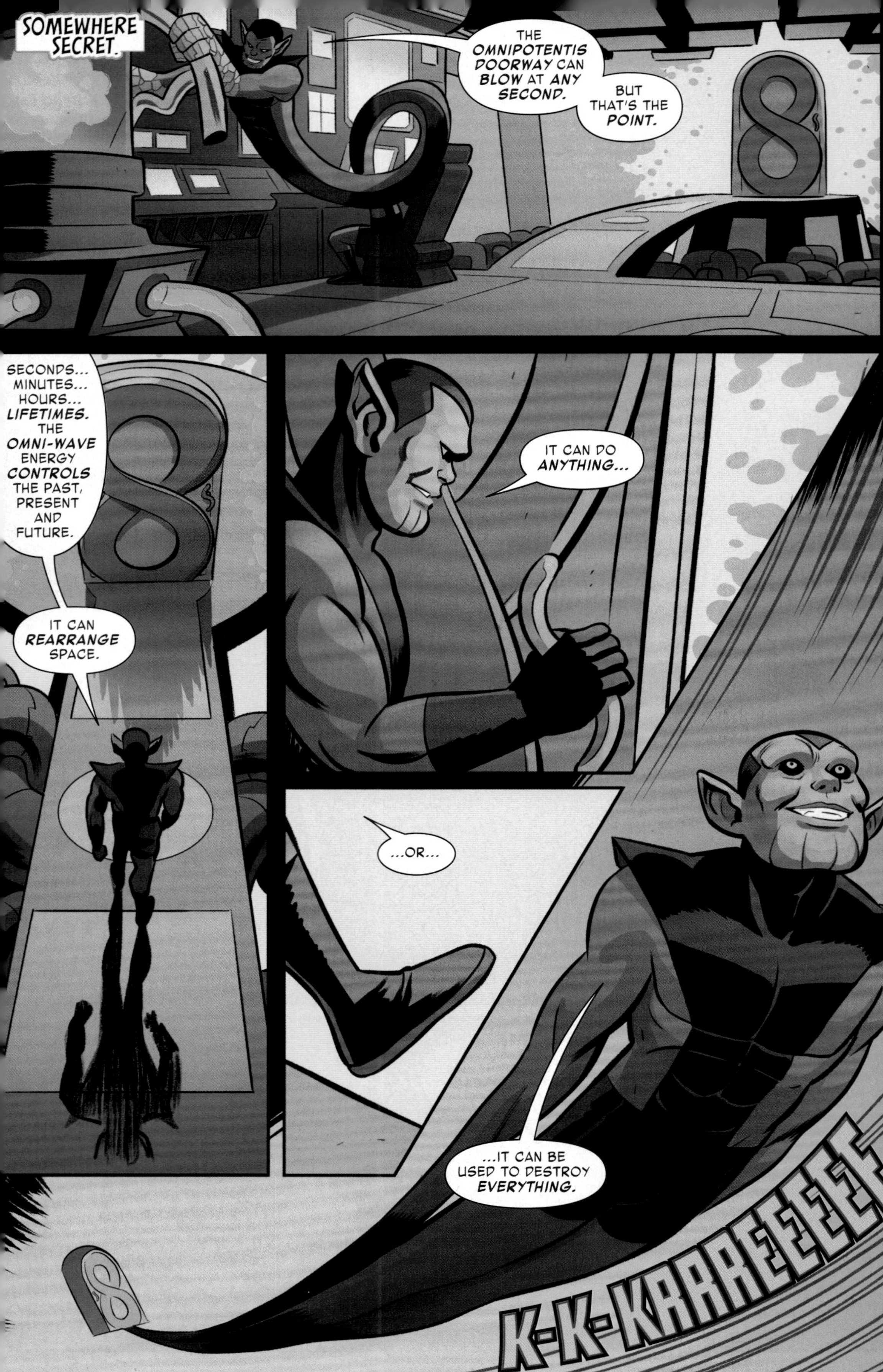

SOMEWHERE SECRET.
THE OMNIPOTENTIS DOORWAY CAN BLOW AT ANY SECOND.
BUT THAT'S THE POINT.
SECONDS... MINUTES... HOURS... LIFETIMES. THE OMNI-WAVE ENERGY CONTROLS THE PAST, PRESENT AND FUTURE.
IT CAN REARRANGE SPACE.
IT CAN DO ANYTHING...
...OR...
...IT CAN BE USED TO DESTROY EVERYTHING.
K-K-KRRREEEEE

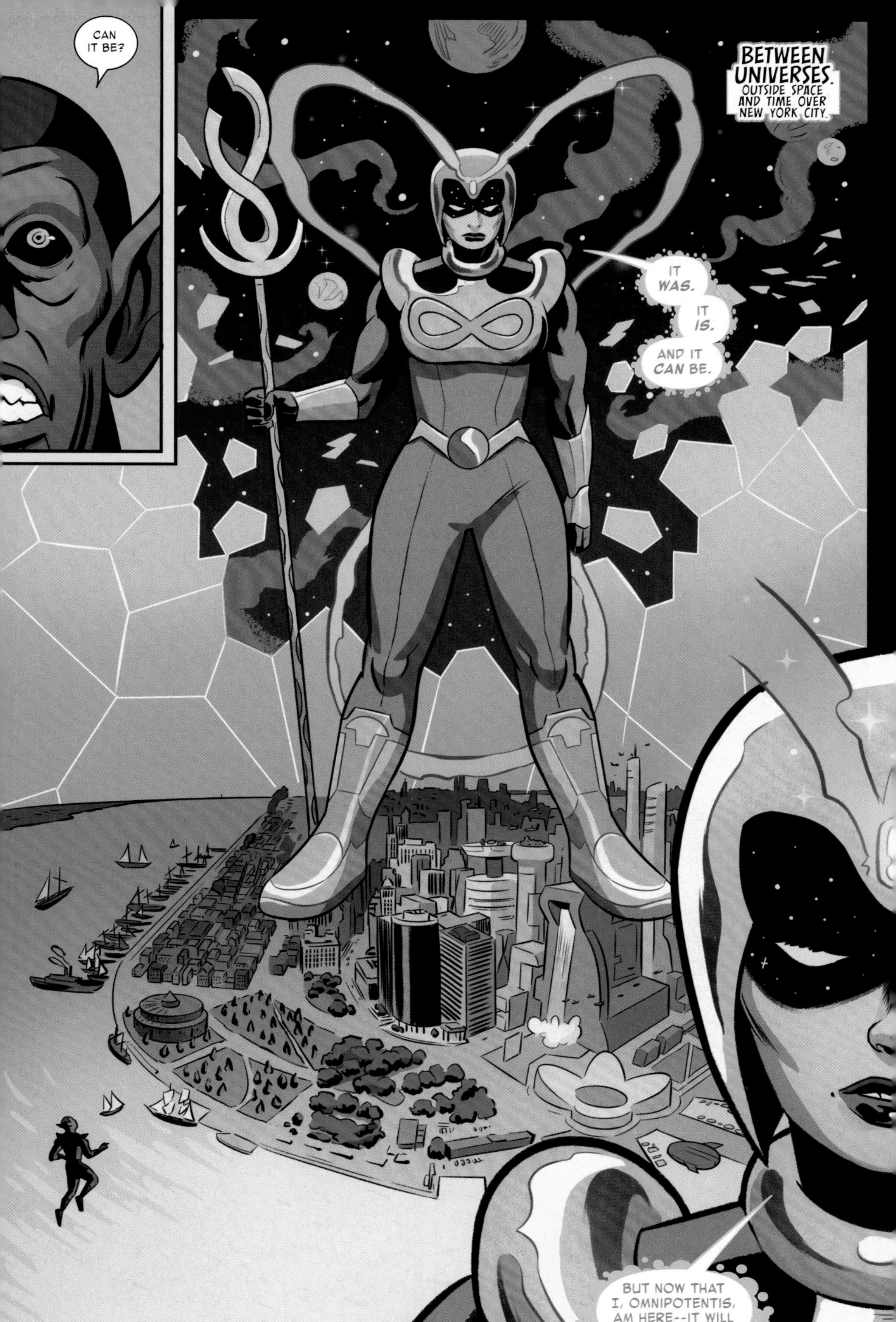
CAN IT BE?
BETWEEN UNIVERSES.
OUTSIDE SPACE AND TIME OVER NEW YORK CITY.
IT WAS.
IT IS.
AND IT CAN BE.
BUT NOW THAT I, OMNIPOTENTIS, AM HERE--IT WILL BE NOTHING.

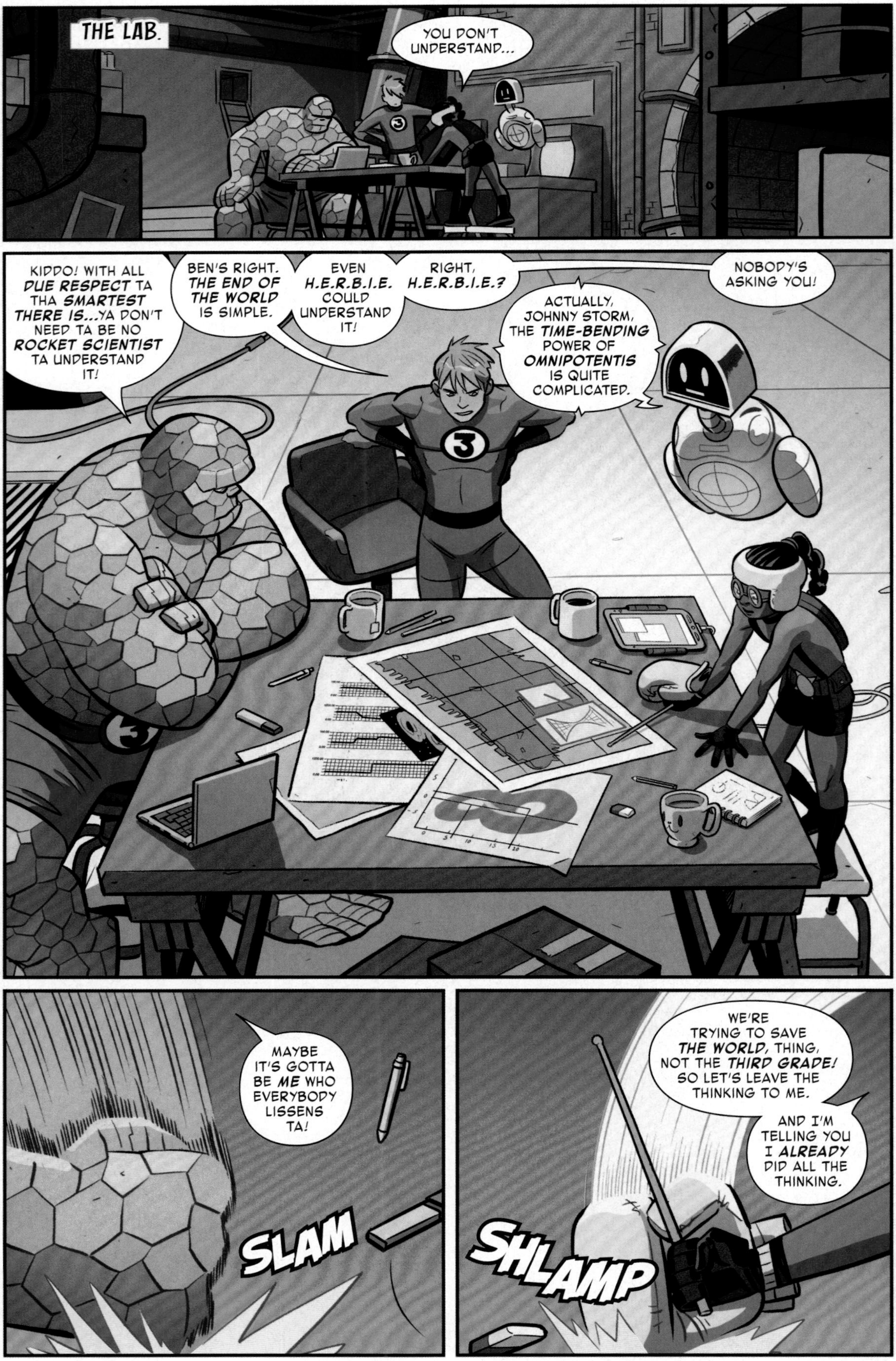

THE LAB.
YOU DON'T UNDERSTAND...
KIDDO! WITH ALL DUE RESPECT TA THA SMARTEST THERE IS...YA DON'T NEED TA BE NO ROCKET SCIENTIST TA UNDERSTAND IT!
BEN'S RIGHT. THE END OF THE WORLD IS SIMPLE.
EVEN H.E.R.B.I.E. COULD UNDERSTAND IT!
RIGHT, H.E.R.B.I.E.?
NOBODY'S ASKING YOU!
ACTUALLY, JOHNNY STORM, THE TIME-BENDING POWER OF OMNIPOTENTIS IS QUITE COMPLICATED.
MAYBE IT'S GOTTA BE ME WHO EVERYBODY LISSENS TA!
SLAM
WE'RE TRYING TO SAVE THE WORLD, THING, NOT THE THIRD GRADE! SO LET'S LEAVE THE THINKING TO ME.
AND I'M TELLING YOU I ALREADY DID ALL THE THINKING.
SHLAMP

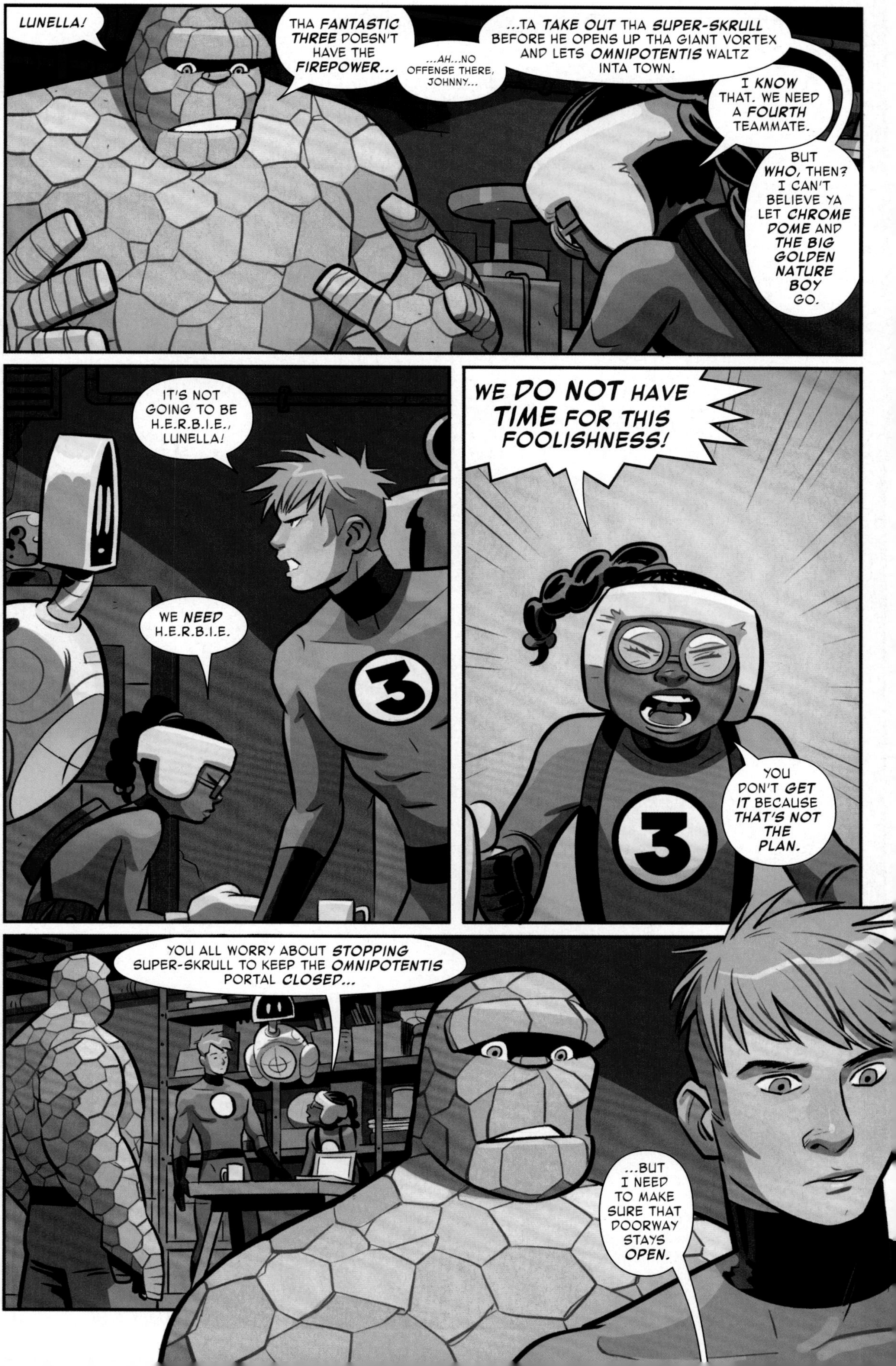
LUNELLA!
THA FANTASTIC THREE DOESN'T HAVE THE FIREPOWER...
...AH...NO OFFENSE THERE, JOHNNY...
...TA TAKE OUT THA SUPER-SKRULL BEFORE HE OPENS UP THA GIANT VORTEX AND LETS OMNIPOTENTIS WALTZ INTA TOWN.
I KNOW THAT. WE NEED A FOURTH TEAMMATE.
BUT WHO, THEN? I CAN'T BELIEVE YA LET CHROME DOME AND THE BIG GOLDEN NATURE BOY GO.
IT'S NOT GOING TO BE H.E.R.B.I.E., LUNELLA!
WE NEED H.E.R.B.I.E.
WE DO NOT HAVE TIME FOR THIS FOOLISHNESS!
YOU DON'T GET IT BECAUSE THAT'S NOT THE PLAN.
YOU ALL WORRY ABOUT STOPPING SUPER-SKRULL TO KEEP THE OMNIPOTENTIS PORTAL CLOSED...
...BUT I NEED TO MAKE SURE THAT DOORWAY STAYS OPEN.

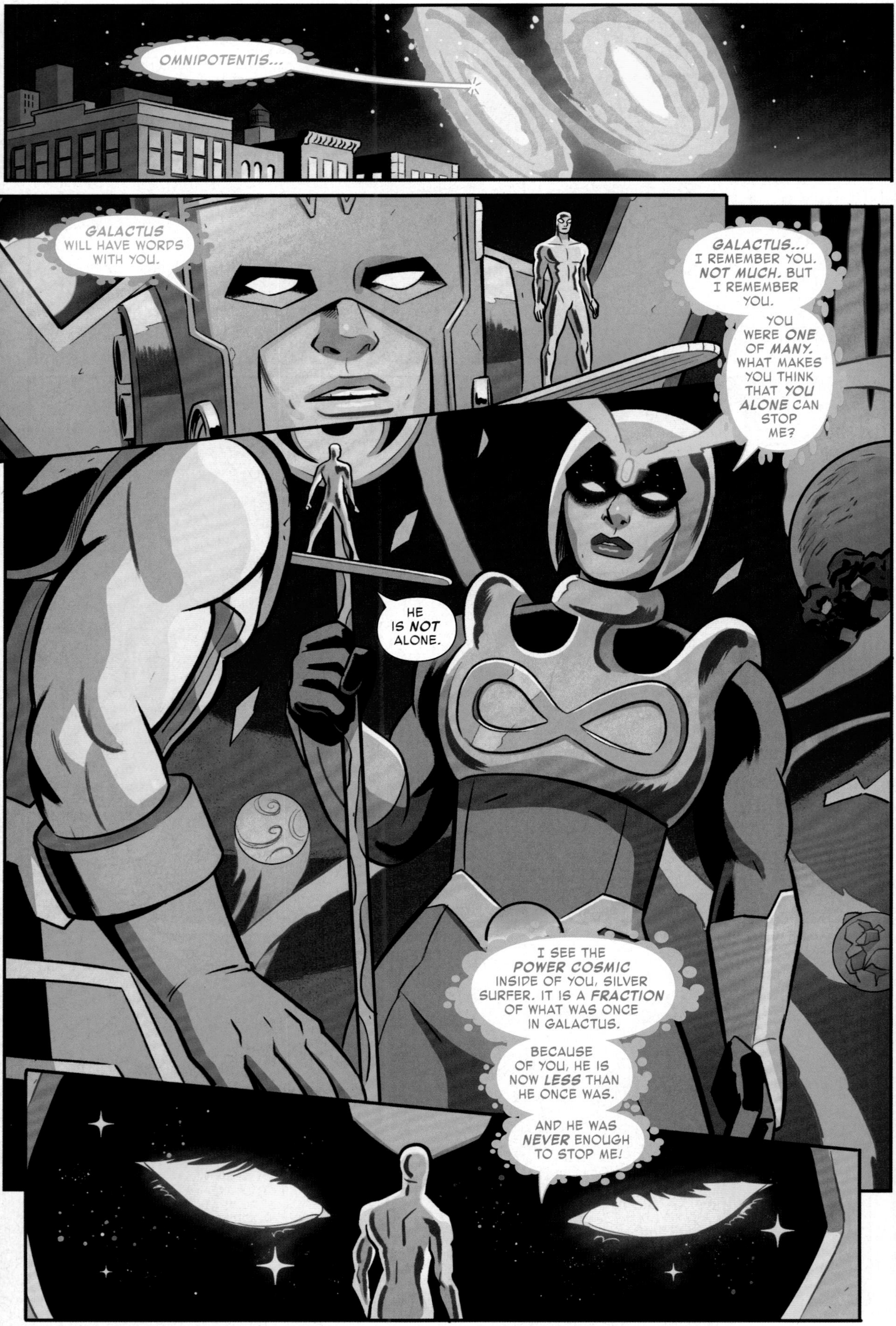
OMNIPOTENTIS...
GALACTUS WILL HAVE WORDS WITH YOU.
GALACTUS... I REMEMBER YOU. NOT MUCH. BUT I REMEMBER YOU.
YOU WERE ONE OF MANY. WHAT MAKES YOU THINK THAT YOU ALONE CAN STOP ME?
HE IS NOT ALONE.
I SEE THE POWER COSMIC INSIDE OF YOU, SILVER SURFER. IT IS A FRACTION OF WHAT WAS ONCE IN GALACTUS.
BECAUSE OF YOU, HE IS NOW LESS THAN HE ONCE WAS.
AND HE WAS NEVER ENOUGH TO STOP ME!

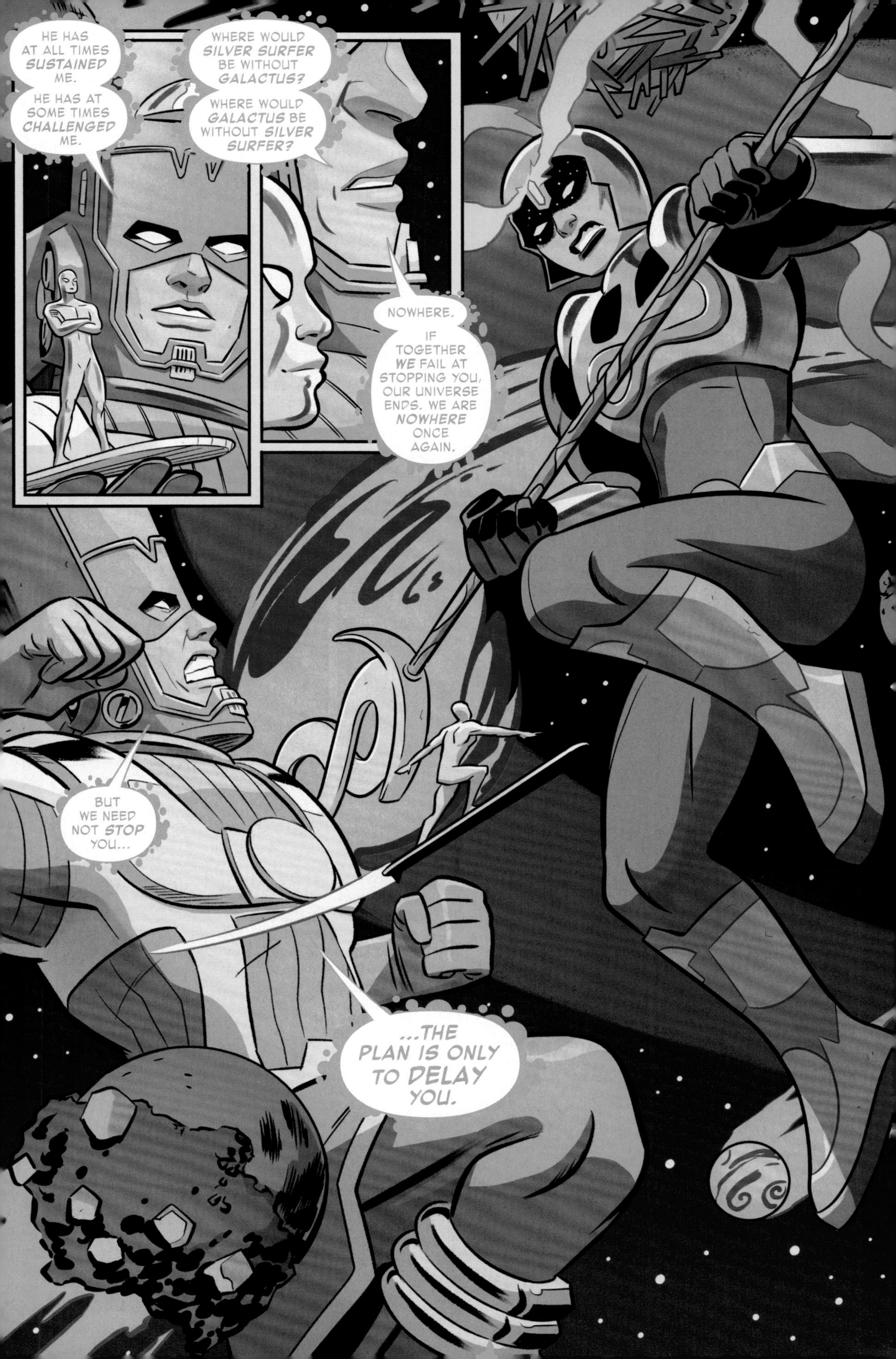
HE HAS AT ALL TIMES SUSTAINED ME.
HE HAS AT SOME TIMES CHALLENGED ME.
WHERE WOULD SILVER SURFER BE WITHOUT GALACTUS?
WHERE WOULD GALACTUS BE WITHOUT SILVER SURFER?
NOWHERE.
IF TOGETHER WE FAIL AT STOPPING YOU, OUR UNIVERSE ENDS. WE ARE NOWHERE ONCE AGAIN.
BUT WE NEED NOT STOP YOU...
...THE PLAN IS ONLY TO DELAY YOU.

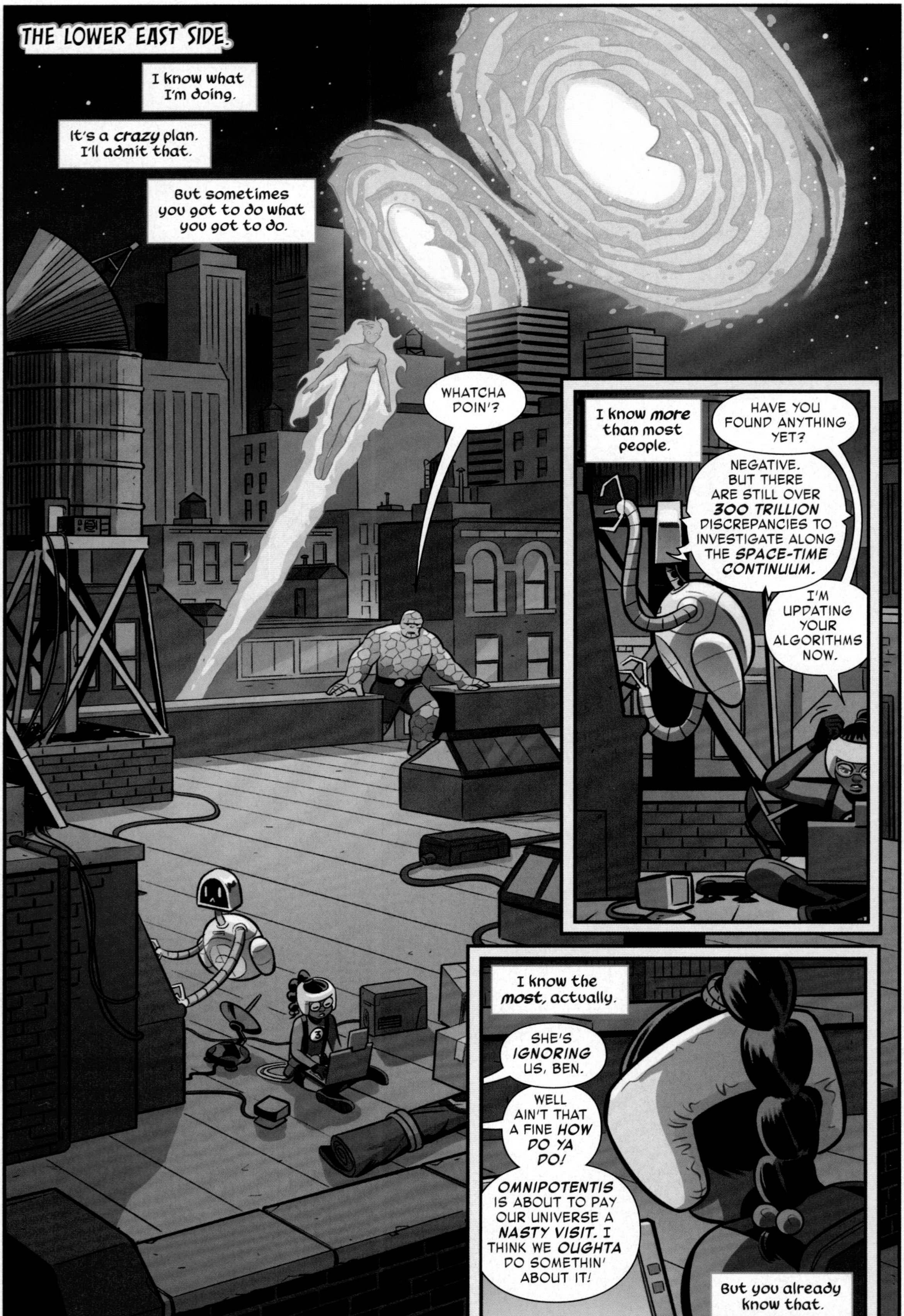
THE LOWER EAST SIDE.
I know what I'm doing.
It's a crazy plan. I'll admit that.
But sometimes you got to do what you got to do.
WHATCHA DOIN'?
I know more than most people.
HAVE YOU FOUND ANYTHING YET?
NEGATIVE. BUT THERE ARE STILL OVER 300 TRILLION DISCREPANCIES TO INVESTIGATE ALONG THE SPACE-TIME CONTINUUM.
I'M UPDATING YOUR ALGORITHMS NOW.
I know the most, actually.
SHE'S IGNORING US, BEN.
WELL AIN'T THAT A FINE HOW DO YA DO!
OMNIPOTENTIS IS ABOUT TO PAY OUR UNIVERSE A NASTY VISIT. I THINK WE OUGHTA DO SOMETHIN' ABOUT IT!
But you already know that.

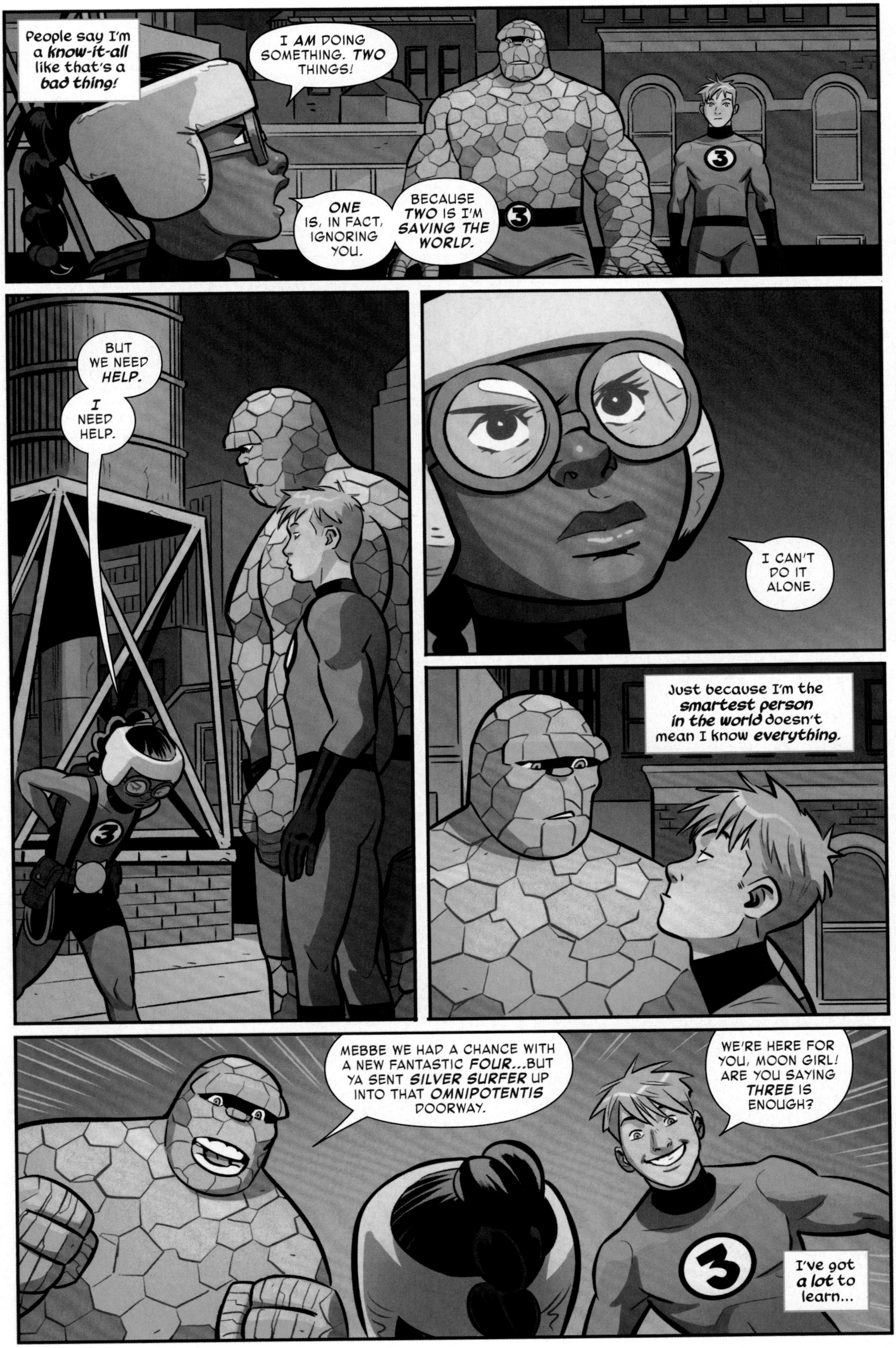
People say I'm a know-it-all like that's a bad thing!
I AM DOING SOMETHING. TWO THINGS!
ONE IS, IN FACT, IGNORING YOU.
BECAUSE TWO IS I'M SAVING THE WORLD.
BUT WE NEED HELP.
I NEED HELP.
I CAN'T DO IT ALONE.
Just because I'm the smartest person in the world doesn't mean I know everything.
MEBBE WE HAD A CHANCE WITH A NEW FANTASTIC FOUR...BUT YA SENT SILVER SURFER UP INTO THAT OMNIPOTENTIS DOORWAY.
WE'RE HERE FOR YOU, MOON GIRL! ARE YOU SAYING THREE IS ENOUGH?
I've got a lot to learn...

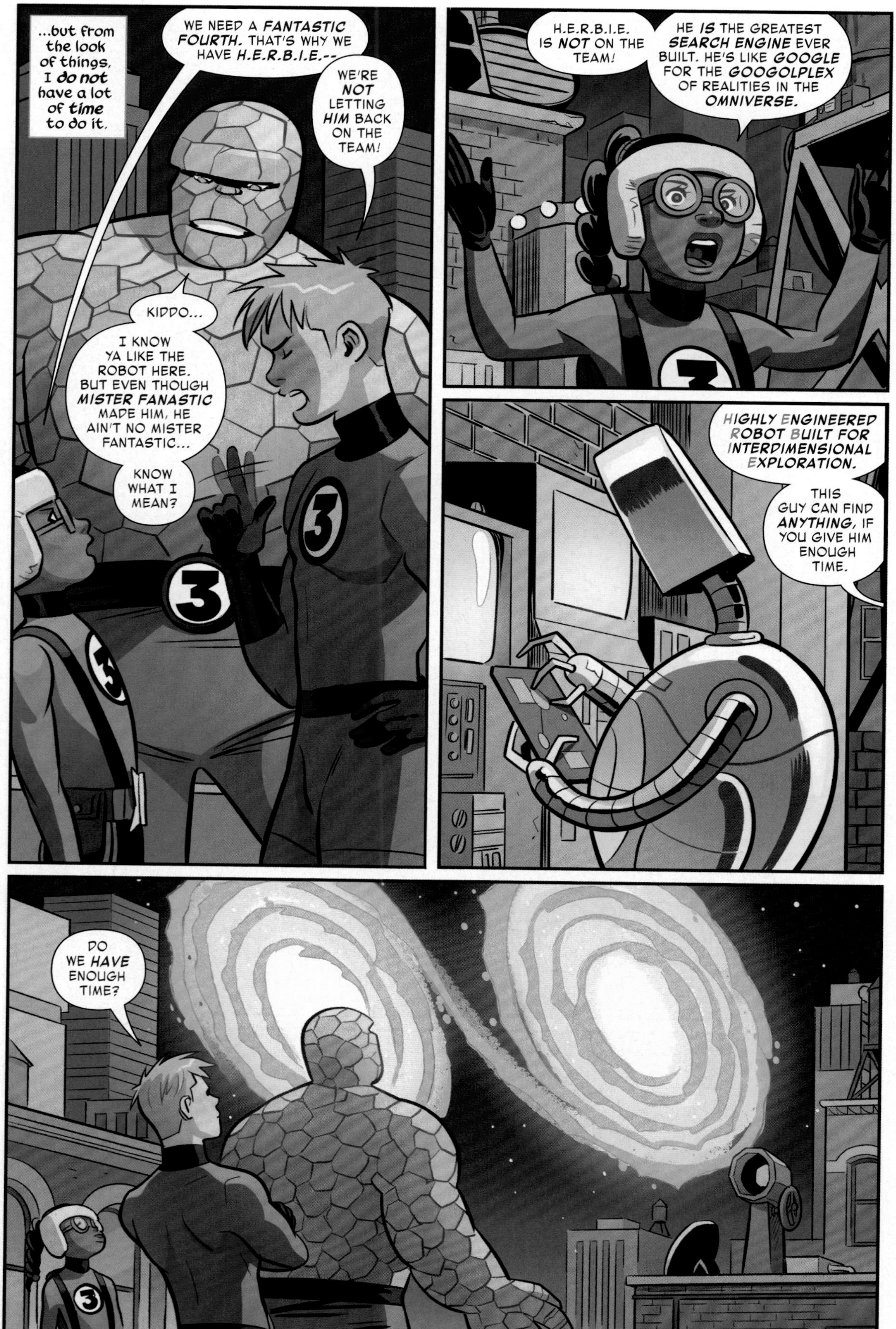

...but from the look of things, I *do not* have a lot of *time* to do it.
WE NEED A *FANTASTIC FOURTH.* THAT'S WHY WE HAVE *H.E.R.B.I.E.*--
WE'RE *NOT* LETTING *HIM* BACK ON THE TEAM!
KIDDO...
I KNOW YA LIKE THE ROBOT HERE. BUT EVEN THOUGH *MISTER FANASTIC* MADE HIM, HE AIN'T NO MISTER FANTASTIC...
KNOW WHAT I MEAN?
H.E.R.B.I.E. IS *NOT* ON THE TEAM!
HE *IS* THE GREATEST *SEARCH ENGINE* EVER BUILT. HE'S LIKE *GOOGLE* FOR THE *GOOGOLPLEX* OF REALITIES IN THE *OMNIVERSE.*
HIGHLY ENGINEERED ROBOT BUILT FOR INTERDIMENSIONAL EXPLORATION.
THIS GUY CAN FIND *ANYTHING,* IF YOU GIVE HIM ENOUGH TIME.
DO WE *HAVE* ENOUGH TIME?

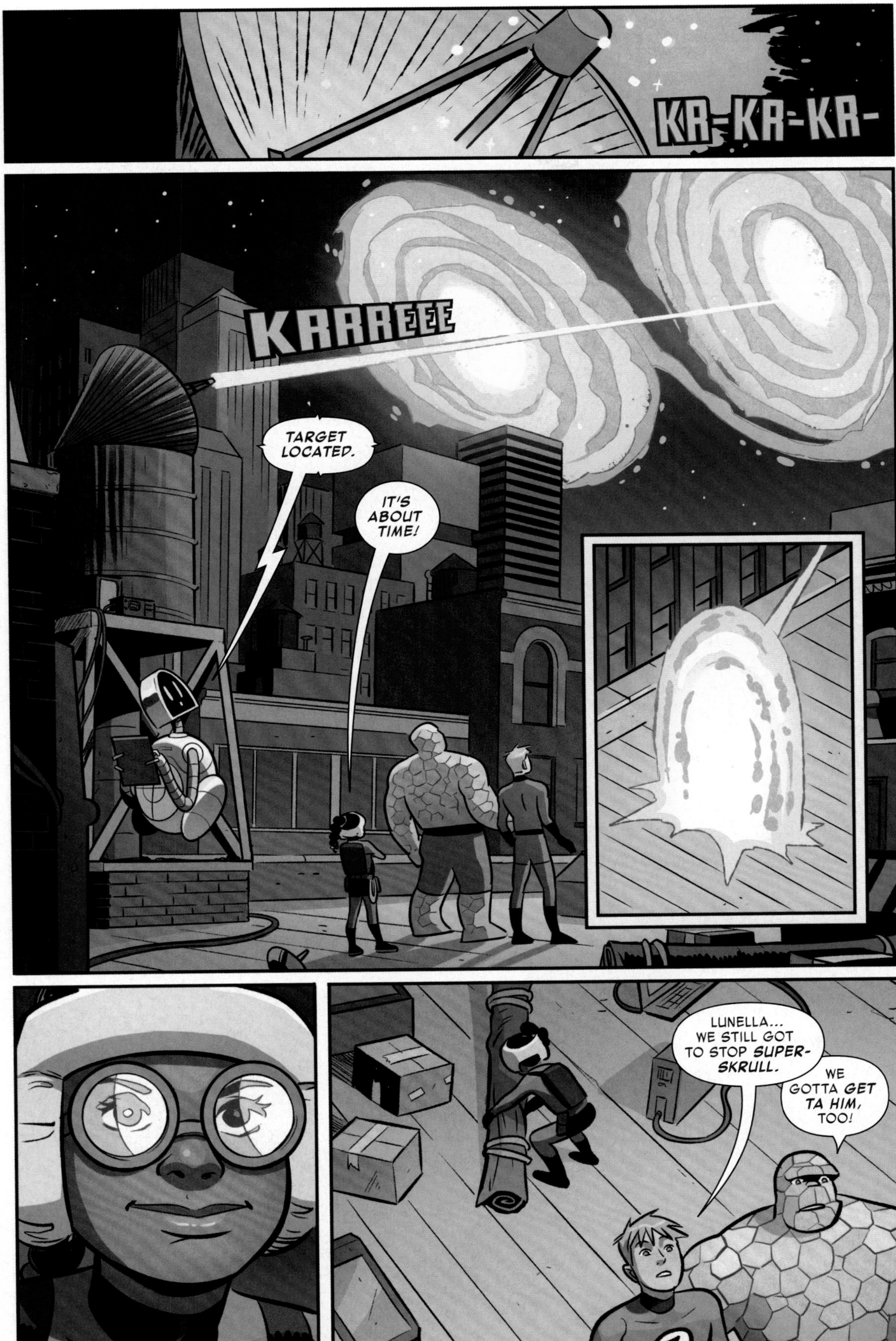
KR-KR-KR-
KRRREEE
TARGET LOCATED.
IT'S ABOUT TIME!
LUNELLA... WE STILL GOT TO STOP SUPER-SKRULL.
WE GOTTA GET TA HIM, TOO!

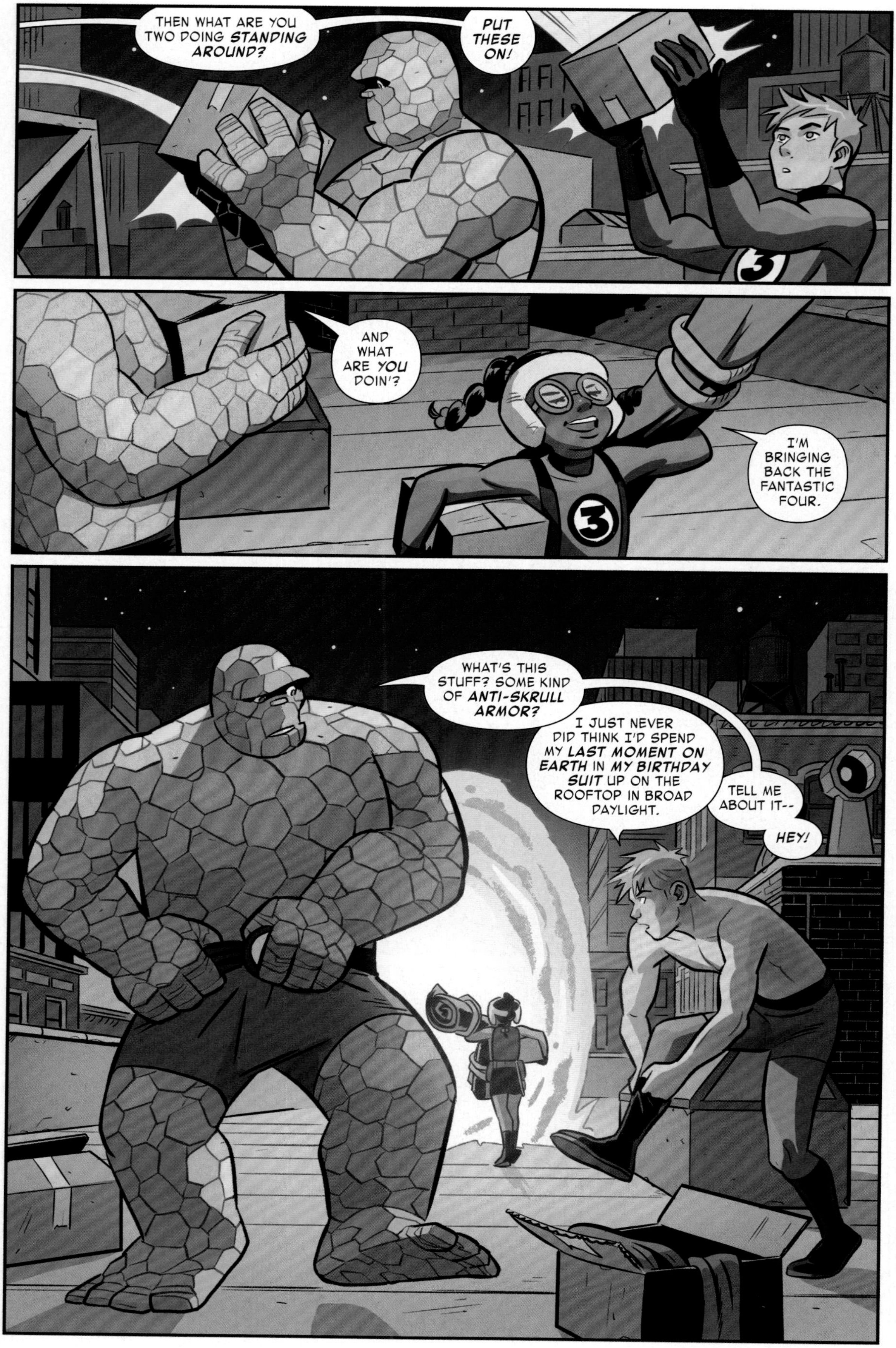
THEN WHAT ARE YOU TWO DOING STANDING AROUND?
PUT THESE ON!
AND WHAT ARE YOU DOIN'?
I'M BRINGING BACK THE FANTASTIC FOUR.
WHAT'S THIS STUFF? SOME KIND OF ANTI-SKRULL ARMOR?
I JUST NEVER DID THINK I'D SPEND MY LAST MOMENT ON EARTH IN MY BIRTHDAY SUIT UP ON THE ROOFTOP IN BROAD DAYLIGHT.
TELL ME ABOUT IT--
HEY!

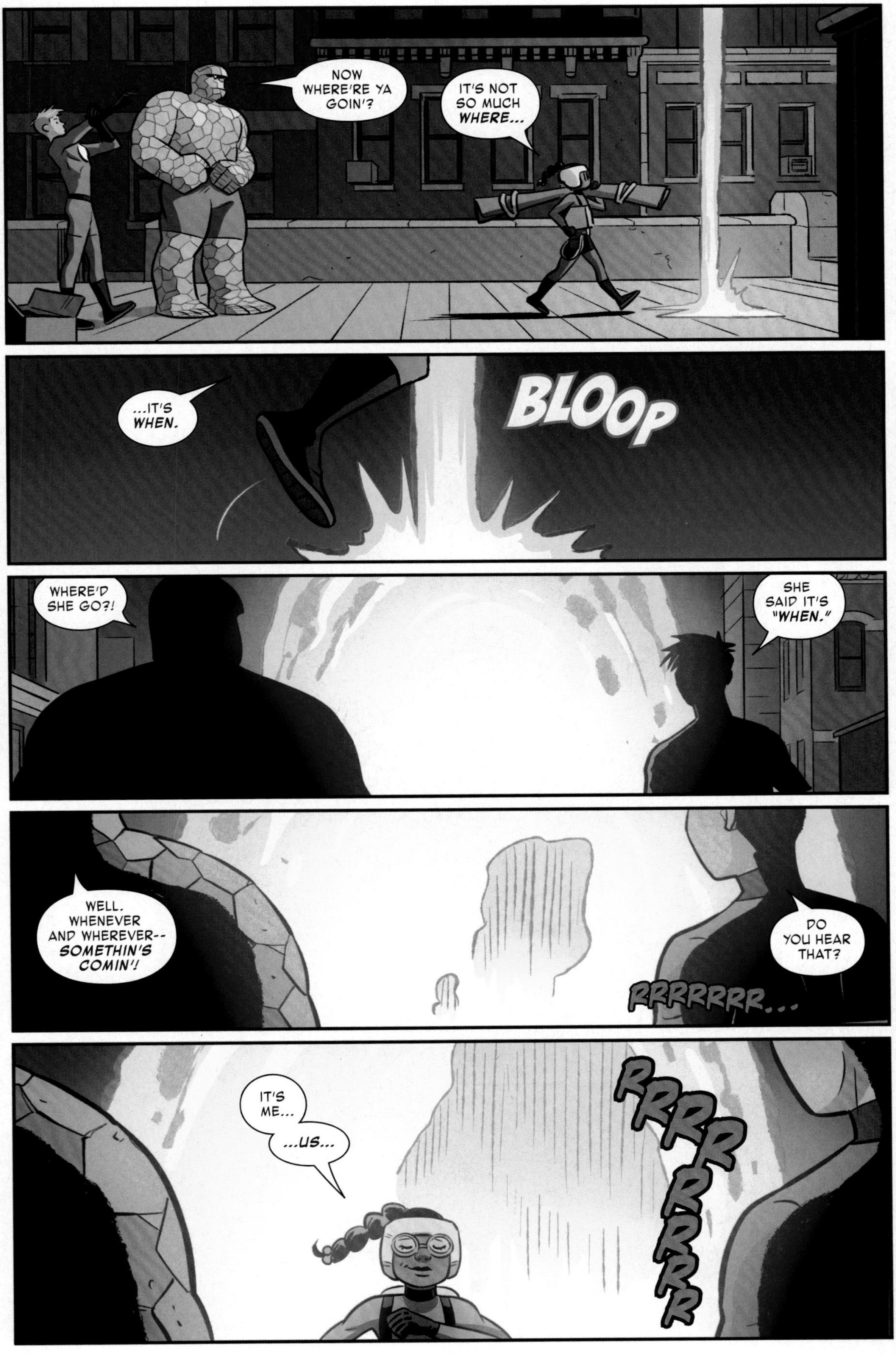
NOW WHERE'RE YA GOIN'?
IT'S NOT SO MUCH WHERE...
...IT'S WHEN.
BLOOP
WHERE'D SHE GO?!
SHE SAID IT'S "WHEN."
WELL. WHENEVER AND WHEREVER-- SOMETHIN'S COMIN'!
DO YOU HEAR THAT?
RRRRRRR...
IT'S ME...
...US...
RRRRRRRRRR

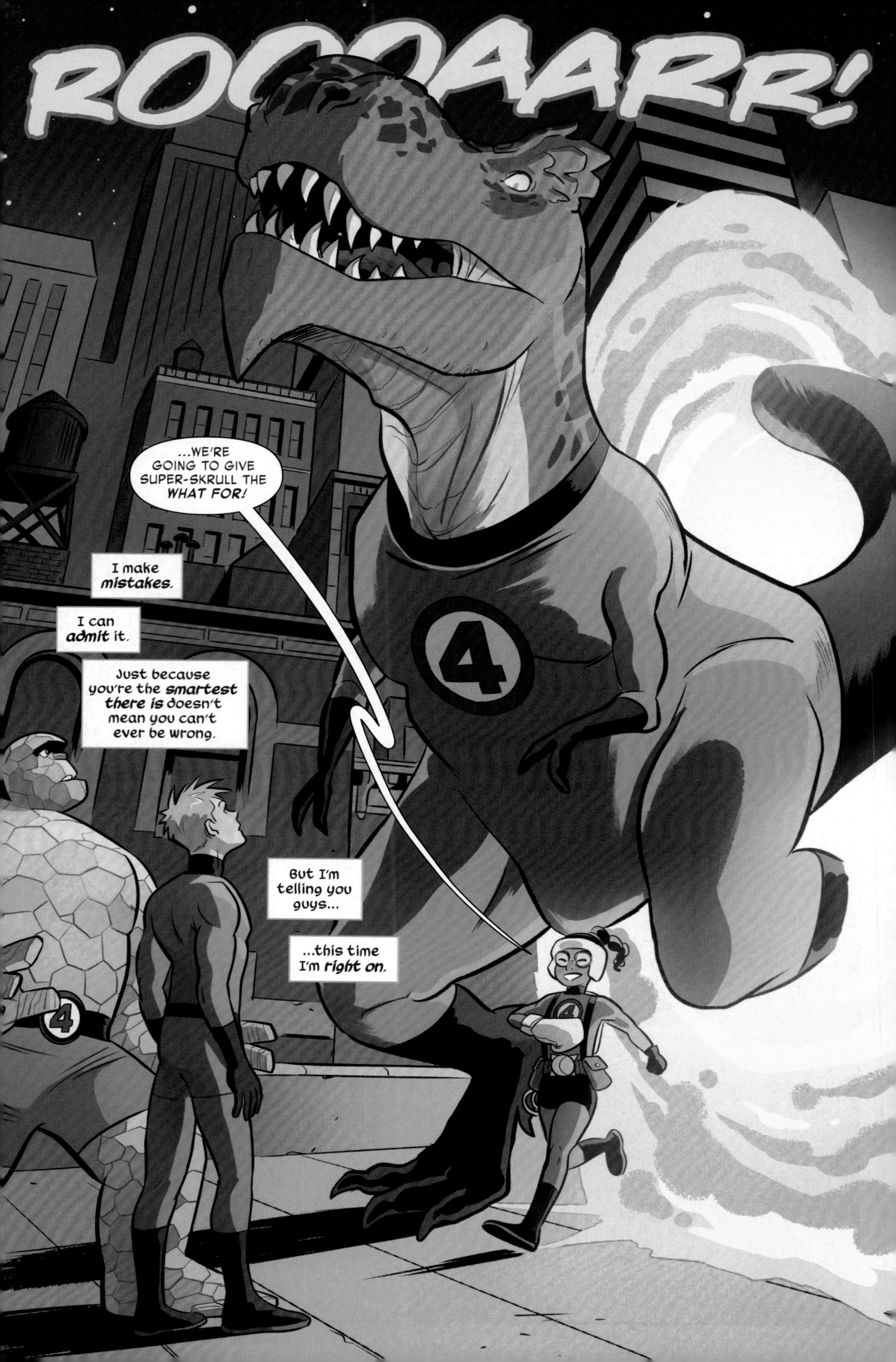
ROOOAARR!
...WE'RE GOING TO GIVE SUPER-SKRULL THE WHAT FOR!
I make mistakes.
I can admit it.
Just because you're the smartest there is doesn't mean you can't ever be wrong.
But I'm telling you guys...
...this time I'm right on.

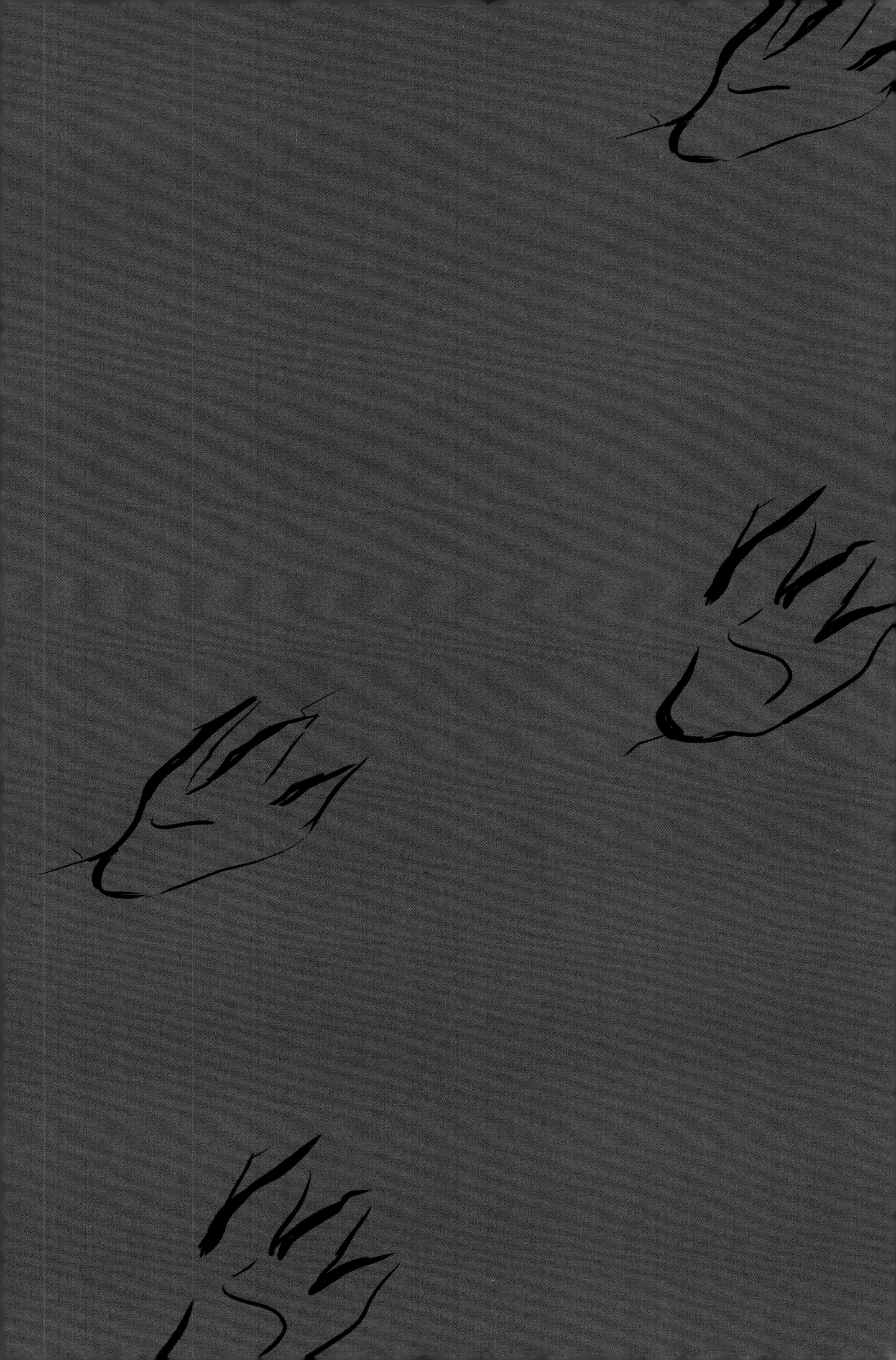

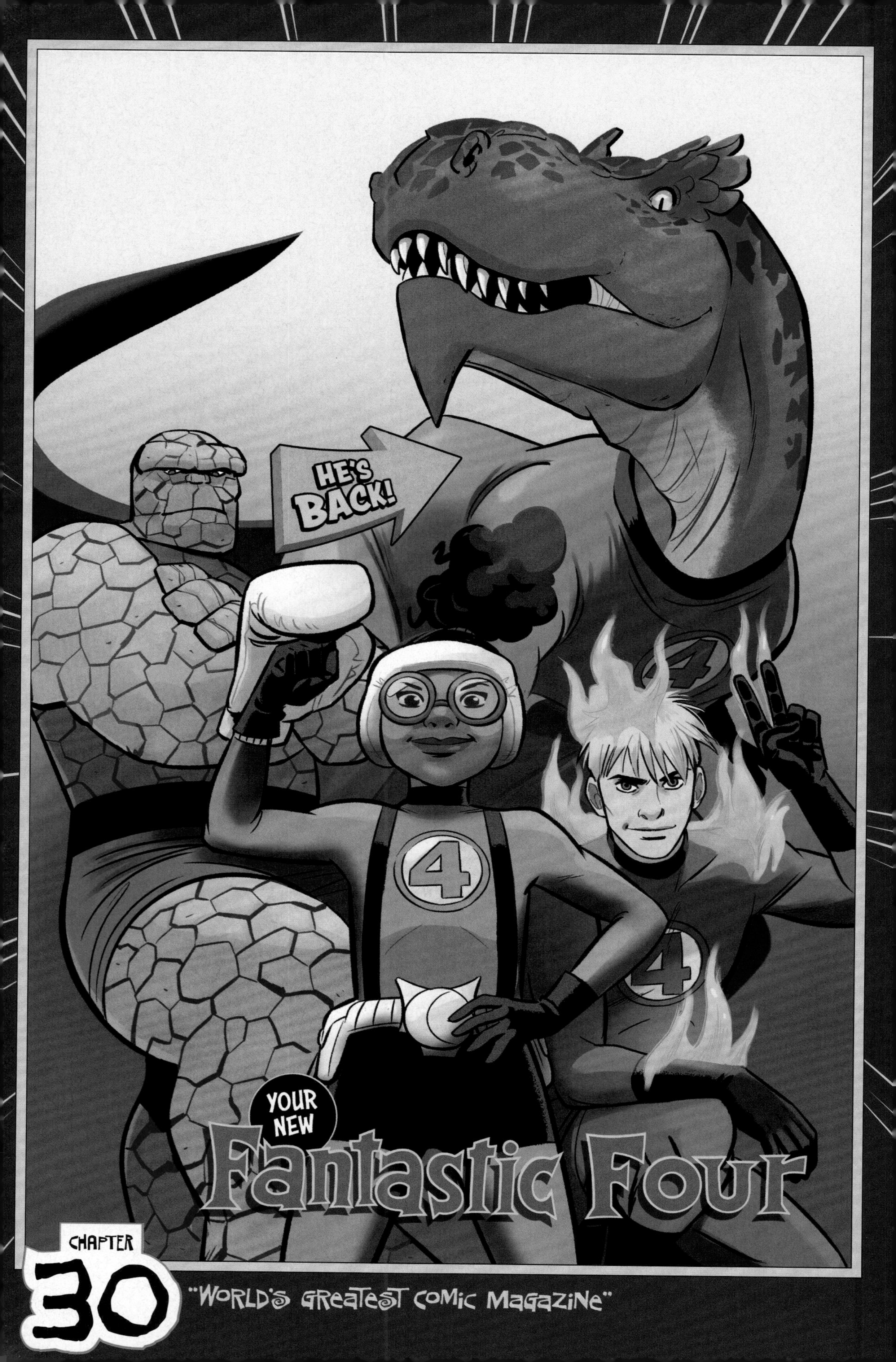
HE'S BACK!
YOUR NEW
Fantastic Four
CHAPTER
30
"WORLD'S GREATEST COMIC MAGAZINE"

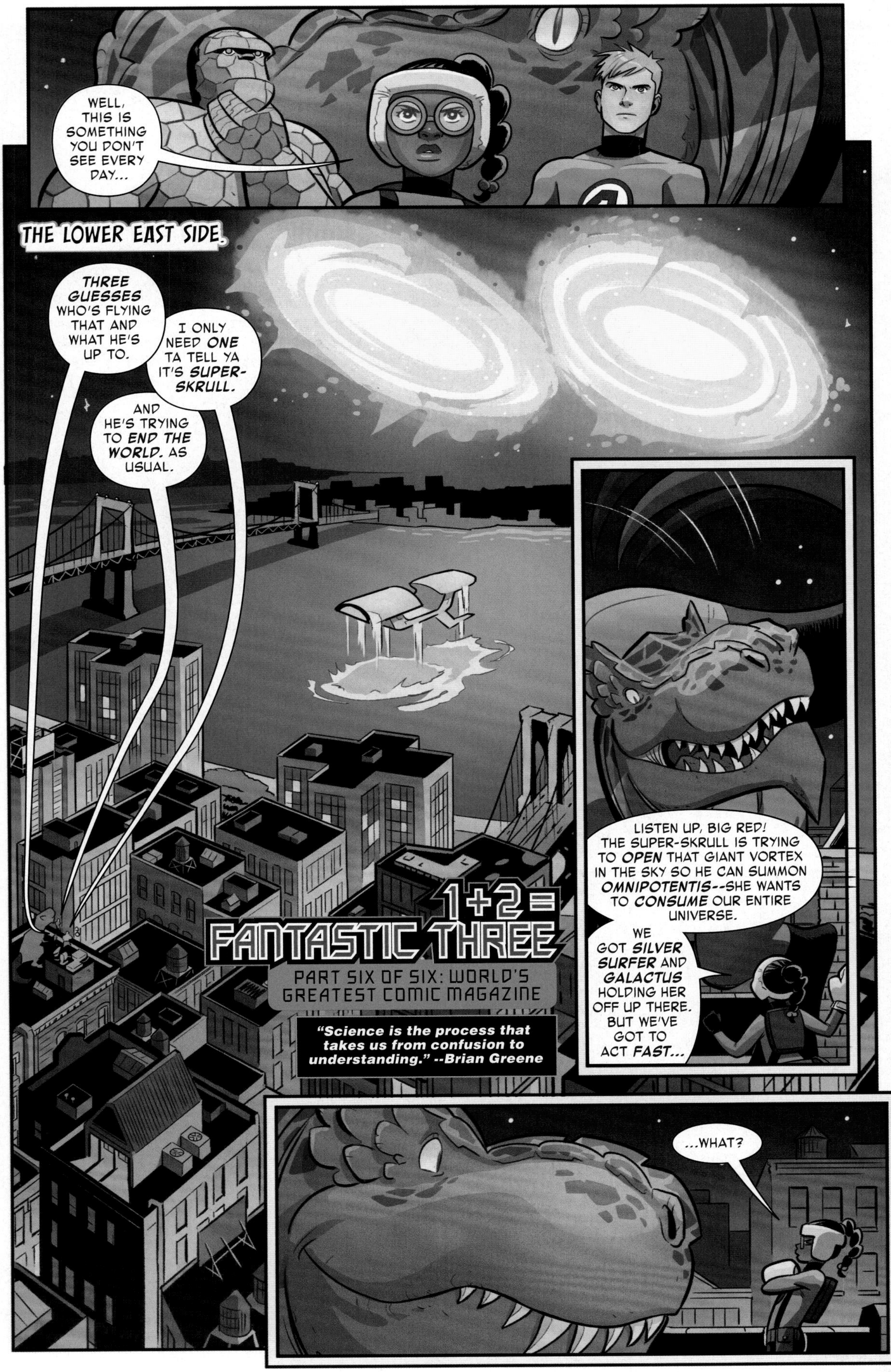

WELL, THIS IS SOMETHING YOU DON'T SEE EVERY DAY...
THE LOWER EAST SIDE.
THREE GUESSES WHO'S FLYING THAT AND WHAT HE'S UP TO.
I ONLY NEED ONE TA TELL YA IT'S SUPER-SKRULL.
AND HE'S TRYING TO END THE WORLD. AS USUAL.
1+2 = FANTASTIC THREE
PART SIX OF SIX: WORLD'S GREATEST COMIC MAGAZINE
"Science is the process that takes us from confusion to understanding." --Brian Greene
LISTEN UP, BIG RED! THE SUPER-SKRULL IS TRYING TO OPEN THAT GIANT VORTEX IN THE SKY SO HE CAN SUMMON OMNIPOTENTIS--SHE WANTS TO CONSUME OUR ENTIRE UNIVERSE.
WE GOT SILVER SURFER AND GALACTUS HOLDING HER OFF UP THERE. BUT WE'VE GOT TO ACT FAST...
...WHAT?

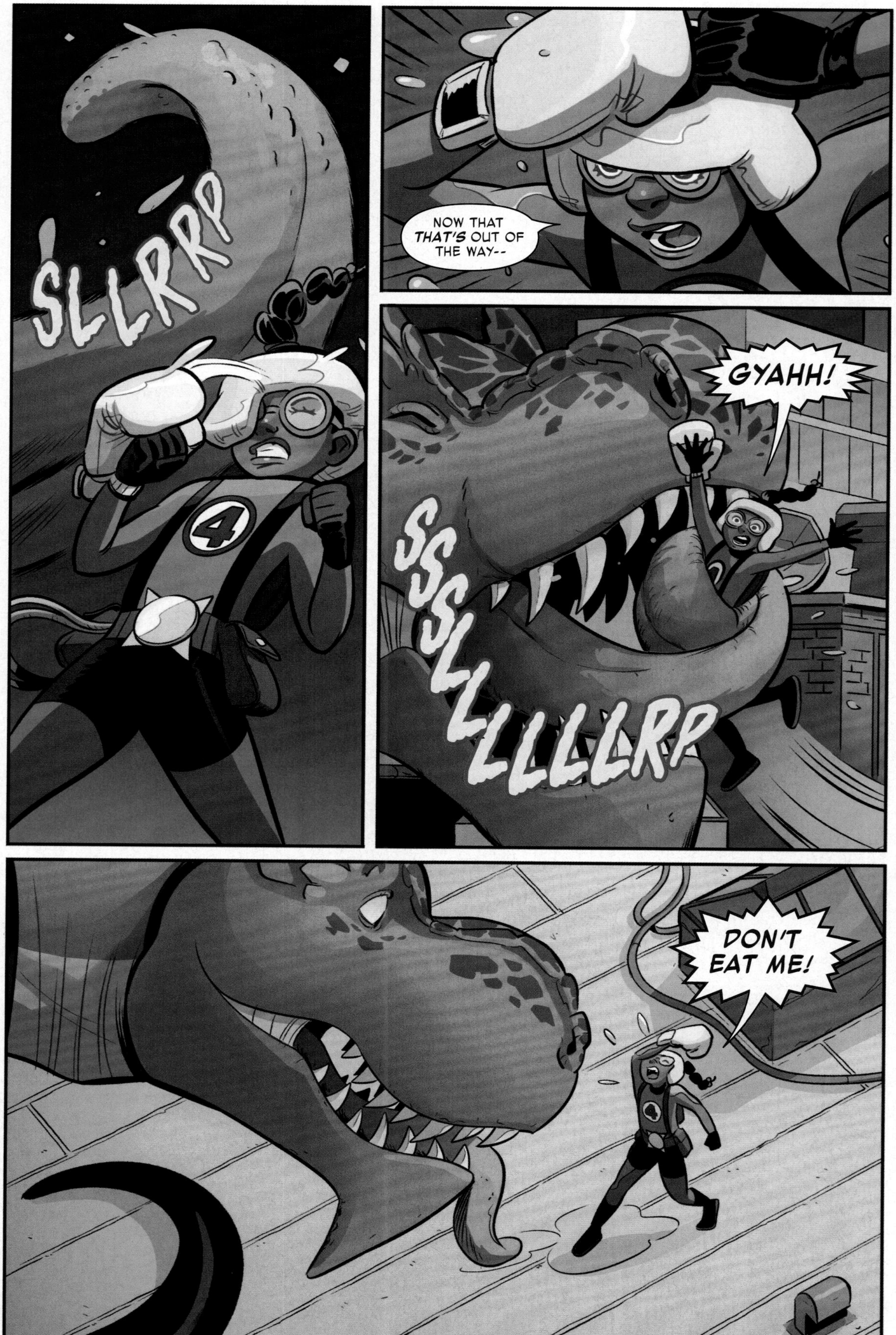
SLLRRP
NOW THAT THAT'S OUT OF THE WAY--
GYAHH!
SSSLLLLLRRP
DON'T EAT ME!

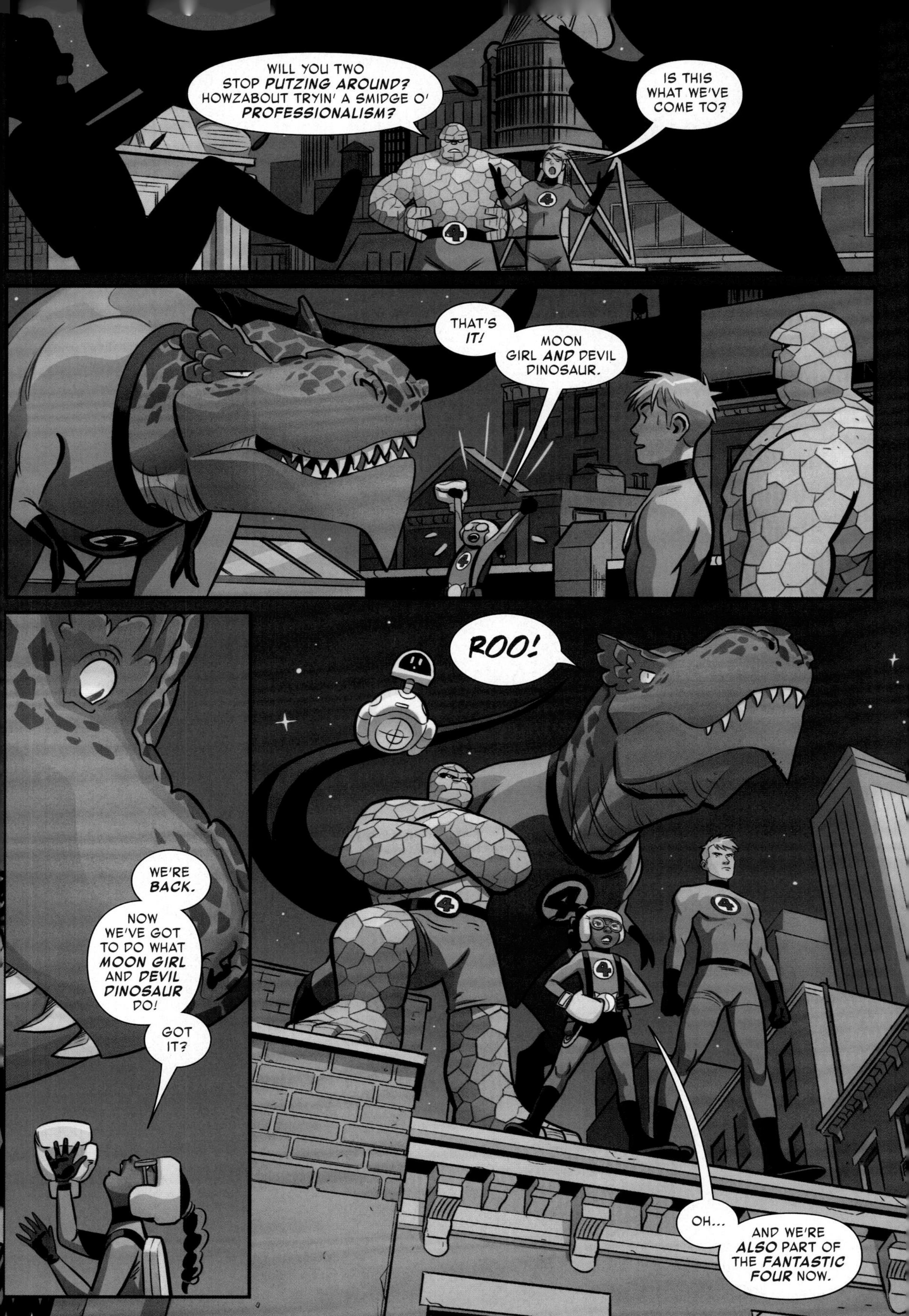
WILL YOU TWO STOP PUTZING AROUND? HOWZABOUT TRYIN' A SMIDGE O' PROFESSIONALISM?
IS THIS WHAT WE'VE COME TO?
THAT'S IT!
MOON GIRL AND DEVIL DINOSAUR.
ROO!
WE'RE BACK.
NOW WE'VE GOT TO DO WHAT MOON GIRL AND DEVIL DINOSAUR DO!
GOT IT?
OH...
AND WE'RE ALSO PART OF THE FANTASTIC FOUR NOW.

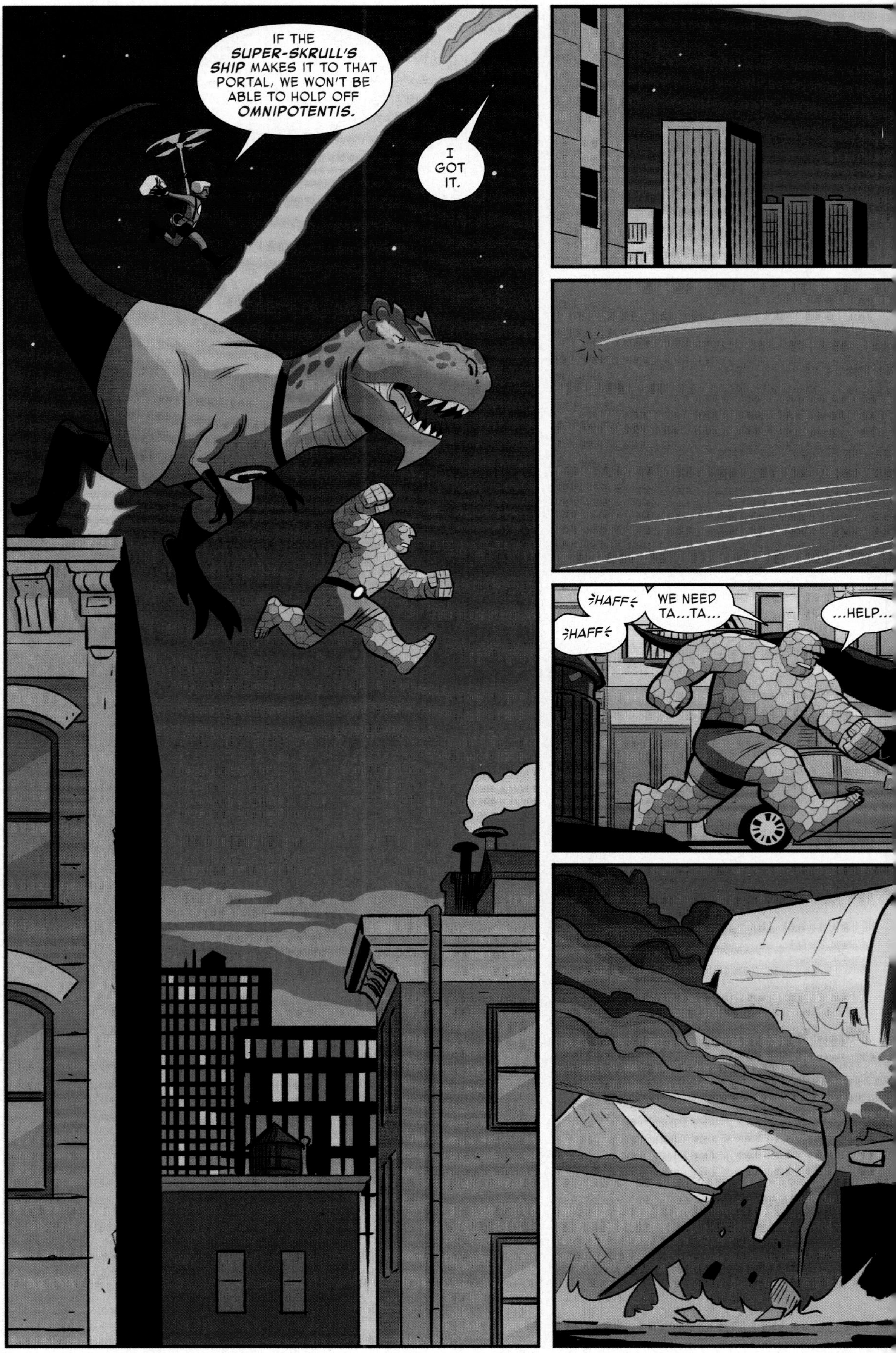
IF THE SUPER-SKRULL'S SHIP MAKES IT TO THAT PORTAL, WE WON'T BE ABLE TO HOLD OFF OMNIPOTENTIS.
I GOT IT.
HAFF
HAFF
WE NEED TA...TA...
...HELP...

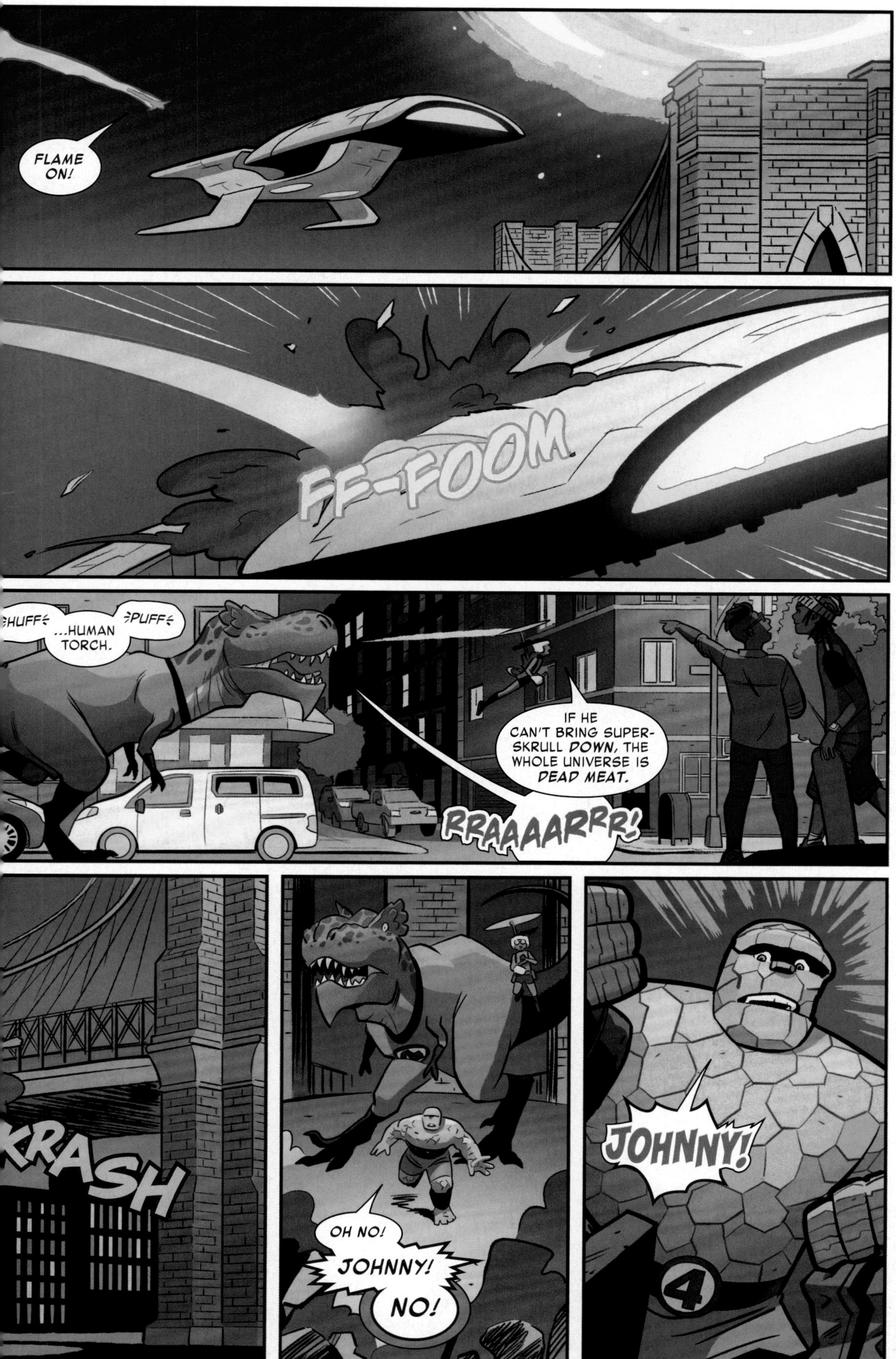
FLAME ON!
FF-FOOM
HUFF
...HUMAN TORCH.
PUFF
IF HE CAN'T BRING SUPER-SKRULL DOWN, THE WHOLE UNIVERSE IS DEAD MEAT.
RRAAAARRR!
KRASH
OH NO!
JOHNNY!
NO!
JOHNNY!

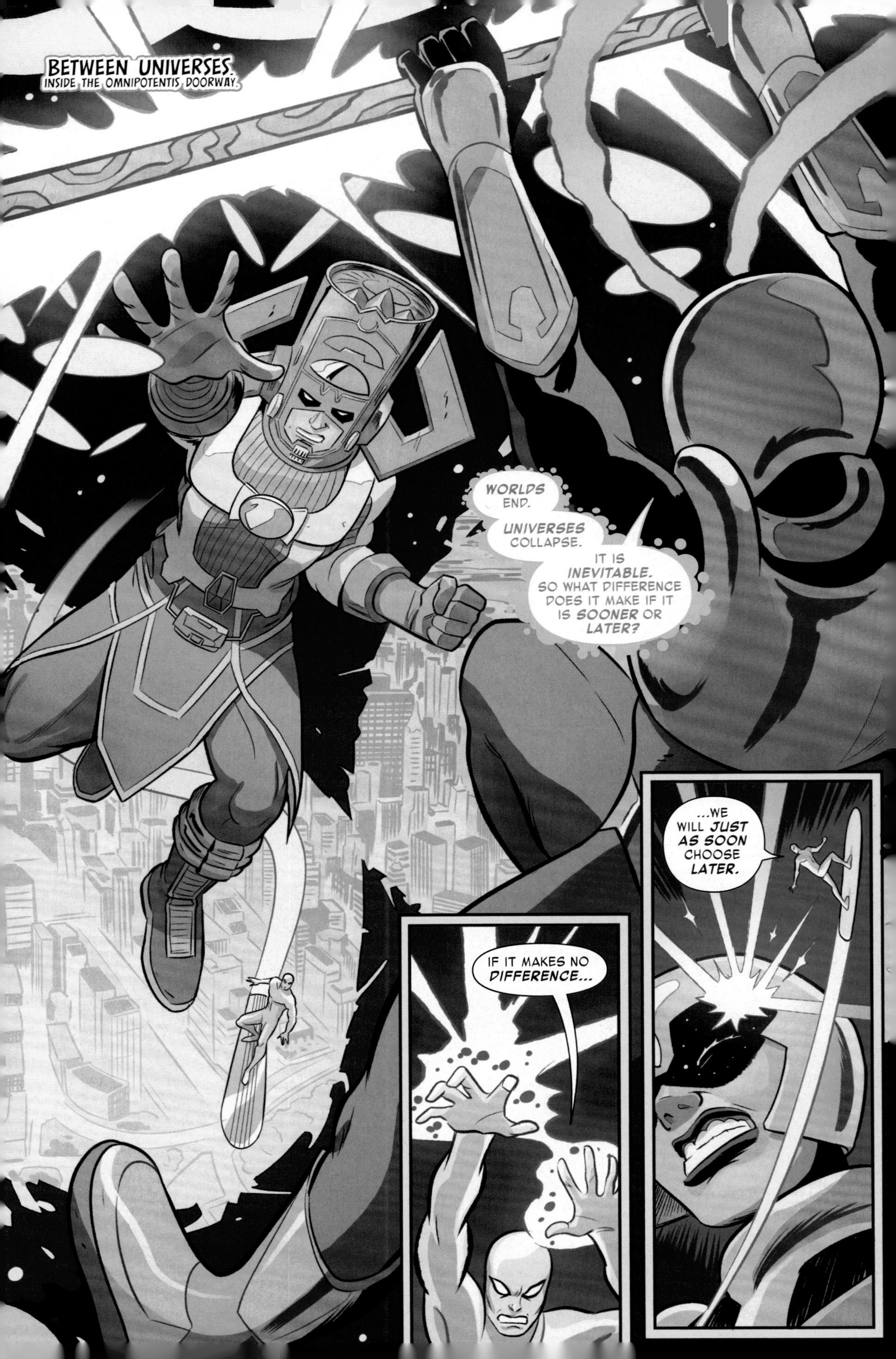
BETWEEN UNIVERSES.
INSIDE THE OMNIPOTENTIS DOORWAY.
WORLDS END.
UNIVERSES COLLAPSE.
IT IS INEVITABLE. SO WHAT DIFFERENCE DOES IT MAKE IF IT IS SOONER OR LATER?
IF IT MAKES NO DIFFERENCE...
...WE WILL JUST AS SOON CHOOSE LATER.

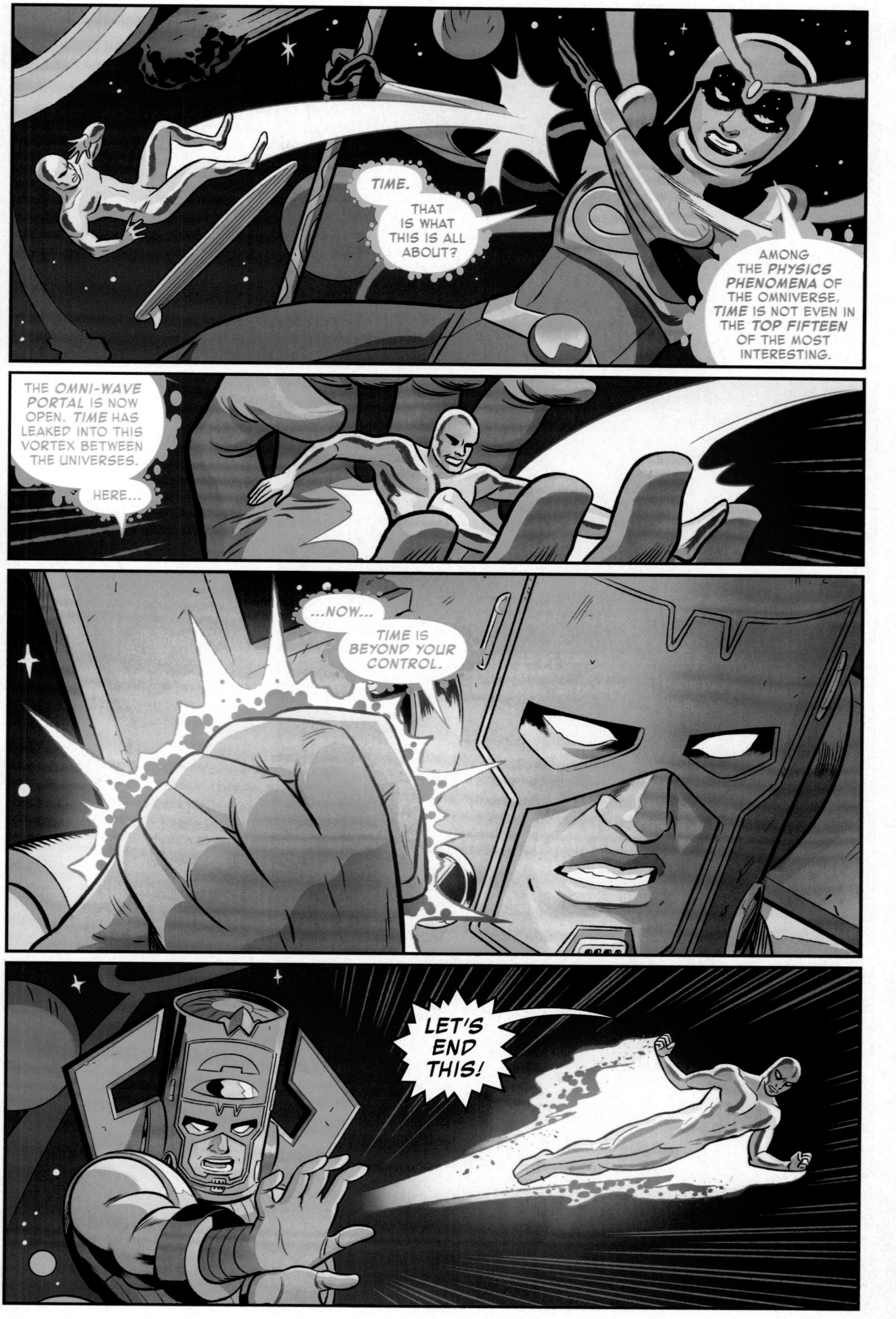
TIME.
THAT IS WHAT THIS IS ALL ABOUT?
AMONG THE PHYSICS PHENOMENA OF THE OMNIVERSE, TIME IS NOT EVEN IN THE TOP FIFTEEN OF THE MOST INTERESTING.
THE OMNI-WAVE PORTAL IS NOW OPEN. TIME HAS LEAKED INTO THIS VORTEX BETWEEN THE UNIVERSES.
HERE...
...NOW...
TIME IS BEYOND YOUR CONTROL.
LET'S END THIS!

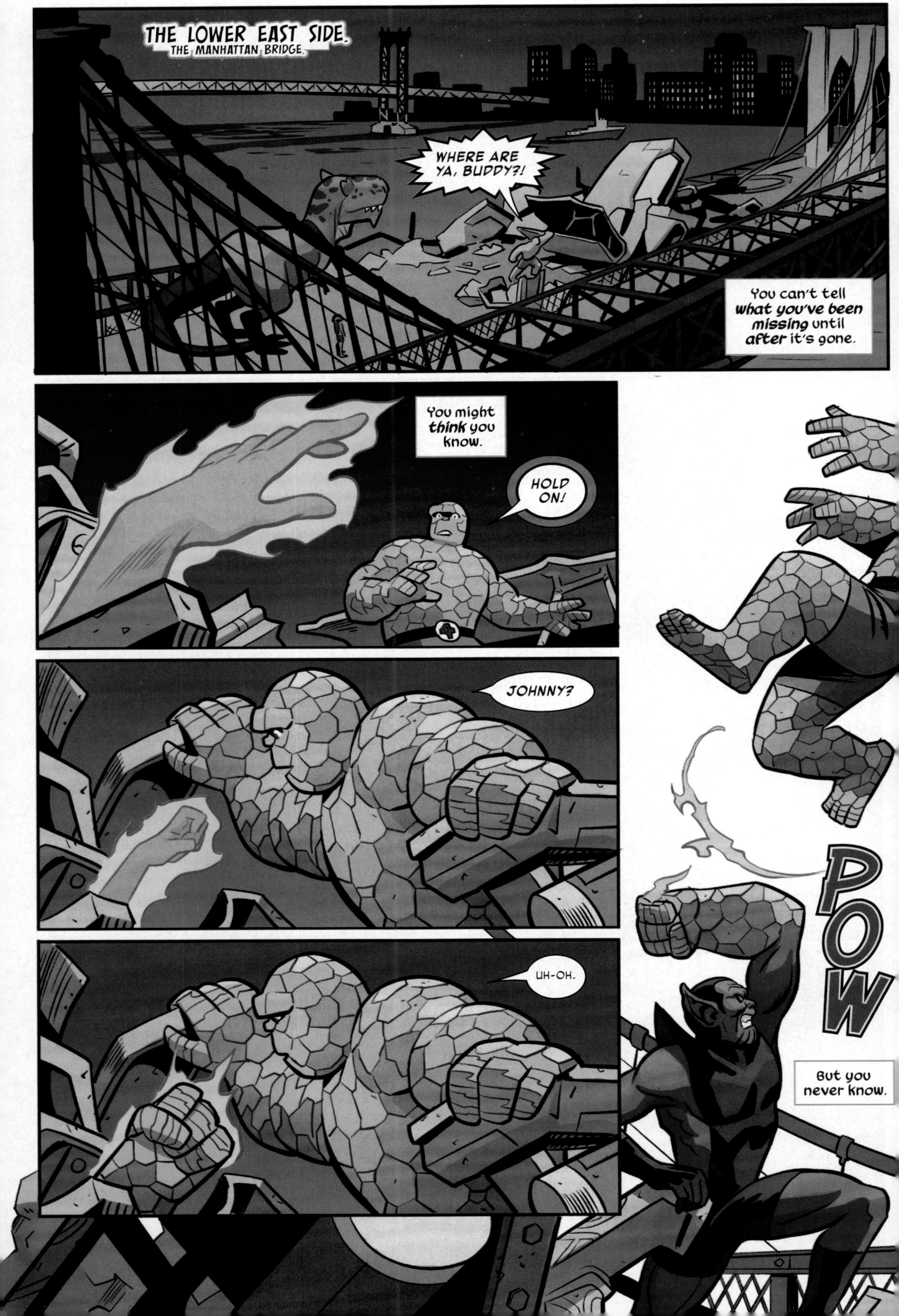
THE LOWER EAST SIDE.
THE MANHATTAN BRIDGE.
WHERE ARE YA, BUDDY?!
You can't tell *what you've been missing* until *after* it's gone.
You might *think* you know.
HOLD ON!
JOHNNY?
UH-OH.
POW
But you never know.

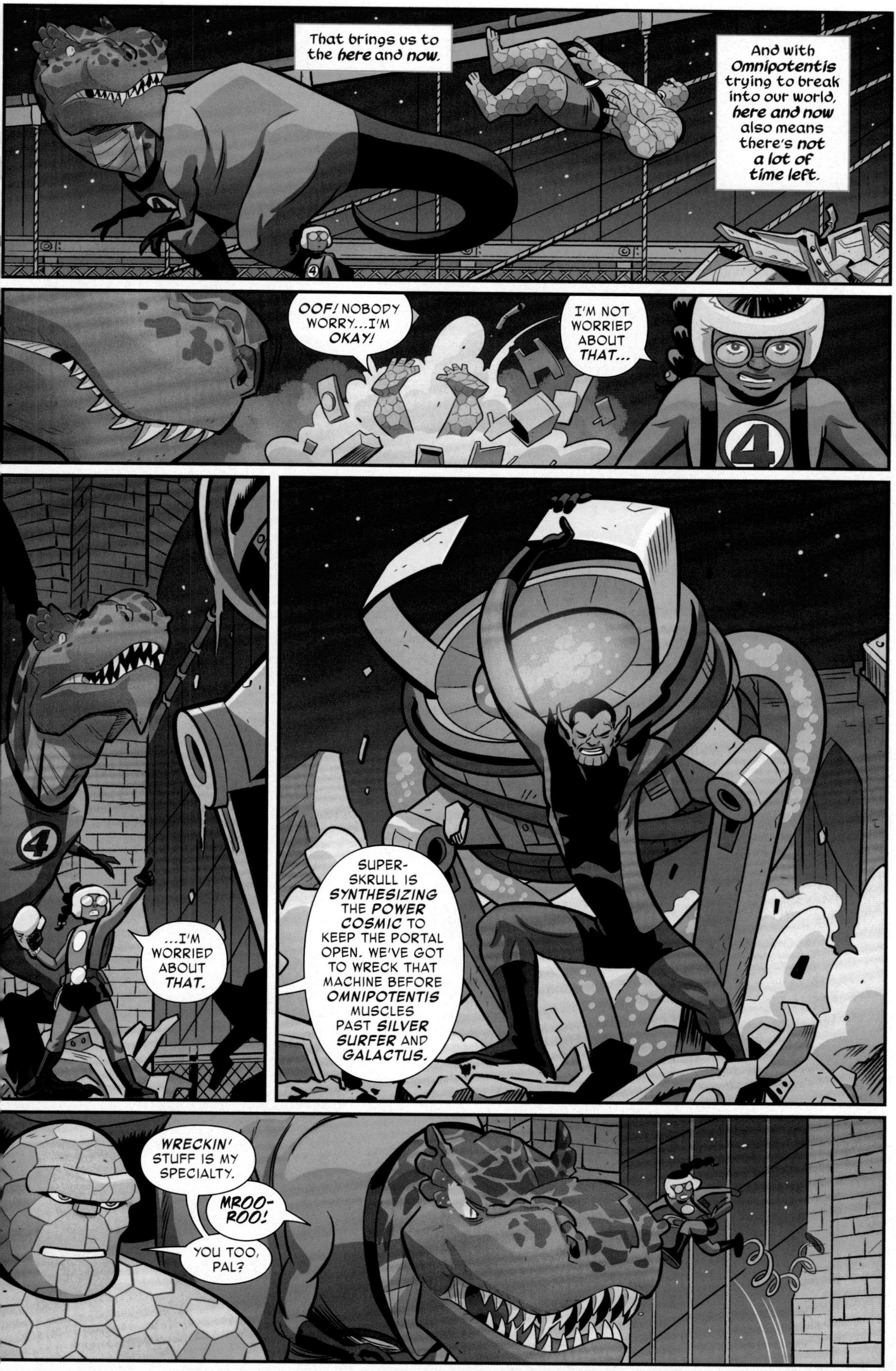

That brings us to the here and now.
And with Omnipotentis trying to break into our world, here and now also means there's not a lot of time left.
OOF! NOBODY WORRY...I'M OKAY!
I'M NOT WORRIED ABOUT THAT...
...I'M WORRIED ABOUT THAT.
SUPER-SKRULL IS SYNTHESIZING THE POWER COSMIC TO KEEP THE PORTAL OPEN. WE'VE GOT TO WRECK THAT MACHINE BEFORE OMNIPOTENTIS MUSCLES PAST SILVER SURFER AND GALACTUS.
WRECKIN' STUFF IS MY SPECIALTY.
MROO-ROO!
YOU TOO, PAL?

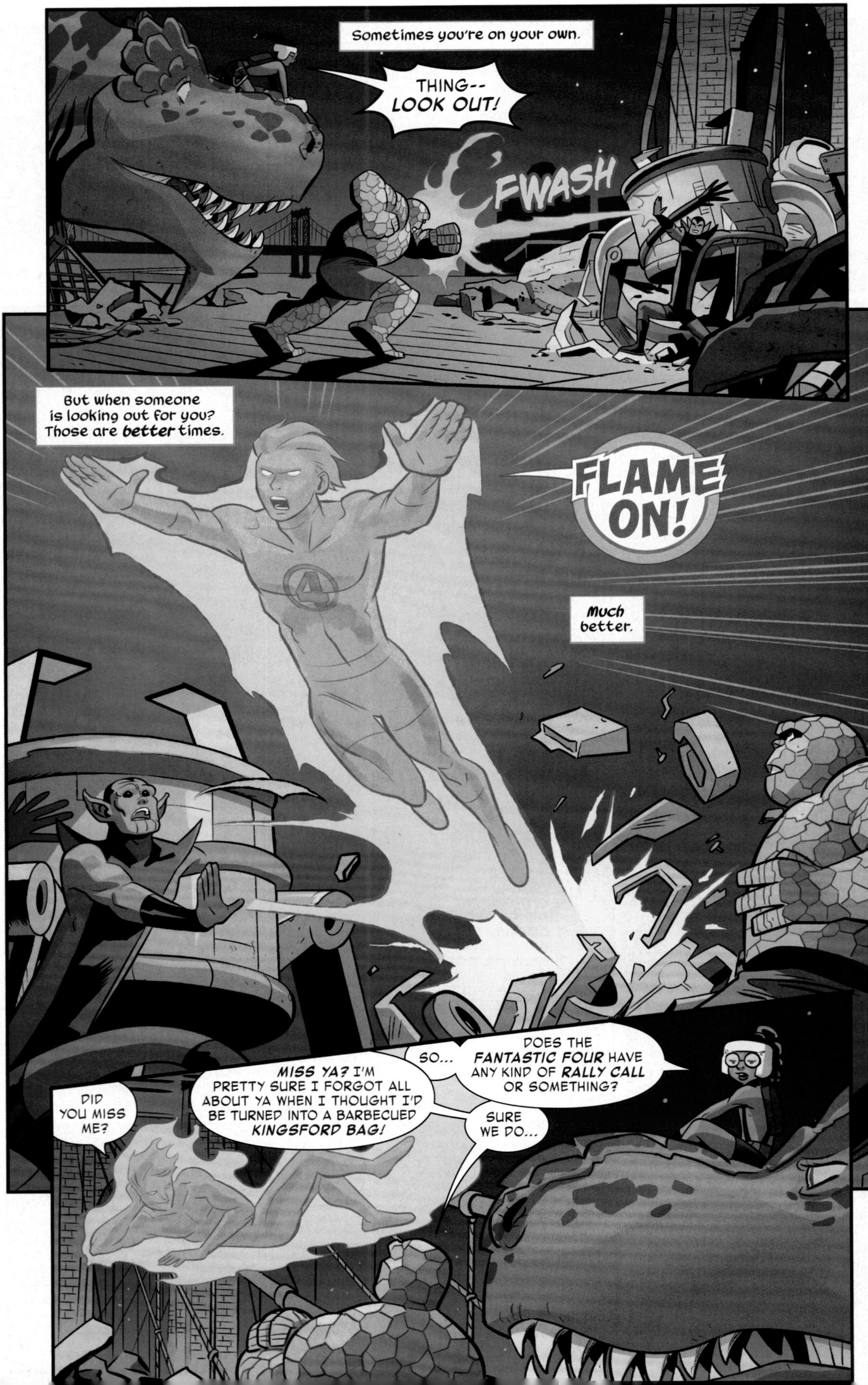
Sometimes you're on your own.
THING-- LOOK OUT!
FWASH
But when someone is looking out for you? Those are better times.
FLAME ON!
Much better.
DID YOU MISS ME?
MISS YA? I'M PRETTY SURE I FORGOT ALL ABOUT YA WHEN I THOUGHT I'D BE TURNED INTO A BARBECUED KINGSFORD BAG!
SO...
DOES THE FANTASTIC FOUR HAVE ANY KIND OF RALLY CALL OR SOMETHING?
SURE WE DO...

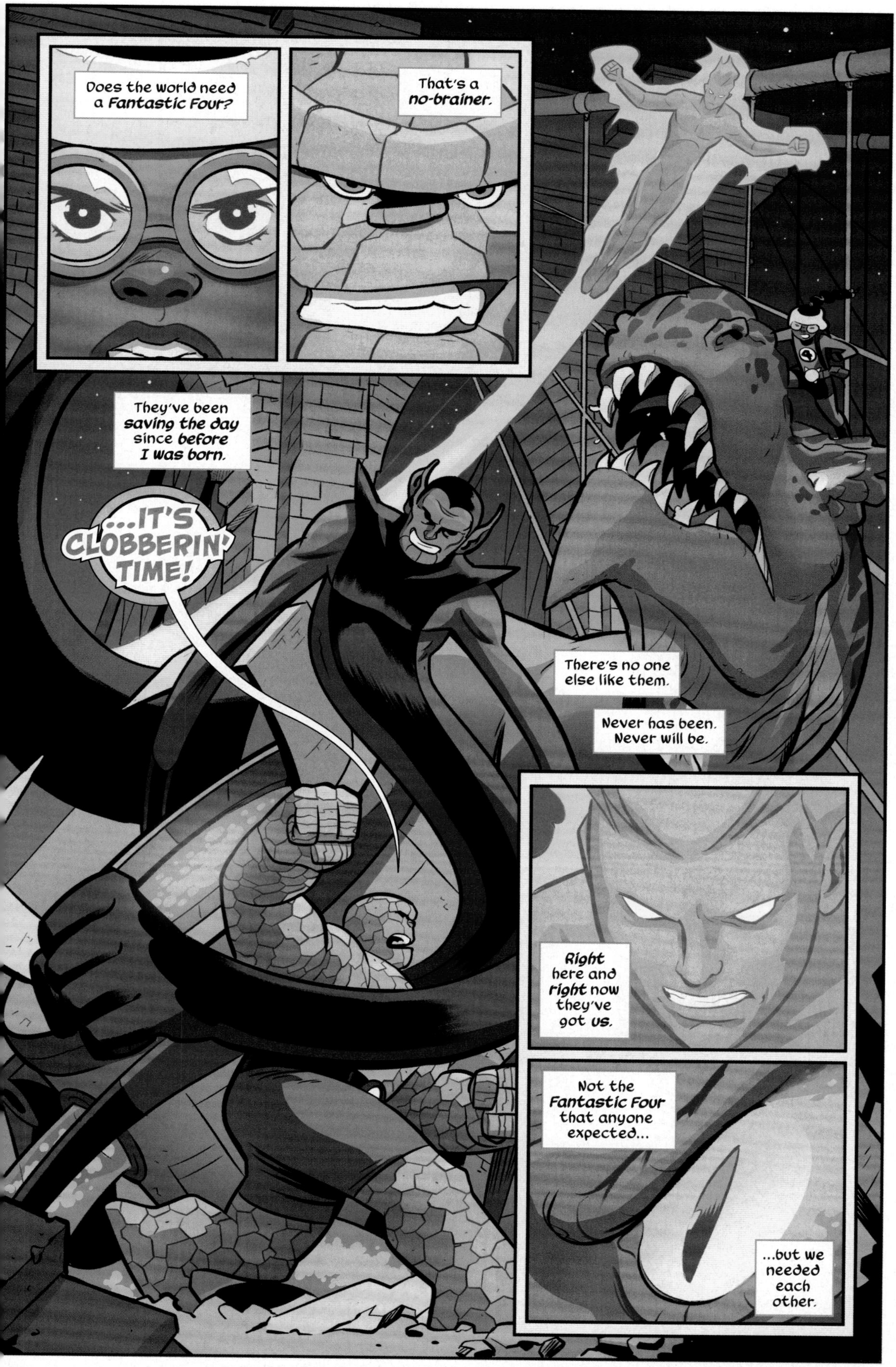

Does the world need a *Fantastic Four?*
That's a *no-brainer.*
They've been *saving the day* since *before I was born.*
...IT'S CLOBBERIN' TIME!
There's no one else like them.
Never has been. Never will be.
Right here and *right* now they've got *us.*
Not the *Fantastic Four* that anyone expected...
...but we needed each other.

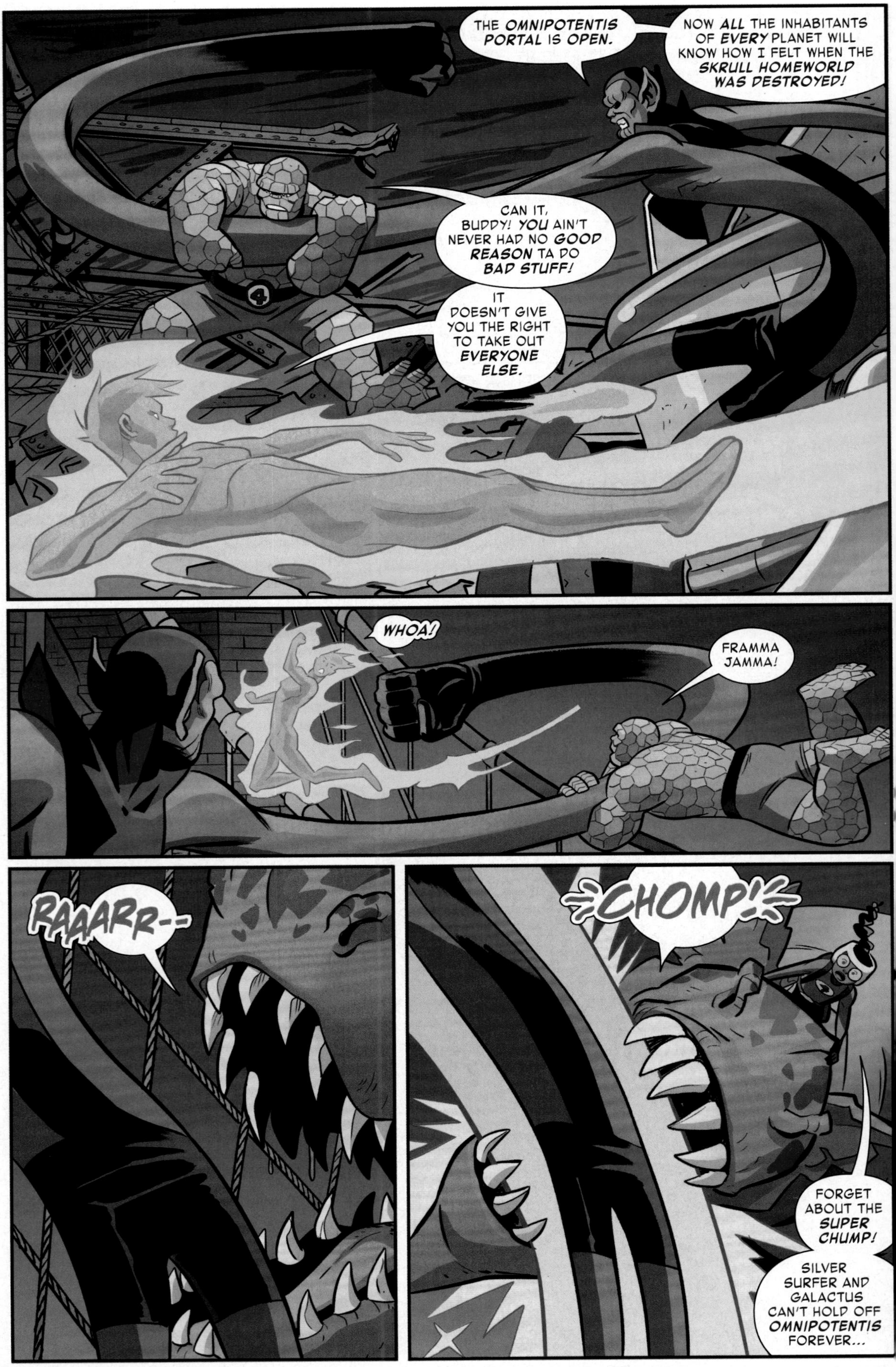
THE OMNIPOTENTIS PORTAL IS OPEN.
NOW ALL THE INHABITANTS OF EVERY PLANET WILL KNOW HOW I FELT WHEN THE SKRULL HOMEWORLD WAS DESTROYED!
CAN IT, BUDDY! YOU AIN'T NEVER HAD NO GOOD REASON TA DO BAD STUFF!
IT DOESN'T GIVE YOU THE RIGHT TO TAKE OUT EVERYONE ELSE.
WHOA!
FRAMMA JAMMA!
RAAARR--
CHOMP!
FORGET ABOUT THE SUPER CHUMP!
SILVER SURFER AND GALACTUS CAN'T HOLD OFF OMNIPOTENTIS FOREVER...

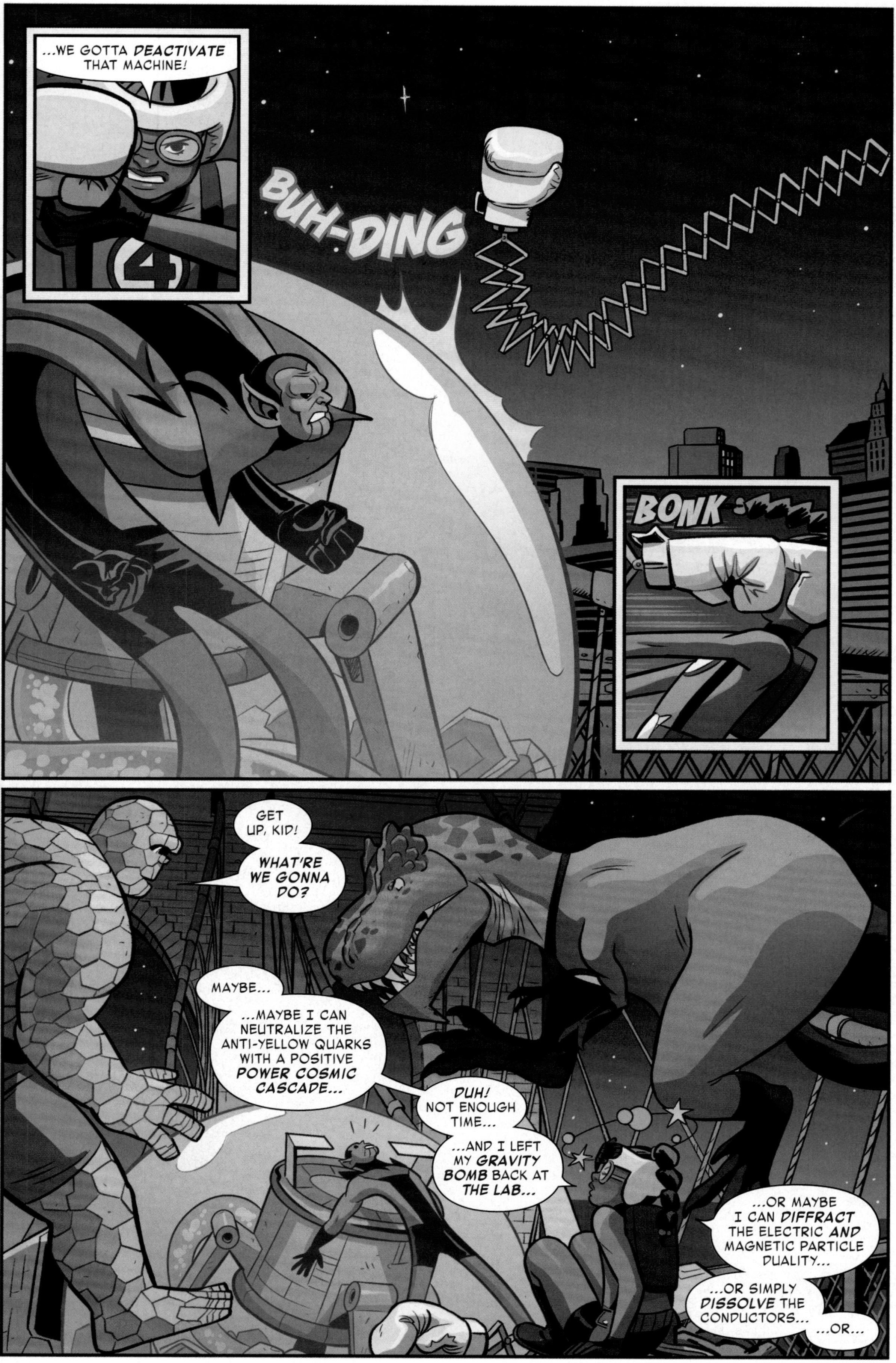

...WE GOTTA DEACTIVATE THAT MACHINE!
BUH-DING
BONK
GET UP, KID!
WHAT'RE WE GONNA DO?
MAYBE...
...MAYBE I CAN NEUTRALIZE THE ANTI-YELLOW QUARKS WITH A POSITIVE POWER COSMIC CASCADE...
DUH! NOT ENOUGH TIME...
...AND I LEFT MY GRAVITY BOMB BACK AT THE LAB...
...OR MAYBE I CAN DIFFRACT THE ELECTRIC AND MAGNETIC PARTICLE DUALITY...
...OR SIMPLY DISSOLVE THE CONDUCTORS...
...OR...

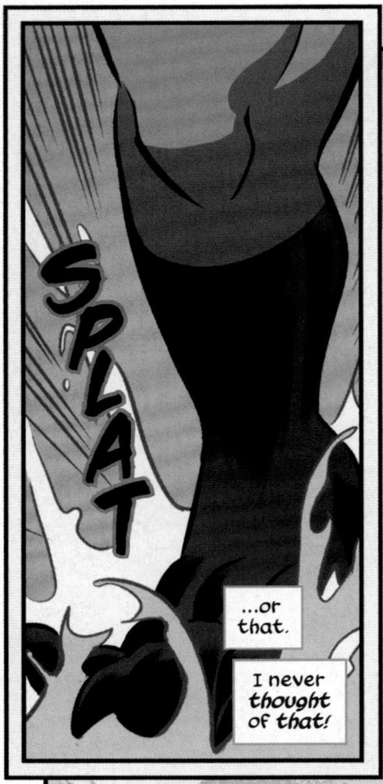
SPLAT
...or that.
I never thought of that!
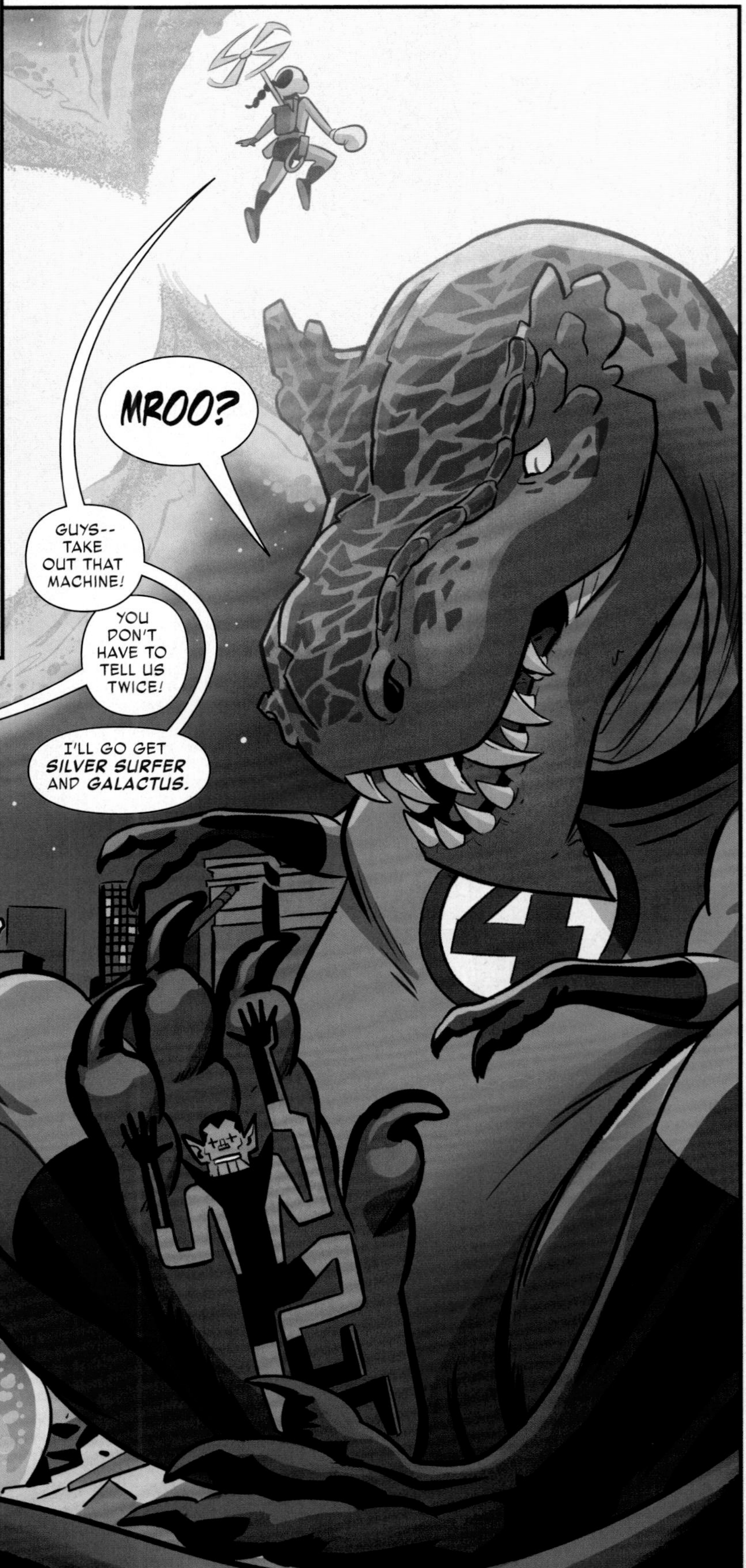
MROO?
GUYS-- TAKE OUT THAT MACHINE!
YOU DON'T HAVE TO TELL US TWICE!
I'LL GO GET SILVER SURFER AND GALACTUS.
FWASH
KLONK

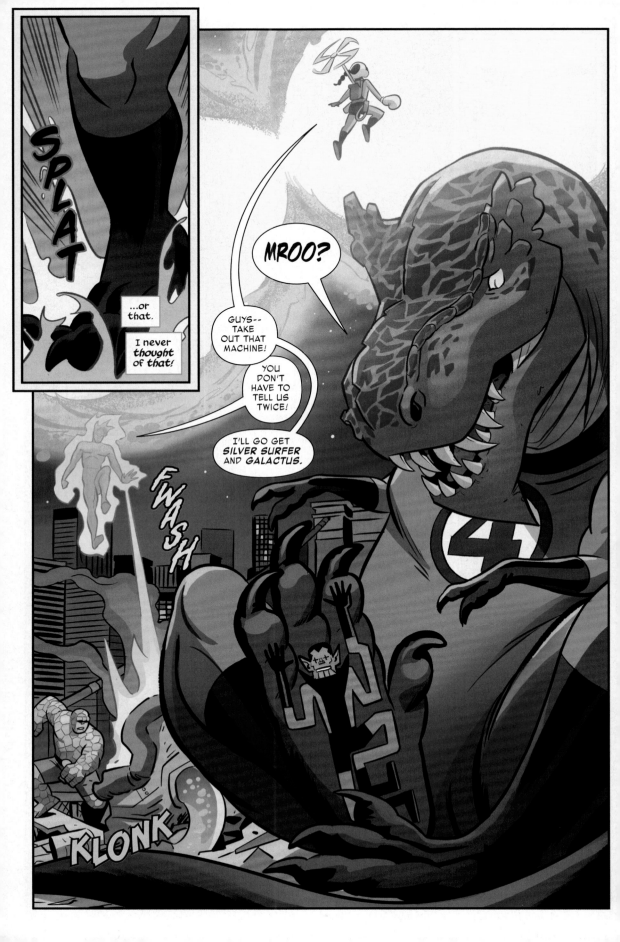

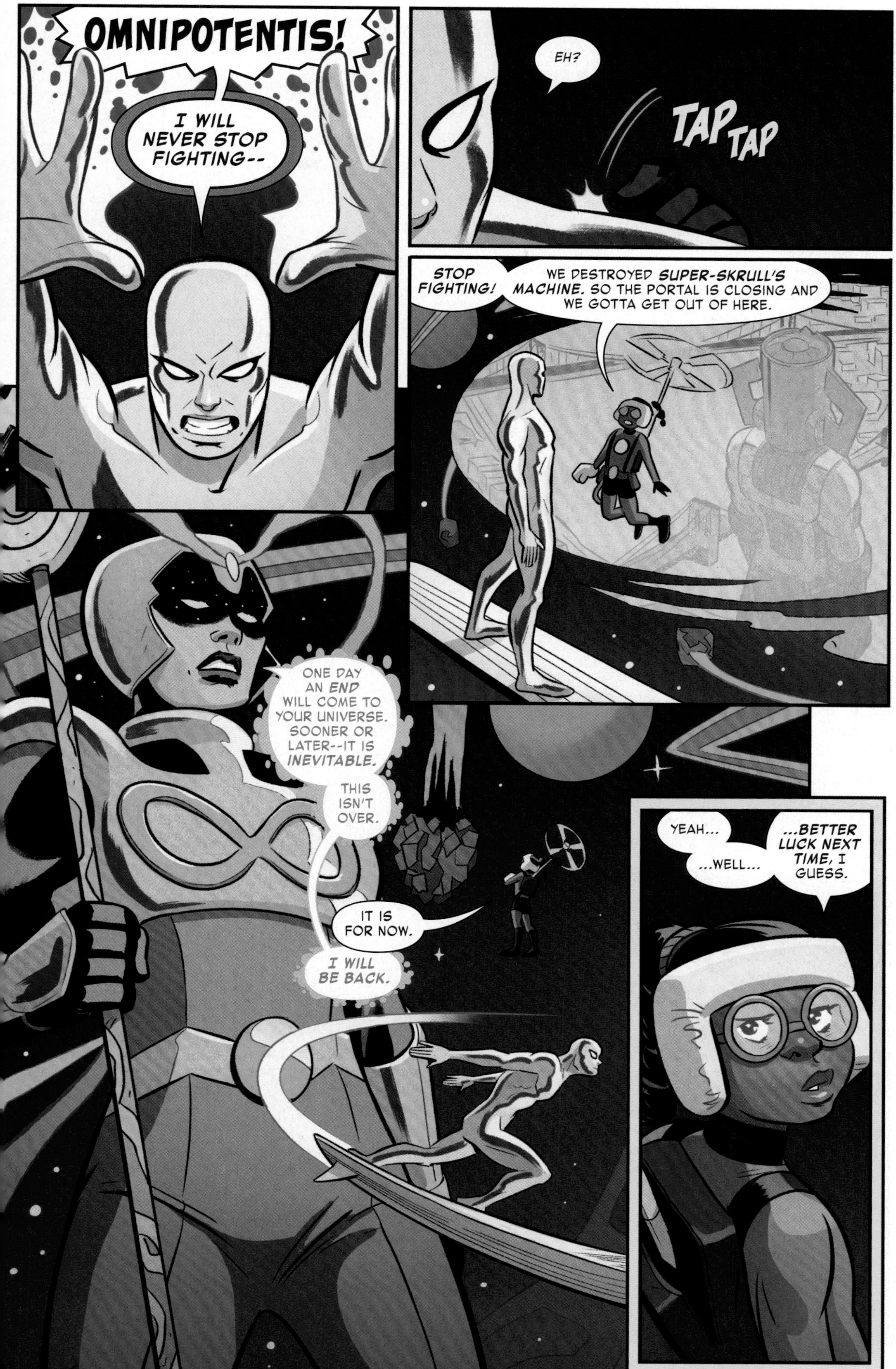
OMNIPOTENTIS!
I WILL NEVER STOP FIGHTING--
EH?
TAP TAP
STOP FIGHTING!
WE DESTROYED SUPER-SKRULL'S MACHINE. SO THE PORTAL IS CLOSING AND WE GOTTA GET OUT OF HERE.
ONE DAY AN END WILL COME TO YOUR UNIVERSE. SOONER OR LATER--IT IS INEVITABLE.
THIS ISN'T OVER.
IT IS FOR NOW.
I WILL BE BACK.
YEAH...
...WELL...
...BETTER LUCK NEXT TIME, I GUESS.

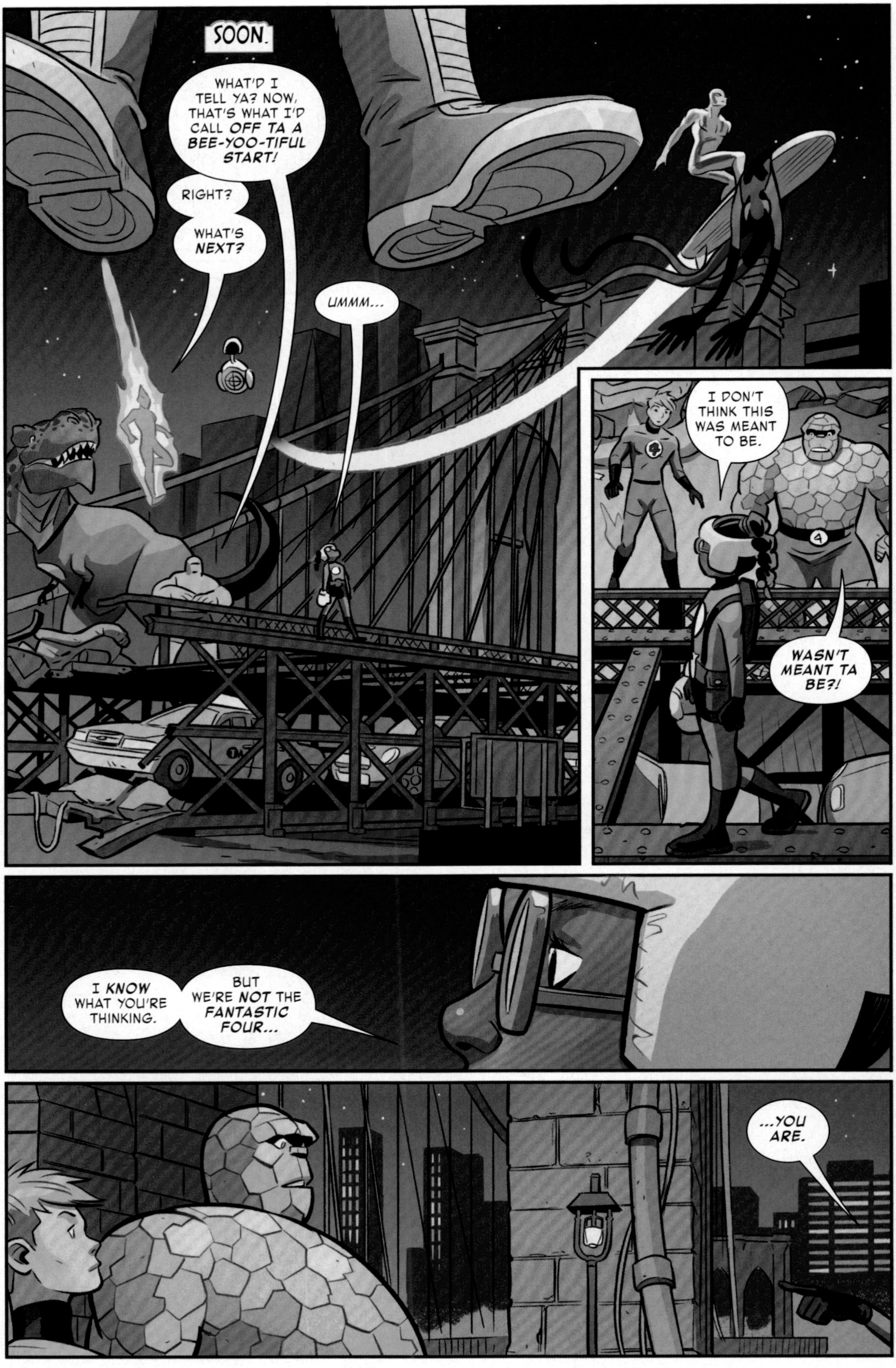
SOON.
WHAT'D I TELL YA? NOW, THAT'S WHAT I'D CALL OFF TA A BEE-YOO-TIFUL START!
RIGHT?
WHAT'S NEXT?
UMMM...
I DON'T THINK THIS WAS MEANT TO BE.
WASN'T MEANT TA BE?!
I KNOW WHAT YOU'RE THINKING.
BUT WE'RE NOT THE FANTASTIC FOUR...
...YOU ARE.

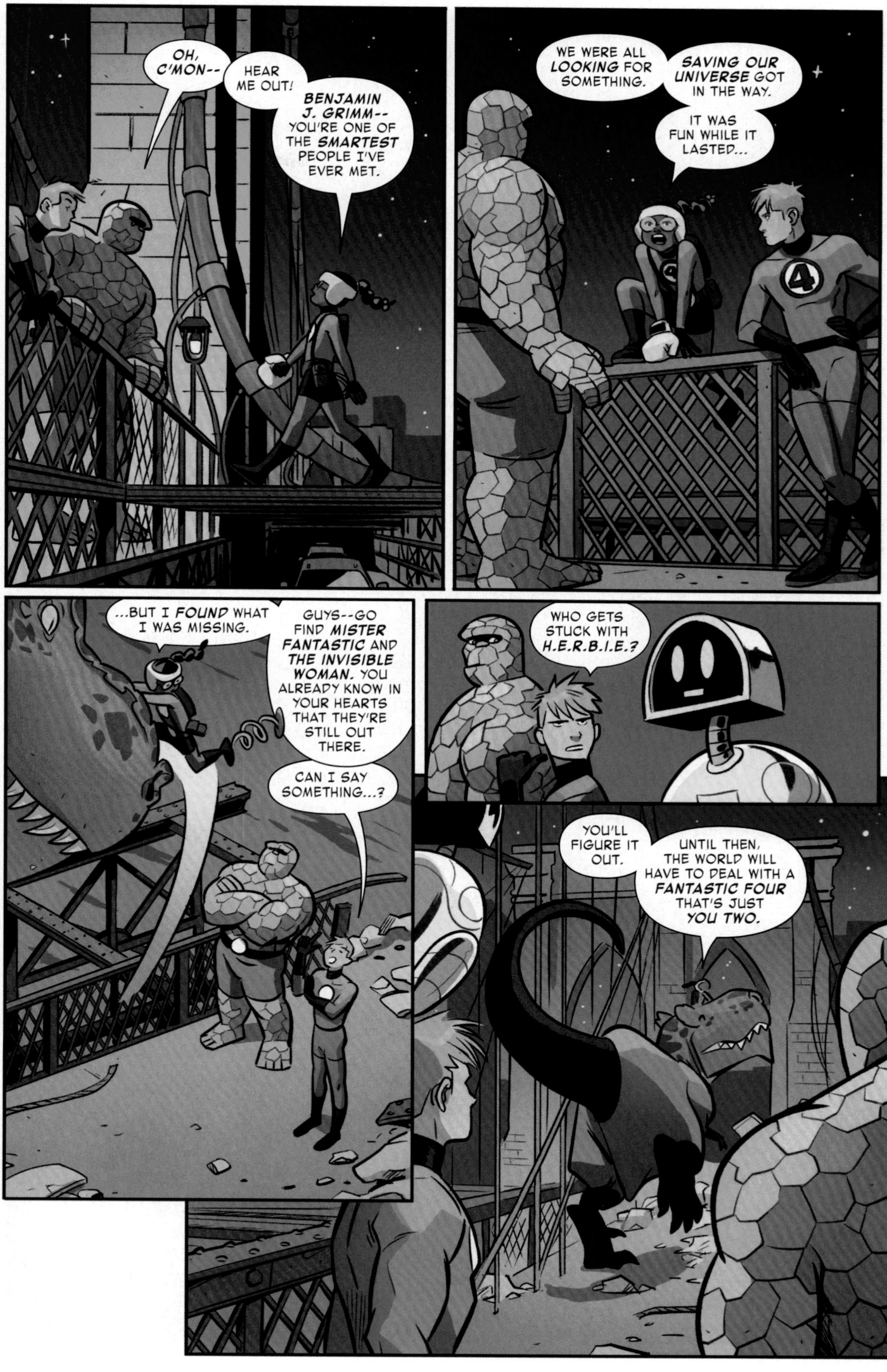
OH, C'MON--
HEAR ME OUT!
BENJAMIN J. GRIMM-- YOU'RE ONE OF THE SMARTEST PEOPLE I'VE EVER MET.
WE WERE ALL LOOKING FOR SOMETHING.
SAVING OUR UNIVERSE GOT IN THE WAY.
IT WAS FUN WHILE IT LASTED...
...BUT I FOUND WHAT I WAS MISSING.
GUYS--GO FIND MISTER FANTASTIC AND THE INVISIBLE WOMAN. YOU ALREADY KNOW IN YOUR HEARTS THAT THEY'RE STILL OUT THERE.
CAN I SAY SOMETHING...?
WHO GETS STUCK WITH H.E.R.B.I.E.?
YOU'LL FIGURE IT OUT.
UNTIL THEN, THE WORLD WILL HAVE TO DEAL WITH A FANTASTIC FOUR THAT'S JUST YOU TWO.

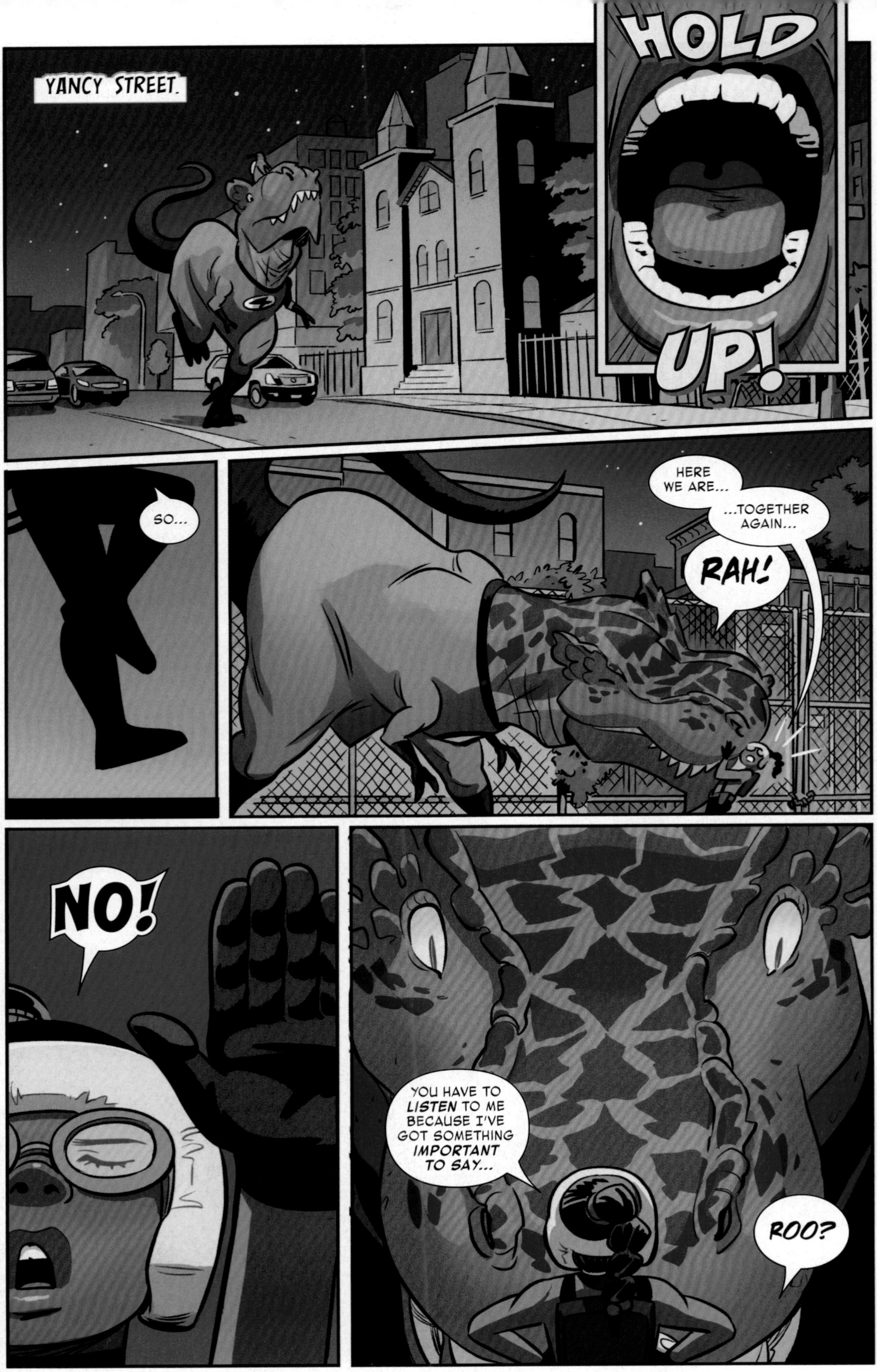
YANCY STREET.
HOLD UP!
SO...
HERE WE ARE...
...TOGETHER AGAIN...
RAH!
NO!
YOU HAVE TO LISTEN TO ME BECAUSE I'VE GOT SOMETHING IMPORTANT TO SAY...
ROO?

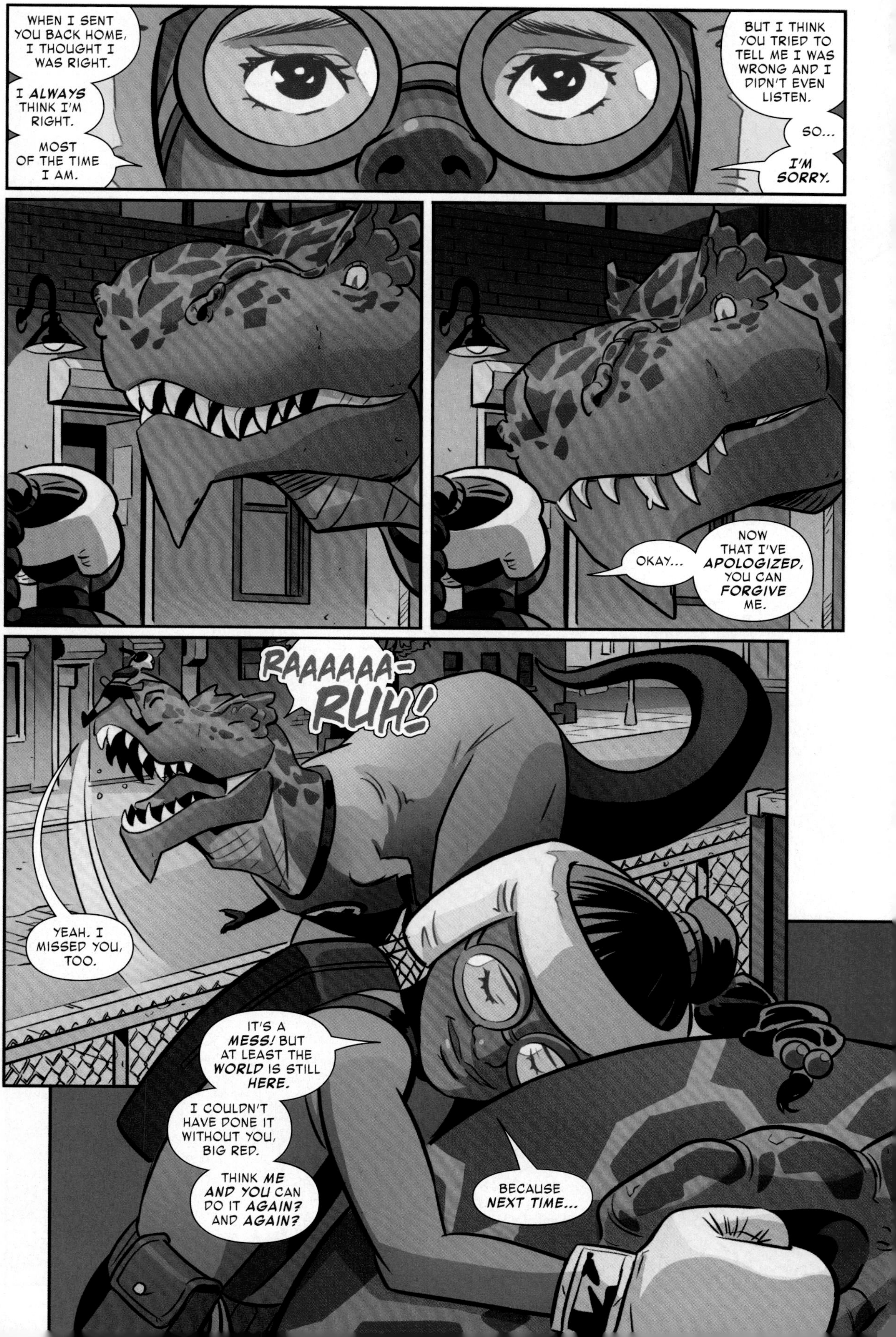
WHEN I SENT YOU BACK HOME, I THOUGHT I WAS RIGHT.
I ALWAYS THINK I'M RIGHT.
MOST OF THE TIME I AM.
BUT I THINK YOU TRIED TO TELL ME I WAS WRONG AND I DIDN'T EVEN LISTEN.
SO...
I'M SORRY.
OKAY...
NOW THAT I'VE APOLOGIZED, YOU CAN FORGIVE ME.
RAAAAAA-RUH!
YEAH. I MISSED YOU, TOO.
IT'S A MESS! BUT AT LEAST THE WORLD IS STILL HERE.
I COULDN'T HAVE DONE IT WITHOUT YOU, BIG RED.
THINK ME AND YOU CAN DO IT AGAIN? AND AGAIN?
BECAUSE NEXT TIME...

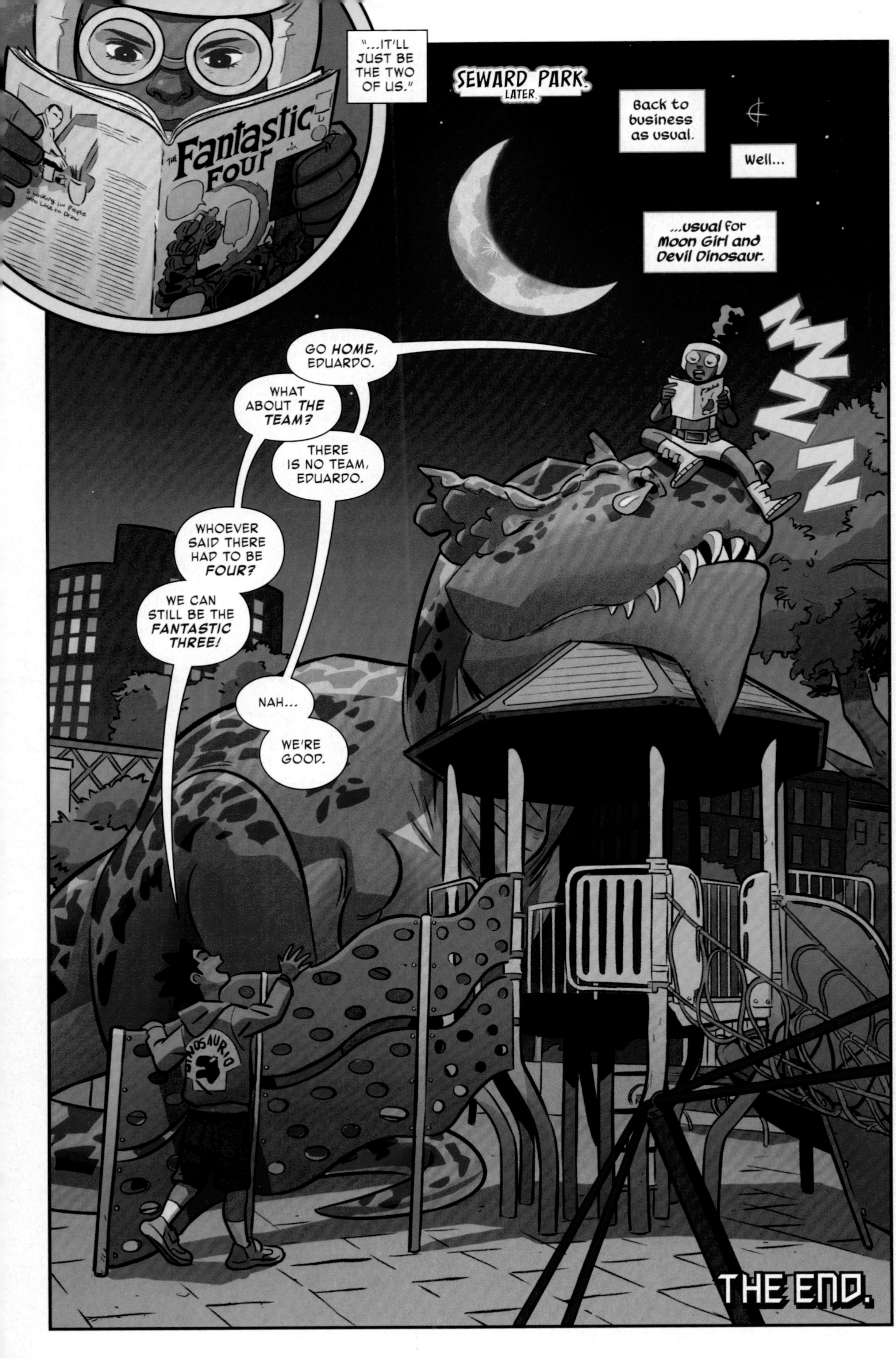
"...IT'LL JUST BE THE TWO OF US."
SEWARD PARK. LATER.
Back to business as usual.
Well...
...usual for Moon Girl and Devil Dinosaur.
GO HOME, EDUARDO.
WHAT ABOUT THE TEAM?
THERE IS NO TEAM, EDUARDO.
WHOEVER SAID THERE HAD TO BE FOUR?
WE CAN STILL BE THE FANTASTIC THREE!
NAH...
WE'RE GOOD.
NNNN
THE END.

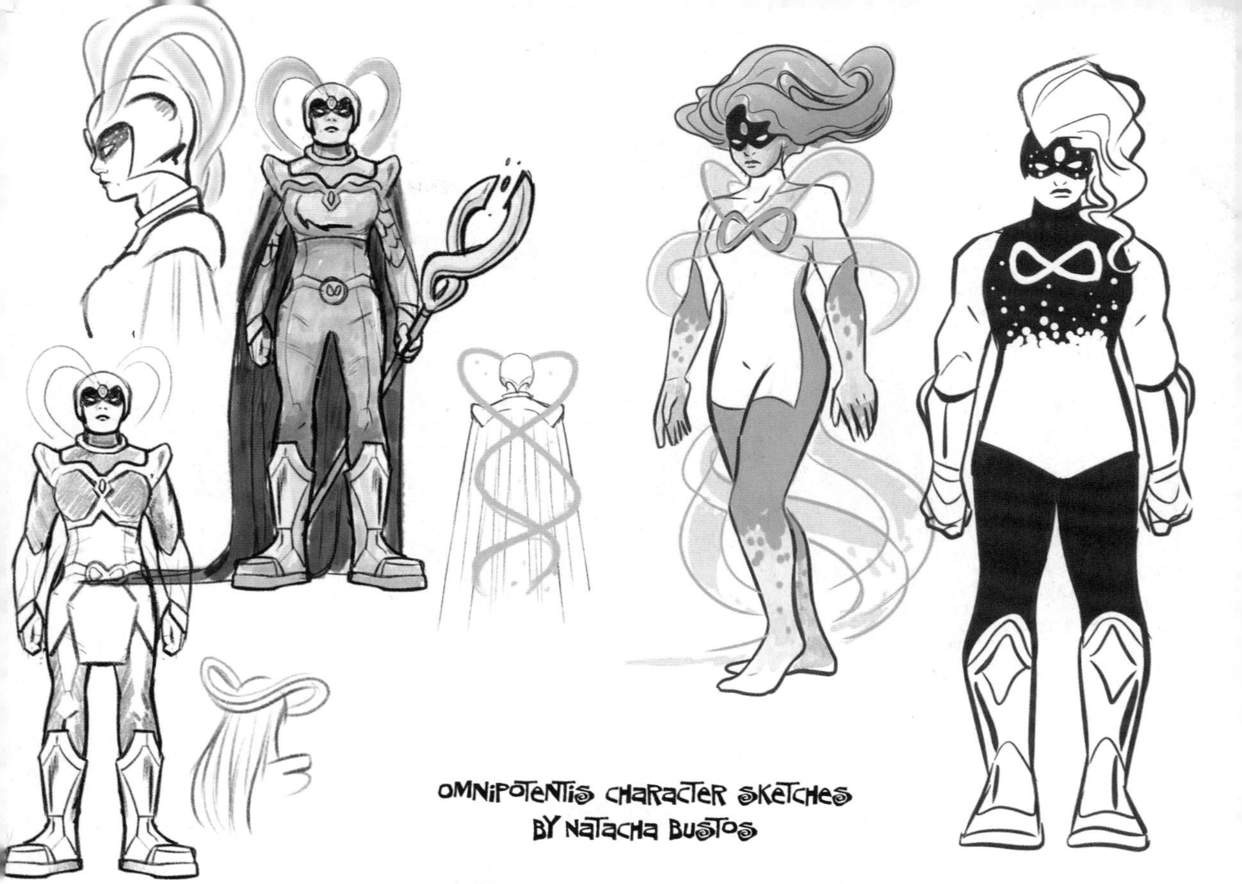

OMNIPOTENTIS CHARACTER SKETCHES
BY NATACHA BUSTOS

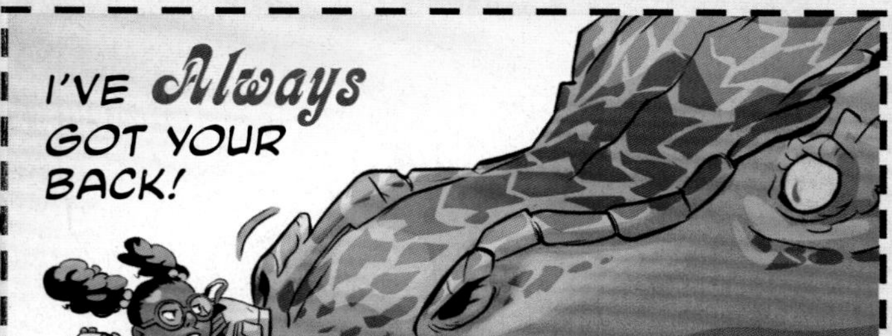
I'VE Always GOT YOUR BACK!

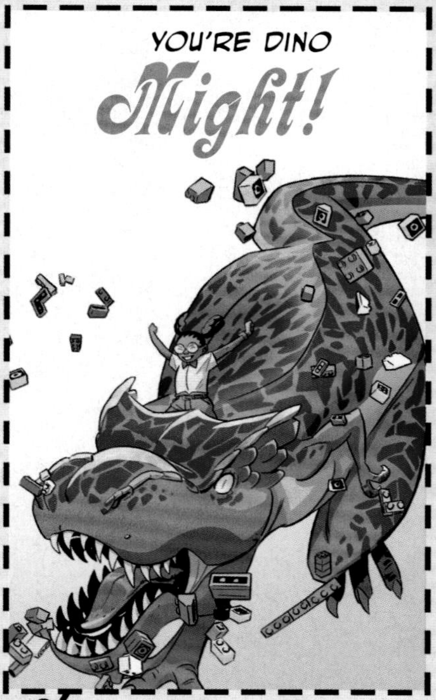
YOU'RE DINO Might!

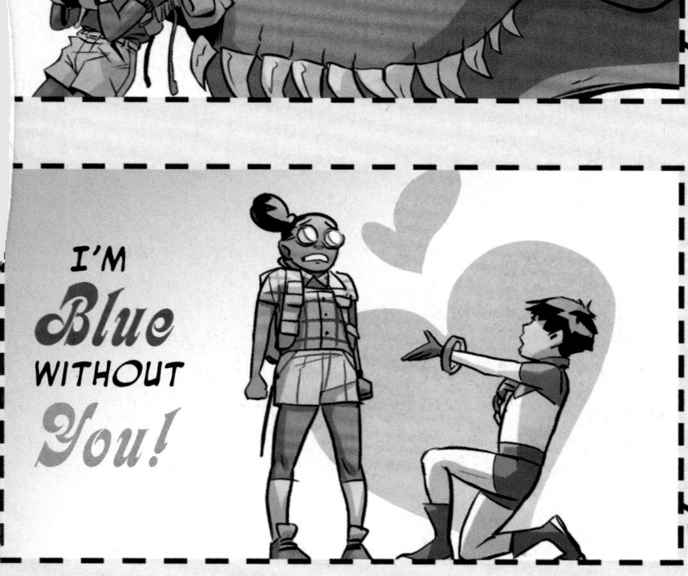
I'M Blue WITHOUT You!

INSTRUCTIONS:
Carefully cut along the dashed line. Ask your parent or guardian for help!

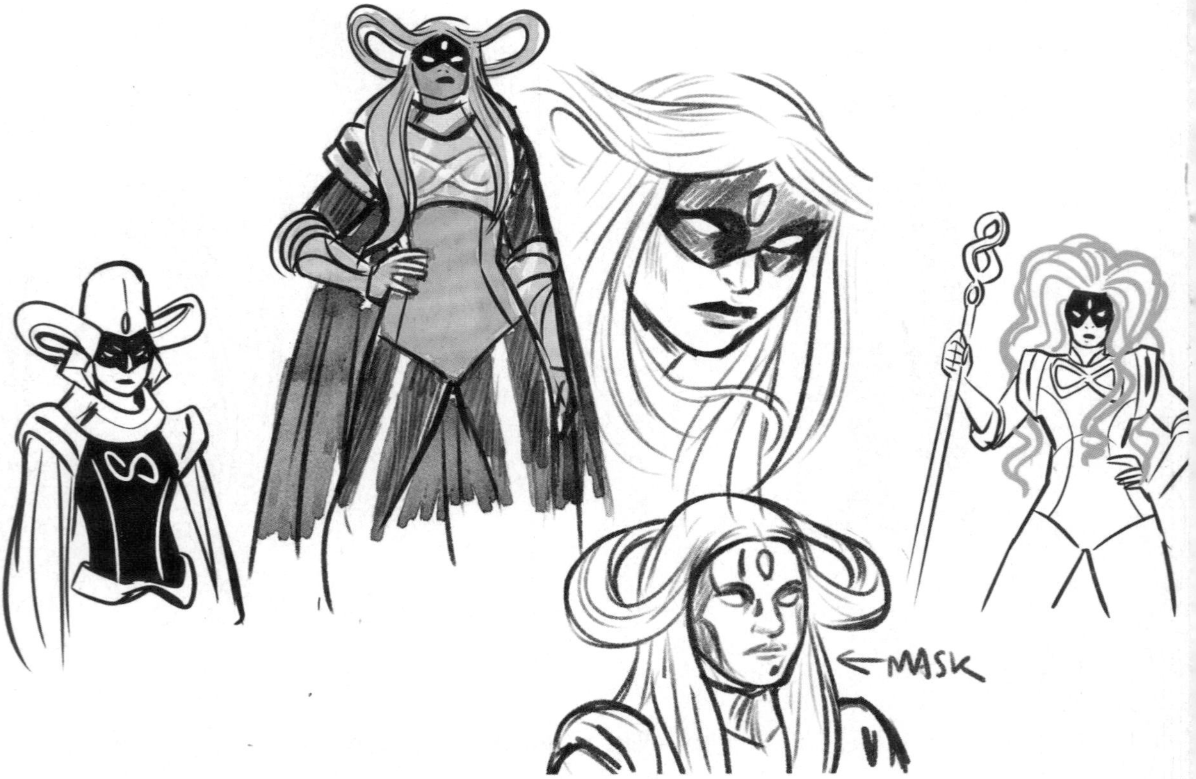
MASK

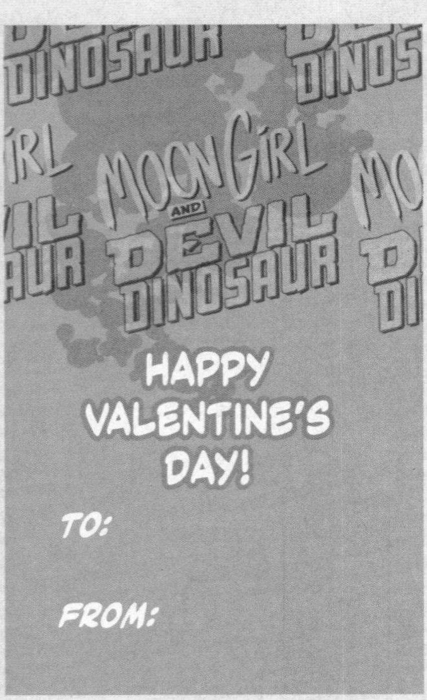
MOON GIRL
AND
DEVIL
DINOSAUR
HAPPY
VALENTINE'S
DAY!
TO:
FROM:

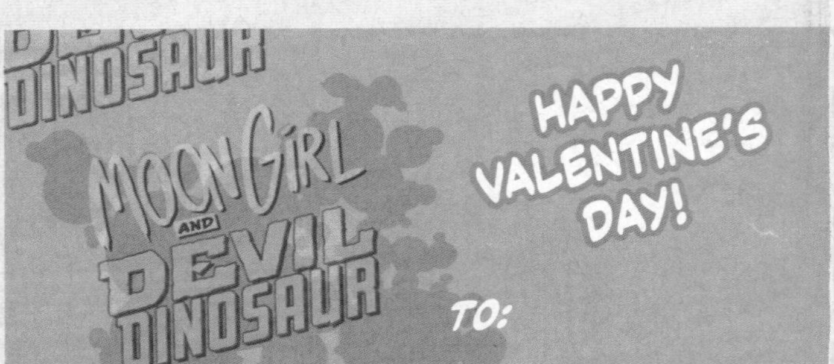
MOON GIRL
AND
DEVIL
DINOSAUR
HAPPY
VALENTINE'S
DAY!
TO:
FROM:

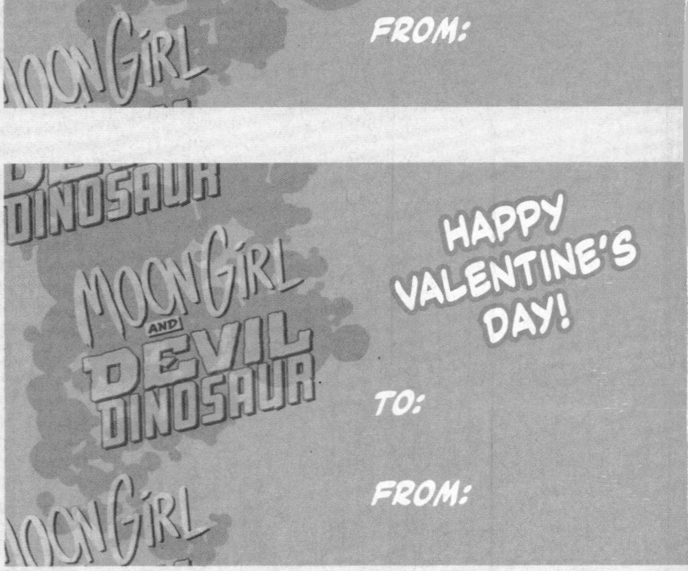
MOON GIRL
AND
DEVIL
DINOSAUR
HAPPY
VALENTINE'S
DAY!
TO:
FROM:

Special thanks to Alyssa Ramos, Mac Paynter, Anthony Gambino, Elissa Hunter and Jacque Porte.